CW00983387

The Superhuman Playbook

18 Proven Strategies to Unleash Unstoppable Growth

A Collaborative Work

Version 1.0 – August 21, 2020

Compiled by Collin Jewett

Illustrated by Daniel Jewett

Published by Increase Publishing

Fort Collins, CO

Copyright © 2020

Library of Congress Control Number:

2020915406

Find resources mentioned in the book at

www.superhumanplaybook.com

All rights reserved, including the right of reproduction in whole or in part in any form.

Dedication

This book is dedicated to all who fear the unknown and run toward it anyway.

Contents

Foreword by Jonathan Levi · 1

Chapter 1: Putting Off Procrastination by Jeff Mesina · 5

Chapter 2: Expanding Your Brain Bandwidth: Getting Rid of Complaints and Excuses and Leveraging Judgement by Antoine Hiolle · 17

Chapter 3: Asking for Miracles by Collin Jewett · 37

Chapter 4: Building Unstoppable Success Momentum by Peter A. Anglin · 51

Chapter 5: The Power of Your Thoughts by Anastasia Kor · 91

Chapter 6: Achieve the "Impossible" Through Visualization by Lorena Compean · 103

Chapter 7: The Sense Audit by Norman Chella · 117

Chapter 8: Habit Building for the "Non-Habit" Types by Meg Zirger · 125

Chapter 9: Performing in an "Agile" Way by Kevin Borrmann · 147

Chapter 10: Productivity is Social by Dahyu Patel · 159

Chapter 11: Repetition, Active Recall, and Reflection for Knowledge Integration and Creation by Rahel Zeleke · 173

Chapter 12: Embodied Learning by Erica Appelros · 185

Chapter 13: From Theory to Practise by Elanor Kloester · 207

Chapter 14: Help! I'm not a Native Speaker! by Andrea Szabo · 223

Chapter 15: Break Free of Damming Liquid by Daniel Lathen · 237

Chapter 16: Get Fit at Home – Even if You Have No Idea Where to Begin by Dylan Peterson · 281

Chapter 17: The Quickstart Guide to Ultimate Performance by Nguyen Tran · 315

Chapter 18: Make Yourself a Priority by Jan Hellwig · 363

Chapter 19: Conclusion by Collin Jewett · 371

Foreword

Less than a decade ago, I was where you probably are today.

All my life, I had sought more. More from my body. More from my time. More from my mind. More from my life. But it wasn't until a chance encounter with an incredible individual - a real-life superhuman - that I realized just how much more there was.

That first encounter - and that individual's willingness to share their wisdom and experience with me - set me on a path that continues to this day. By acquiring the skills of accelerated learning and improved productivity, I was able to unlock an entire pandora's box of personal growth and development. I began improving my fitness, my relationships, my mindset, my outlook, my finances, and much, much more. No stone was left untouched. No area of my life unaffected. It seemed as if there were no longer any limits on what I could achieve - or become.

Today, I'm blessed to be known all over the world for my courses, podcasts, books, and content. I've spoken to major corporations, packed auditoriums, and worked directly with some of the world's most influential people. Most importantly, I'm proud to say that my team and I have empowered over 300,000 people to become better versions of themselves - and completely changed quite a few lives along the way.

But it all started with that one encounter. That first domino that set off a chain reaction.

In this book, you'll find a plethora of such encounters, each one with the capacity to become your first domino. In it, you'll meet the SuperLearner® Certified Coaches; a cadre of exceptional individuals from all walks of life, ranging from technology and finance to social sciences and medicine. Over the last year, I've had the great honor and pleasure of personally selecting, working with, and training each of these exceptional individuals as they expand our mission to positively impact a million lives worldwide. What's more, I myself have learned a great deal from their diverse experiences and unique perspectives. And above all, I've been deeply inspired by their passion for personal development, and their deep-rooted commitment to empowering others.

This book is not the be-all end-all of personal development, because as you already know, personal development is a never-ending journey. What it is, however, is a jumping-off point; a treasure map that leads to other treasure maps. As you read it, you'll discover topics and perspectives that will change the way you go about your daily life. When a particular subject does pique your interest, then, I encourage you to do what any good SuperLearner would and pursue that interest. Dig deeper. Ask questions. Do your research. Get your hands dirty. Try new things. From there, you'll no-doubt discover other topics of interest - other treasure maps - creating a never-ending cycle. That cycle is your journey towards continuous improvement.

Who knows? Perhaps, a few years from now, we'll be reading all about it?

I know that the authors of this book (and I) would love nothing more.

Never Stop Learning!

-Jonathan Levi

Founder, SuperHuman Academy®

Putting Off Procrastination

Jeff Mesina – Sydney, Australia

With two master's degrees in education and over 15 years' experience helping his students and clients reach and surpass their learning goals, Jeff is excited to help you identify and implement the small changes you can make to unlock big results.

Let's Do It! Later…
We've all done it.

Heck, you might be reading this chapter right now as a cheeky way to avoid working on something else that you know you should be doing.

Hopefully, you've decided to read this to gain some insight into why people procrastinate. You want to learn to overcome procrastination and finish the projects you've been putting off.

In writing this chapter, I'll admit that I went through some extreme levels of procrastination. I'm not sure why it was more intense than usual, but if you're reading this, it means I found a way to overcome it. And by following some simple steps, you too can take your procrastination gremlins, finally get to "that thing", and turn your desires into realities.

I'm not sure what it's like for you, but when I'm gripped by procrastination, it can be all-encompassing. It might begin with a quick check of the sports scores and then, an hour or more later, I'm in bed watching a video of the "Ten Cats I Might Meet in Heaven". In moments like this, not only do I feel guilty about the time I've just wasted, but the anxiety of having to accomplish what feels like more in less time begins to build. A few more episodes like this and I'm in full-blown shutdown and have wholly identified with the procrastinator that exists in all of us. Why would I even start when it's virtually impossible to do at this point? What's the point in anything? What dogs would I meet in heaven? That's when having the ability to recover and get back on track feels like being reborn—another chance at life.

I look at the process of going from initial thought to frustration to achievement as a form of alchemy. Because being able to take the spark of an idea and manifest it into being, simply by taking small but focused steps, is truly a form of magic. What would you do if you could overcome procrastination today? What projects could you finally ship? What open loops would you close? And most importantly, what new life would you create for yourself?

I share with you the top tools and questions that help me manage my procrastination and create routines that help me to stay productive through the siren calls of impulsivity and distraction.

What is procrastination?

Procrastination comes from the Latin prefix pro-, which means 'forward' and crastinus, which means 'of tomorrow'. On the first pass, it doesn't seem that bad. Sometimes we need to put things off so we can focus on what is essential now. The process of delaying can be a good thing. When we delay our gratification, forgoing short-term gain for long-term results, it seems like we've set ourselves up for success. Wasn't that what the whole delayed-gratification marshmallow experiment carried on about? Yes, there are positive aspects to intentionally delaying activities.

Unfortunately, procrastination is an entirely different form of delay. It is the voluntary delay of an intended action which brings adverse consequences. So, despite the reward of instant gratification, the immediate comfort granted by procrastinating, you are left worse off. When we procrastinate, we already know the result is going to be harmful, and yet we still do it.

When you learn to overcome procrastination, you can move forward on your health goals, allowing you to create a body full of energy, strength, flexibility and endurance. When you move forward with your wealth goals, you might begin your investment portfolio or build that business that you've been talking about for years. When you move forward with your learning goals you develop the capabilities that could transform your life.

Piers Steele, one of the leading researchers on the science of motivation and procrastination, authored the book *The Procrastination Equation*[1] which shared factors that can influence a person's motivation towards a task which can impact their level of procrastination

$$MOTIVATION = \frac{EXPECTANCY * VALUE}{IMPULSIVITY * DELAY}$$

MOTIVATION	=	HOW ENERGIZED YOU FEEL TO ACCOMPLISH SOMETHING
EXPECTANCY	=	HOW LIKELY YOU BELIEVE YOU WILL RECEIVE THE PAYOFF FROM TAKING ACTION
VALUE	=	HOW HIGHLY YOU VALUE THE PAYOFF FROM TAKING ACTION
IMPULSIVITY	=	HOW EASILY DISTRACTED YOU ARE WHILE TAKING ACTION
DELAY	=	HOW MUCH TIME THERE IS UNTIL THE DEADLINE

We can improve our level of motivation towards a task by increasing the value and likelihood that we will receive a payoff from taking action. By decreasing our impulsivity and how far we've set our deadline, we can also enhance our level of motivation. Each of these action points can be manipulated to change the level of motivation for a task. You might turn up the value dial by reflecting on how accomplishing your goal actually has several knock-on benefits in other areas of your life. You could also decrease your impulsivity by deleting apps and blocking websites that you use to distract yourself from completing your goal. Simply turning the dials on these factors, so we have the maximum amount of motivation possible, is a great place to start on your journey to overcoming your procrastination.

Now that you have the ability to drive up your motivation by adjusting the dials of expectancy, value, impulsivity, and delay, what do you do about the times when having motivation still isn't enough. Have you ever been highly motivated to accomplish something and yet you still found yourself procrastinating? Why would we choose to delay when we know it makes us worse off? Because we dislike discomfort. So, to avoid a task we dislike or have anxiety over we simply replace it with something else that we find pleasurable. It's an easy and accessible strategy for getting what we want (to enjoy ourselves), in the short term.

Dr Timothy Pychyl, the author of *Solving the Procrastination Puzzle*[2], shares that in some situations your choice to procrastinate may not be a result of low motivation or poor-time management skills but rather actually an emotion-focused coping strategy. Many people attempt to overcome their procrastination by trying to improve their time-management effectiveness or by increasing their motivation for a given task which can yield some results. Unfortunately, even tasks approached with a detailed schedule and high levels of motivation can be subject to procrastination. If avoiding a job still provides a large enough amount of emotional relief, then a person may choose to procrastinate. Couple this with the dopamine-releasing activities that are available to us from technology, and you have a recipe for building up anxiety with simultaneously self-gratifying and self-destructive behaviour.

So how do we go about overcoming procrastination with what we now know?

One technique that we can start with is to stop asking ourselves "What will make me feel better now?" and start asking, "What will be better for me in the long-term?" If we can create clarity on how taking action on what really matters gives us a greater benefit in the long run, we are more likely to take action on it. But of course, knowing that the long-term benefits are better is not enough to change behaviour alone, as evidenced by the number of people knowing the foundations of good health and financial independence and not actually living it. It can be useful to imagine your Desired Possible Self, the person who you could be if you took the positive daily actions that you know you could, with the Feared Possible Self, the person you might become if you continue on the path of inaction. For some, being able to see the stark contrast in potential futures brings a greater sense of motivation and urgency to acting in the now. Once we've identified the future self that we want to create, we can begin to take aligned, committed actions in service to our important goals.

Another way to help relieve the anxiety caused by procrastination on big projects is to break the project down into simple, discrete tasks. When faced with overwhelm and resistance towards your goal, you can ask yourself "What is the first step of this task?". Being clear on what to do helps relieve overwhelm and then, as Timothy Pychyl says, "Just get started." This is in contrast to Nike's slogan "Just Do It!" as the emphasis is not on the completion of the task, but on initiating it. Taking the time and effort to clearly break down and schedule the essential elements of a project goes a long way in making completion of a goal manageable. But what do we do when things don't go according to plan, or when we're surprised with new projects, or find ourselves behind in our tightly scheduled calendar? Asking ourselves "Now, what *needs* to be done?" is a great way to pause, reset and reprioritize the most crucial task to take action on. Once the next key action has been identified, the next step is to start the task, and when you inevitably become distracted, ask yourself again what *needs* to be done and to start again.

Despite all of this preparation and organization, there will be times when you still don't feel like starting the important task that you've identified. During these situations, it's beneficial to realize that our attitudes can flow from our behaviour, not just the other way around. Rather than waiting for your attitude to lend itself to taking action, you can take action to modify your attitude. By taking action, we have the ability to transform how we feel towards a task or project. Furthermore, the practice of taking action, *despite* how we feel about a project, produces an antifragile mindset towards difficult work. Each time you take action when you want desperately to procrastinate, you become a little more durable.

I've found that it is useful to reflect at the end of each day and each week on the actions that I have or haven't taken. It is a great opportunity to get curious about what factors have influenced my behaviour. I can check if there are some environmental changes and behaviour algorithms I can put into place to help me do the things I want to accomplish. Small adjustments might not seem that potent in the short term, but these incremental improvements, compounded over weeks, months, and years, yield exponential growth.

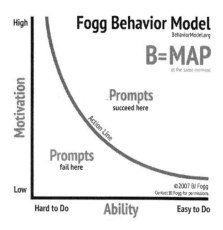

Learn more at www.behaviormodel.org

BJ Fogg, PhD, the founder and director of the Stanford Behavior Design Lab and author of the New York Times Bestseller *Tiny Habits*[3], shares, in the Fogg Behavior Model, how we can prompt a behaviour by keeping the combination of motivation and ability on or above the action line. For example, even if we possess a very low level of ability for a behaviour, if we are sufficiently motivated, that behaviour will happen. If we move along the action line towards the right, prompted behaviours will happen even with very low levels of motivation, if the behaviour is easy to do.

Breaking our projects into smaller tasks that are so easy to accomplish that we would choose to do them, despite our fluctuating levels of motivation, is a powerful tool in overcoming procrastination. I may not feel like I have the motivation to head to the gym for a 45-minute workout, but I can manage two pull-ups every time I pass the bar installed on the door to my home office. Regardless of my levels of motivation, I could easily do three squats after entering the kitchen or a couple burpees when I enter my bedroom. I can begin to create what Fogg calls Tiny Habits[3] around my home that help me take action on the goals I've set for myself, regardless of the swings in my motivation levels throughout the day.

There are some subtleties to behaviour design, but you can begin by following this simple template outlined in *Tiny Habits*[3].

"After I..., I will..."

It could be something as simple as "After I sit down at my desk, I will switch my phone to airplane mode."

You've identified a prompt that regularly happens and have linked it with a micro-action that you can take regardless of your motivation. The actions and events that reliably happen in your life act as anchors to which you can bind new beaviours.

"After I wake up, I will…"

"After I walk into the kitchen, I will…"

"After I pour myself a cup of coffee, I will…"

"After I get in my car, I will…"

"After I hear my phone ring, I will…"

"After I brush my teeth, I will…"

"After I put my head on my pillow, I will…"

It's quite powerful to build awareness around the anchors that already exist in your day. These are actions or events that happen on autopilot, without extra effort. I invite you to spend 10 minutes to identify at least 30 anchors that automatically occur during your day. Once you've identified them, you can begin to link them with the aligned actions you discovered your future self would benefit from.

As silly as it may sound, it is important to celebrate each time you accomplish one of your Tiny Habits. Fogg summarizes his research in three words: "**Emotions create habits.**"[3] When we celebrate after a behaviour, we create positive feelings and wire the new routine in our brains. Instead of building the procrastination habit by getting the positive emotion from avoiding discomfort, we get the positive emotion from taking the tiniest step forward. And the beauty is that we can do it again and again and again.

It takes some time and experimentation to tweak and refine your Tiny Habit recipes so that they work on auto-pilot, but doing so not only builds momentum and confidence in the achievement of your goals, it also helps you create an identity as someone who takes necessary daily actions to create the life you desire.

You've done it. You've finished this chapter.

Hopefully, you've learnt some new tools that you can immediately begin testing and tweaking to apply to your personal goals. Give yourself a pat on the back. You've earned it.

Now excuse me while I celebrate.

Expanding Your Brain Bandwidth: Eliminating Complaints and Excuses and Leveraging Judgement

Antoine Hiolle - Braga, Portugal
Antoine is a Software Engineer, building the next generation sensors for autonomous driving, and Superhuman Academy coach. He focuses on the study and mastery of new technologies, human optimisation by self-experimentation, and the constant growth of the people he coaches.

The Three Behaviours

We all want to focus on the activities and projects that make our lives more exciting and fulfilling. Learning new skills and applying them to our work and private life requires motivation and commitment. We need to focus our time and energy on the behaviours and activities that move the needle in the direction of growth and happiness. There are many obstacles on that road. Growth and progress come from hard work. As Josh Waitzkin states in the *Art of Learning:* "Growth comes at the point of resistance"[4].

Pushing through this point, this wall, is the necessary step to transformation. It helps us build resilience and experience the feeling of success on the other side. But the resistance brings with it an immediate negative experience. The experience is even worse when not in a state of mind prepared to cope with its negativity. Many outside events can prevent us from keeping the focus and dedication required to overcome resistance and the patience to continue working on ourselves and challenging projects we want to complete. Externalities consume our mental energy and impede us from attacking our work with a clear focus and a positive mindset. This leads us to lose motivation, become depressed, postpone essential deliberate practice, and view our work and private life in a negative light.

Whether we can control these external events or not, we can control how we respond. We need not internalize them nor let them define us. We can take control of our response, we can recapture our focus, and we can redirect our paths.

This chapter tackles three specific behaviours, three common responses to externalities, that cripple our performance and stunt our development.

The first is our urge to complain about the people and events in our lives.

The second is the compulsion to make excuses for our failures instead of bettering ourselves.

The third is the tendency to pass unnecessary judgement on people and subjects instead of keeping a fluid opinion and position until we are well-informed and need to take action.

These three behaviours have three characteristic properties.

First, they multiply. Complaints lead to more complaints, excuses breed excuses, and judgment invites judgement.

Second, they cost us valuable brain bandwidth during stressful times.

Third, they consume our time and yield no long-term benefit.

How can we substitute or eliminate these self-destructive behaviours?
What does a life free of complaining look like?
Who could we become if we stopped making excuses and took ownership of our actions?
How might we transform if we let go of unnecessary judgement?

The tactics presented here demonstrate how complaining, making excuses, and judging can be optimized for success and happiness or entirely eradicated.

Why We Complain
Why do we complain?
Well, not you specifically, because you never complain...
But how are you so sure?

Consider the following definition.

"A complaint is a verbal statement expressing your dissatisfaction about something or someone without providing next steps to fix the problem."[5]

This definition distinguishes complaining from honest, constructive feedback. Feedback is different as it aims at producing immediate, productive change in a perceived event or behaviour. Complaining only provides an outlet for negative thoughts and feelings without any effort to correct the situation.

Here are some typical examples:
"The food in this restaurant was bland", "This place is too loud", "This guy cut me off on the highway", "You don't listen to me", "the trains are always late", "It is too hot", "It's too cold", "John is always rude to me", "I don't like my job", and so on.
Sound familiar?

These examples fulfil the definition. They also have a distinct feature. They are worthless. The world does not bend to accommodate you when you complain. Your mood does not lighten as you air your dissatisfaction. Neither you nor the people around you are positively affected.

Then why do we do it?

Sure, complaining allows us to verbalize, externalize, and even "vent" a bit. Complaining makes us feel as though we have taken action. They give us the illusion of control. We "retaliated against injustice". Words. Just words that we assembled and sent crashing into the void.

This is a widely accepted behaviour. Take note of how many conversations start with a complaint. Where do they lead? Nowhere.

We bond with our friends and relatives by complaining about the same events and people. How backwards is that? Our closest relationships are founded on shared discontentment!

We vent to our friends and family. They understand. They like it! It is an invitation to blow some steam of their own. We listen. We agree. The cycle repeats.

On the other hand, complain to the wrong person, someone who disagrees, and you unleash endless debates and arguments where no good is produced.

The truth is, complaining kills happiness.

Complaining as a means of release and bonding reveals a profound misunderstanding of the process. It is useful to identify objects and agents that cause discomfort, distress, and dissatisfaction; however, if you leave the process at this step, you release nothing - you improve nothing. Your complaints accumulate to haunt you and undermine your relationships.

How to Stop Complaining?

The answer may surprise you. A Kansas City minister named Will Bowen came up with a simple system, and it works. Popularized by Tim Ferris in his world-renowned self-improvement blog[5], the elegant solution takes an unlikely form: a bracelet.

To eradicate complaining from your life, all you need to do is slap on a bracelet and follow one simple rule: Whenever you catch yourself complaining, take the bracelet off your wrist, and place it around the other. Do this until you have gone 21 consecutive days without switching the bracelet. That's it. Easy.

Why a bracelet? First, it is always within reach. It is always visible. You can do it under a table. No one will take offence if you do this; most people won't even notice. You can use any bracelet, but it is best if the switch takes between 10 and 30 seconds. Consider a watch or bracelet with a clasp that is difficult to secure with your non-dominant hand.

Capitalize on these moments, as you make the transfer. Use this time to look inside, reflect on what happened, accept it, and let it go.

This isn't a form of negative reinforcement, like wrapping your knuckles with a ruler; the bracelet is a constant reminder of your commitment to change and the switches provide you with the time to reprogram. You are converting complaints from a hindrance to a trigger to generate positive change.

If you have ever meditated and managed to watch your thoughts come and go without clinging to them, this should sound familiar. Our thoughts come and go, if we let them, so will your urge to complain.

What happens next?

Depending on how often you used to complain, swear, or criticize unnecessarily, in two days, you will feel the need to stop it as it happens; you may even catch it sneaking up on you. You then have a choice. Go through with it, share your grievance with the world, even if you are alone, and watch as nothing improves. Or, let it go.

When you choose the latter, the effects are profound. Your relationship with complaining will change, both inside and out. Internally, you will see that nothing is gained, and the relief you may have felt, or the entitlement you thought you had will appear brittle and empty. Externally, people will notice what you are doing. Some will think it is great and reinforce the positive outcome of such a behavioural change experiment. Others might think it silly - that trying to get rid of or reduce one's complaints is pointless or even detrimental. Either way, I encourage you to invite them into your challenge. Just say "I am studying how to deal better with negative thoughts and how I express them. I want to see what life is like without complaining. Can I ask a favour? Whenever you catch me complaining or being negative, can you call me out? If you do, I'll move the bracelet and my streak resets!"

Suddenly, it's a game. People will try to catch you complaining to make you move the bracelet. The results are twofold. First you will have a veritable army of accountability partners helping you in your efforts. Second, the people around you will become conscious of their own negativity and some will rethink their own outlook and behaviour. Do not be surprised if your entire environment begins to positively transform.

After three days, you will be much better at spotting complaints forming in your mind. Everyone around you will be invested in your success or failure, either way, they will hold you to your commitment.

21 days is a long time to go without complaining. To many, unthinkable. Depending on your baseline, this might be a hard goal to reach. But most worthy goals are.

In any case, the reduction in negative thoughts and voiced complaints will change you. That much is guaranteed.

First, by taking on this challenge and seeing it through, you will begin to believe in your ability to do hard things. You will also discover your triggers and the environments in which you are most likely to curse and complain. This could be your workplace, doing chores, dealing with relatives, shopping, queueing, working out.

Knowing this, you will be prepared to handle yourself carefully and deliberately, with tolerance and self-compassion.

Second, after a week or so, your mind will provide you with shortcuts.

This is where all of this becomes a powerful tool for anyone who wants to achieve great endeavours. Anything significant and worthwhile will be hard. By being hard, it will lead to quick and frequent failures. These failures bring negativity, which can often turn into complaints and criticism, turning you away from the goal.

After a couple of weeks of switching the bracelet from wrist to wrist, having trained your mind to anticipate negative thoughts, and avoiding uttering them, your mind will give you a way out.

The few seconds you used to switch this bracelet from one side to the other will be provided to you before you trigger any negative reactions. These few seconds of stillness, calm and silence, allow you to let it go and forego the bracelet switch. That is a win.

A few days later, the switch will provide your mind the time and motivation to go one step further.

Instead of merely exhibiting the behaviour less, your mind will provide you with options to stop the onset of the negative feeling at its source if at all possible.

You will automatically work to solve the problem if it is something you can solve or accept and cope with the inevitable if it is outside your powers.

Your mind will have discovered the "default aggressive" mode that Jocko Willink speaks about in his book *Extreme Ownership*.[81]

The aggressive part has nothing to do with being rude or violent towards other people. It pushes you to tackle what you can tackle now. Handle it instead of complaining about it or waiting for someone to fix it for you. Change the way you will approach this specific problem next time, write it down if you need to, ask for help - anything that may help you avoid the avoidable.

I learned the bracelet trick from Tim Ferris three years ago and I use it to this day. I did not consider myself a chronic complainer. After all, what did I have to complain about? I was not living in particularly dire circumstances. My work was compelling, my marriage was stable, we enjoyed frequent vacations, I was practicing the sports and activities I loved, my social life was vibrant. No one would describe me as a negative person. And yet, as I observed my behaviours more closely, I was shocked to find complaining in every social interaction. Nothing drastic, just a few comments here and there that I had considered useful criticism. Life wasn't perfect after all. When you work and live with people in our uncertain world, things will often go wrong. But an honest examination showed me that my "useful criticism" was, in fact, complaining, and it was running unchecked. Every meeting and every discussion had a complaint or a negative comment in it.

That is when I decided to start wearing the bracelet.

The first day was a challenge. I needed to remember to check myself. That took a while, but after I involved my friends and coworkers, it got easier. The real challenge was to count the number of times I switched the bracelet. The first day I was above fifty, not counting the times I didn't catch. That was a painful eye-opener. But soon, it turned into a fun game.

The more people I exposed to the experiment, the better feedback I got. After a week, I was switching the bracelet less than five times a day. I included swearing, gossiping, and any negative verbal output that was not constructive.

The result was total transformation. In a few weeks, the counterproductive behaviour began to disappear. My conditioning was being reversed. When some hardship presented itself, and I needed to communicate it, my mind and will had changed their reactions. My brain went straight for the design of a solution and its immediate implementation.

My conversations became shorter yet far more pleasant. I did not need to explain the negative setting, complain about it, get someone to agree with me, distribute blame, and then propose a solution. I just got straight to the solution.

I reduced my swearing to almost nothing, even when alone. I changed the way I use sarcasm – which is fun to me – limiting it to an audience and subjects where the negativity would not spread or contaminate my life or relationships.

I replaced complaining about people with direct and timely feedback. If someone did something unpleasant leading to unwanted consequences, I just started mentioning it directly (most often in private) in a clear way. Feedback is simple. Describe the event or behaviour then explain what negative consequences it has and propose your wish for change. Most often, people are grateful.

I stopped gossiping. Talking negatively about people without them present is useless.

I have not managed to stop complaining entirely. It still sneaks up on me sometimes when extremely tired, surprised, or scared by something dangerous or new. That is OK. I just acknowledge it, move my bracelet, and never complain about it again.

More Good

As in meditation practice, this moment that your brain gives you before you give outlet to the negativity will occur during or before most negative episodes. You will probably feel the same feeling before someone else complains, gossips, or curses without funny intent. You can use this time to douse the fire before it takes. This is a gift for yourself, as you will not experience the other side of the flow of negativity and you will be able to redirect conversations before things turn unpleasant.

You might also notice an increase in your pain tolerance. The onset will feel the same, and you can apply the same mindset to it. Most pains go away. And the ones which do not, need to be taken seriously.

Your clarity and attitude towards these small adverse events that happen daily will increase, and you will discover new ways to be resilient and face ever-growing challenges.

You will discover and redefine your limits as well. What can you tolerate? What will you choose to endure?

A Bracelet for Everything

I wrote the prior section about complaining because that is where the bracelet challenge originated, but the bracelet trick can be used to analyse and curb any negative behaviour. Any action that is conditional and triggered by external and internal stimuli can, in theory, be studied and changed using this methodology. It is especially true if the behaviour is automatic and compulsive; the bracelet trick opens a valuable time window to analyse and alter your behaviour.

Whether you want to tackle smoking, drinking, procrastinating, or attention lapses, the same technique applies. When you spot yourself doing or wanting the behaviour you are trying to curb, switch the bracelet, take your time to look inside and ask if this is really what you want for yourself.

Excuse Me

No one likes excuses, and yet not a day passes without hearing them. Maybe you are a fluent user.

Here is the truth. Excuses undermine progress and personal development. Imagine you are late for a professional appointment - there was traffic. Fair, right? You use the traffic as an excuse, and people "understand".

But what do they understand really? You were unable to cope with a phenomenon as common as traffic. Are you new to town? Are you new to cities and their problems? Could you not plan ahead better?

These are just a few examples of what credit you may have lost using such an excuse.

Of course, there might be real, horrible events outside of your control.

"I am in the hospital; I broke my leg in a car accident"

"There was a death in the family"

If someone asks you for the reasons for a particular outcome, feel free to share it. One negative event has many causes, but don't use events that could have been planned for or avoided as an excuse for breaking commitments; this is just failing to take responsibility for your own incompetence.

The bottom line is this: making excuses is a nasty habit for your brain. Something does not pan out as you planned; your brain will find every excuse. Skipped a workout? "It was raining, and instead I kept reading this book and prepared a nice meal for my partner... and I did not sleep well last night so I might have gotten injured; by skipping I will be in better shape and I will go tomorrow."

This is a colossal waste of brainpower, not to mention miserable conditioning for your mind. The more you produce and use excuses, the better you will become at making them. Your brain will have a laundry list prepared to explain any failure.

Instead of going down this road, there is an easier path that is akin to how we dealt with complaining. Let your brain take one more step and skip the excuse. Do not even mention it. Do not think about it - even if it is true.

Whatever commitment you did not manage to fulfil, let yourself come up with a way to fulfil it, now. Reduce scope. Extend the deadline with something else on top. If you could not and needed help, ask for help and tell the truth.

"We are not ready to deliver yet. To be sure your project would be successful, I pivoted and got help, we will deliver in a week's time instead of tomorrow. This will be worth it."
And make it worth it.
"Hey, I will be late to our meeting, can I arrive 20 minutes late or can we reschedule for 3PM tomorrow?"
"I did not do my full workout today so I will go cycling for an hour."

And so on. You have to mean it though, and not use this tool to cover for your laziness, procrastination, or lack of foresight. Delays and problems happen. If you aren't failing frequently, you aren't doing enough hard things. If your failure has a reason based on facts that are worth sharing, you should. Everybody will learn from it. If you mess up, it happens, just clean it up and do not make and use excuses. Ever.

I stopped this behaviour some years ago. I realised I was saying "sorry" too many times. I rarely was sorry. Things happen. Good and bad. When bad things happened that compromised the outcome of a task or commitment to someone else, I used to come up with a well-crafted excuse, completely unavoidable, wrapped up in a beautiful argument to deflect any possible blame. That took a fair amount of brainpower and worked most times. If a project was late, I had to do this to feel better about it, and prevent my counterparts from associating me with my failures.

Since then, I have avoided using the word "Sorry" unless I step on someone's foot. I take responsibility instead. I try to come up with a solution that will prevent or address the situation in the future. If I cannot, I ask for help. This is how collaboration occurs.

The crucial difference is that it happens right when needed and not after spending time and energy trying to look like it is not my fault.

Open Judgement

Judgement is a word with many uses. We use it every day in many different ways.

Where will you eat? Who do you trust? Which colour suits you best? Which career do you want to follow? Is this person a worthy partner? Should I eat out?

Judgement has one simple trait that makes it powerful and dangerous. It is final.

What we are exploring here is not the absence of judgement and its final nature; we need this. This section is about unnecessary judgement.

We get asked our opinions on topics on which we are far from being an expert, and yet we deliver them as though they are final and correct.

We define ourselves by what we do, we label people we don't know, we pick sides at every chance without any real purpose other than picking a side.

Sometimes we are wrong. Usually, we are wrong. In these cases, we defend ourselves, spend enormous mental energy to work out a path to still being right or not-that-wrong in light of some new evidence. We debate others based on these judgements to no avail. They do not know either.

We spend our judgement credits like they are free. But are they?

Imagine all positions you have taken, all opinions you have defended, and all the debates you entered as though they meant something to you. You will be held to those positions by others. You spent your credits. Unless it is your profession or you just enjoy debating for its own sake, it is rarely productive.

Imagine you reserved judgements only for subjects that truly matter. Right Now. To you. To your family or relatives who need your opinion to take action.

There would be only a few of those. Imagine the extra brain bandwidth you are creating, the time you are freeing, and the flexibility you are giving yourself.

How? Simple, yet not easy.

One simple rule. If your opinion or judgement does not need to be final, do not make it so. Keep it open. Try: "I don't know. I need to check." Or better, if there is no need to care, don't. Keep your credits.

When to use and keep a final judgement? Once more, a simple answer: just before you need to act on it.

If you need to act, you need a solution, a path, or a plan. This comes out of your judgement. This is when we use expressions such as "good" or "bad" judgement.

Good judgement comes from a few sources: preparation, humility, and time.

Your Next Steps

We have covered the negative consequences of three common yet powerful behaviours that drain your brain bandwidth with no positive outcome. Complaining is a master thief of time and a positive attitude is required daily when you are committed to your unbounded personal growth. Excuses are a distraction that draw your focus from the solution space and train you to worry about appearances. Final judgement is only needed if immediate action needs to be taken, not whenever we engage in conversation or explore a new subject.

You do not want to be this person: "Hey man, I am late to meet you. There is horrible traffic where I am. God I hate this part of town. People really cannot drive, I am so tired of this, I will move to the countryside."

Instead, embrace the following recipe:
- Get yourself a bracelet and start wearing it now.
- Tell family and friends you are giving up complaining.
- Switch the bracelet every time you complain.
- Approach every failure by finding a solution and not an excuse. Get help as soon as you can if you need to.
- Do not make judgemental statements in conversations.
- Finalise your judgement only before actions.
- Enjoy the time and peace that comes with these changes.

Once you commit to this approach to deal with negative experiences and associated behaviours, you will increasingly improve your focus on what is important and consequently accelerate your growth and personal success. As a bonus, your social interactions and outlook on life and its hardships will transform for the better. You will still face negative experiences and resistance the more challenges you take, but you will be better prepared to deal with these than ever before.

Asking for Miracles

"The most incredible thing about miracles is that they happen."

- G.K. Chesterton

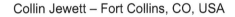

Collin Jewett – Fort Collins, CO, USA

Collin Jewett is an engineer, author, and Director of the Superhuman Academy Coaching Program. When he is not coaching others to rediscover the joy of learning, Collin can be found playing guitar, writing his next book, practicing Brazilian Jui Jitsu, or exploring the world with his wife and adventure partner, Jess.

The Nature of Miracles

There are 2 components to a miracle; a miracle is inexplicable, and it is welcome.

A miracle is an inexplicable, welcome event.

What is fascinating about this definition is that it means both components of miracles are subjective. And if miracles are purely subjective, it follows that their occurrence is entirely dependent upon one's perspective. This isn't a wholly novel idea. My favorite quote from the English Philosopher G.K. Chesterton illustrates it nicely "An adventure is only an inconvenience rightly considered. An inconvenience is only an adventure wrongly considered." In other words: your perspective is your reality. This idea, while enticing, had never been

37

tangible to me before a moment of internal collapse. It was a pleasant thought, but it wasn't something I could do anything with, other than try to be more easy going. But after that fateful day in 2016, strange things began to happen, welcome events that I could not quite explain: miracles. It wasn't until years, and many miracles later, that I recognized the cause of this change. This is the cause, the story, and the secret to invite miracles into your life.

"Time's up! Pencils down!" 700 pencils clattered on lapboards throughout Elliot Hall. 700 test packets shuffled back into the correct page order. 699 students clambered over folding chairs and eachother to turn in their work. I sat, staring dumbly at the stack of pages on my lap. 2 weeks. That was all I could think of. 2 weeks, I studied for this every night. I thought of the late nights, the friends I had turned down, Jess's worried face. The theater was beginning to empty. If I stayed much longer the teaching assistants would suspect me of cheating, so I rose slowly from my seat and drifted down the long hall to the stage. My unfinished exam slid into the pile and disappeared.

I remember the walk home. It was dark out, wet, and cold. The streets were bustling, as usual, but I didn't notice. I felt numb. It was hard to believe that just a year earlier, I was a rockstar. I graduated high school with straight A's, no problem, I had been accepted to the only university I applied to, the engineering program no less, one of the top schools in the world. I was one of only 12 applicants to get into my choice fraternity. I had a car, family, friends, girlfriend... the future was bright. 4 years of cruising through college and I'd be living the American dream with a wife, a cushy engineering job, and a nice house in the richest suburb in America. Yet here I was, neglecting my friends, girlfriend, and newly divorced parents to study all the time, stepping in puddles on my way home from my third failed exam in 4 days.

That night I wrote the following email to my academic advisor:

Date: 11/8/2016

Subject: SOS

Dear Ms. _____,

I just got home from a Calculus 3 exam and, like the last three or four exams I have taken, I think I failed. I am working extremely hard, my social life is dwindling to nothing, but I just can't seem to make ends meet academically. I don't know if I can afford tutoring and my class schedule and house responsibilities have prevented me from being able to attend SI or go to office hours. I am getting desperate. Do you have any advice or guidance for a willing, dedicated student who is failing miserably?

Thank you,

Collin Jewett

The events that followed changed my life forever...

Slow is the New Fast

I trudged out of the room, embarrassed, but hopeful. My academic advisor had referred me to the Disability Resource Center and, after basically crying in front of a stranger for an hour, I was told that I had severe testing anxiety and I was to be given extra time and a quiet space for all my future exams. I had officially been diagnosed as a mess and was prescribed some chill pills. My grades improved a bit after that, and I thought maybe everything was going to be ok. But something had changed. You see, up until this point, I had clung to the belief that I was smarter than everyone else, that I was somehow uniquely capable, endowed with a special gift of clarity and intuition. In that meeting, as I cried like a baby in front of the stranger at the DRC, I stopped believing that. That meeting marked a shift in my identity. I believed I was special only in that I was especially weak under pressure, that I was uniquely incapable of facing the challenges all my fellow students seemed to overcome with ease. For the first time in my life, I accepted that I was the "slow kid." That identity shift changed everything: the way I thought and spoke, the way I interacted with others, the way I communicated, the way I saw the world. I didn't adopt a victim mentality, I just decided I was really stupid. While I don't generally recommend philosophical implosion as a path to success, it played an important role in my life at that time. First, it broke my pride. And while the resulting lack of confidence wasn't great, it forced me to take a deeper look at who I really was. Second, it made me question. Prior to that identity shift, I believed that I had gotten to where I was by having answers. Younger me was always full of "sage" advice and happy to dispense such unsolicited wisdom at a moment's notice. The truth is, my answers had never brought me anything but disappointment. Everything I had was handed to me; the most I had done for my success was not turn down the gifts that were showered on me by friends, family, teachers, and God. As a newly minted "slow kid," I started to ask questions again. That's when it began.

"When nothing is sure, everything is possible."

- Margaret Drabble

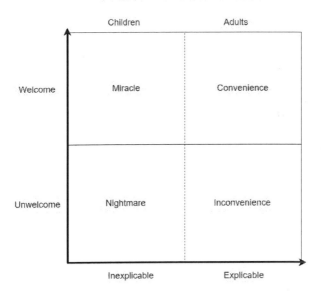

Explicable vs. Welcome

	Children	Adults
Welcome	Miracle	Convenience
Unwelcome	Nightmare	Inconvenience
	Inexplicable	Explicable

Closets are for Clothes

Adults live in the realm of convenience and inconvenience; children live in the realm of miracle and nightmare. For a child, nothing is sure and therefore, everything is possible. For an adult, everything is sure and therefore, few things are possible. This is not to say that adults know everything and predict the future, but rather that they are experts in their own opinions and wizards of backfilled reasoning and rationalization. "Inexplicable" is, for an adult, an explanation in and of itself. It is used to describe events that surely have a logical explanation but are too tedious or tragic to explore. "Inexplicable" is the end, rather than the beginning, of inquiry. The opposite is true of children. Inexplicable events are objects of wonderment, even obsession. They are mysteries to dive into and swim around in. They are both the monster in the closet and the princess in the tower. Children understand intuitively that you cannot have one without the other. At some point, adults throw the princess out with the monster. The closet is for clothes and the tower is for guided tours on holiday. The consequences to this transition are many and diverse. On the one hand, it is important to acquire grounding principles in order to be a functional, contributing member of society, on the other, it is critical to retain a sense of wonderment to go on extraordinary adventures and live a life filled with miracles. When I lost myself, I found both.

The Obstacle Mindset

I stated at the beginning of the chapter that miracles are inexplicable, welcome events and are therefore subjective and perspective dependent. Consequently, your mindset determines your miracles.

Some people have a problem for every solution. They don't have original ideas, but they can shoot holes in anything and feel great about their contribution.

Some people have a solution to everyone else's problems. You know the type. Complexity and nuance be damned, their approach worked for them; it will work for you.

Ironically, these people are often one in the same. They were certainly me; maybe they are you.

If you relate to one or both of those descriptions, you have adopted an Obstacle Mindset, and you are in good company. The Obstacle Mindset is an unnecessary side effect of the necessary process of growing up. As children, most of us are taught to behave a certain way, to speak a certain way, and to treat others a certain way. These rules governing speech and behavior are designed to help us become functional adults, to act in a manner that is socially acceptable. To use a bowling analogy (because, why not?) these rules are like bumpers placed over the gutters to keep the ball (our behavior) in the lane (within the boundaries of what is socially acceptable). Over time, external guidelines are internalized and become mental filters; what we cannot say and do becomes what we cannot think or imagine. As we grow into adulthood, rather than remove these bumpers, many of us pile on additional filters. Not only do we not bowl into the gutters, now we roll the ball down a slide so that it stays dead center in the lane every time (we develop ingrained patterns of thoughts and behavior and do not deviate). "Look mom, no effort!" This is an oversimplification and I  am certainly not suggesting that people do not change over time – they do – or that they always live by the same rules instilled in them as children – they often don't. My point is that the Obstacle Mindset, which manifests in perfectionism, close-mindedness, and a lack of creativity, has deep roots and, while it is not healthy, it is normal. The good news is, there are simple and immediate actions you can take to trade your Obstacle Mindset for a Possibility Mindset and rediscover miracles in your life.

The Possibility Mindset

The Possibility Mindset is key to inviting miracles into your life. If a miracle is an inexplicable, welcome event, the world must become less explicable, and you must become more welcoming. I am not suggesting that you become willfully ignorant and lower your standards, rather that you run towards the unknown and accept yourself. There is infinite mystery in the universe. We do not become cynical, uncreative adults because we learn all there is to learn, we become cynical, uncreative adults because we learn enough to "get by" and ignore the rest.

Therefore, decreasing the explicability of the world is not about ignoring what we know, it is about acknowledging and exploring what we don't. "When nothing is sure, everything becomes possible." When I lost my self-confidence, I began to doubt my answers. By doubting my answers, I returned to the questions: deep questions, basic questions, downright "stupid" questions. The more I asked, the more I realized there was to ask. The more I learned, the more I realized there was to learn. And so, paradoxically, the more I expanded my knowledge, the more the infinite mystery of the universe expanded. Creativity is the art of coming up with answers. Not the answers, just answers. The uncreative person sees one answer for every question; the creative person sees endless possible answers to every question. So, creativity is not about correctness, it is about possibility. This is why the Obstacle Mindset prevents creative thinking. The Obstacle Mindset tells us that there is one correct way and that all other ways are fraught with difficulty and error. The Possibility Mindset tells us that there are infinite ways and encourages us to explore.

How to Ask for Miracles

Through a string of miracles in my own life, I went from failing student with no job prospects, to successful student with companies fighting over me, to senior level engineer, to accelerated learning coach, to coaching program director in 4 years. As a coach, when I would start working with a new client, we would first focus on improving memory. Sometimes this worked well, often it did not.

Many of the techniques involved creative visualization and some people simply weren't creative. Not one to give up on vast swaths of the population, I began incorporating creativity exercises into the early phases of training. I had the clients do things like think of as many alternative uses for an object as they could in 5 minutes. This yielded some improvement, but not much; turns out, uncreative people are bad at creativity exercises. The exercises helped slightly in that they forced uncreative types to push themselves, but they did not lead to the giant leap in original, lateral thinking I was hoping for. Then I had an idea. To help them think of more uses for an object, for example, I provided a list of questions that they could ask.

1. *What are the key geometrical features of the object? -> What else shares those features?*
2. *What is the fundamental purpose of this object? -> What else shares that purpose?*
3. *What other objects could I replace this one with?*
4. *If you were in [X situation] how could this object help you?*
5. *What are the components of the object? -> how could they be used separately?*
   ...

All the sudden, clients who had previously been able to think of only 12 uses in 5 minutes, could come up with 25+! Breakthrough! There was only one problem: I had come up with the questions. And, furthermore, these questions were only useful for this exercise; this sudden improvement didn't represent an increase in creativity overall. But the problem had shifted. I had just proven that, if the "uncreative" people had the right list of questions, they could generate ideas nearly as fast and effectively as their more naturally creative counterparts. So, the problem wasn't with their ability to come up with answers, but with questions. If creativity is the art of coming up with answers, they didn't have a creativity problem; they had a problem with coming up with questions. They had a curiosity problem.

I recalled a journaling exercise I had learned at some point, used for self-reflection, called "100 Questions." The point of the exercise was to explore your thought patterns and desires by writing 100 questions, whatever came to mind, in one sitting, without stopping. The point of the original exercise wasn't to get good at asking questions, but it was worth a shot. I had all of my clients (about 20 people at the time) try it the next day. Sure enough, the ones who excelled at the creative exercises were able to perform the task in 20 minutes or less, while members of the "uncreative" group took 40 minutes - 2 hours! The correlation was 100%. How well they did on the creativity exercises mapped exactly to how well they did on this new "curiosity" exercise. This result was interesting, but I wasn't sure what it meant.

I spoke to each of my clients about their performance to see if any insights would present themselves. Thankfully, they did, loud and clear. Despite clearly stating in the instructions that there were NO bad questions and that they should write anything and everything that came to mind AND that they didn't have to share their questions with me (in case it would prevent them from writing anything embarrassing), everyone in the "uncreative" group sent me their list of questions and asked if they were good enough. When I asked them about the exercise, each shared that the exercise had been extremely difficult and exhausting and they wanted to know if they had done it right. I explained, again, that the only goal was to write 100 questions as quickly as possible and that there were no other rules, no bad questions, and no grades.

And then, I had everyone do it again.

Those who had excelled the first time, excelled again, those who had struggled the first time... *cut their times in half.* All I had done between trials 1 and 2 was reassure those who had struggled that they were doing the exercise correctly. And, after this initial, massive improvement, they continued to make incremental progress until they could generate questions nearly as fast as the original creative group. What had held these clients back, more than anything, from accelerating their learning, was not a bad memory, it wasn't even a lack of creativity, it was an Obstacle Mindset that manifested in perfectionism and fear of open inquiry. Once overcome, the gap between the "creatives" and "uncreatives" dwindled from a canyon to sliver.

People are different, and differences in ability level and outcomes are to be expected, but this experience and my own story taught me that most of the time, when it comes to learning, and when it comes to miracles, mindset plays a much larger role than genetics. While your ability to change your total creative capacity may be limited, your ability to access that creative capacity is not. By simply asking questions and generating a burning, fearless curiosity, you can unlock your creativity, your memory, and your superhuman learning ability.

Since this first experiment, curiosity and mindset training have become the bedrock of our accelerated learning coaching program. By asking questions without fear of judgement, you can break free from the Obstacle Mindset and adopt the Possibility Mindset. By asking questions, you can rediscover the wonder of childhood and invite miracles back into your life. But, what about the nightmares? What about the monster in the closet? Shutting out the unknown doesn't make it go away. The fact is, the darkness, the monsters, and the nightmares are all real and they are worse than you thought they were as a kid. But fear is a choice. You can let fear run your life. You can choose to give it free rein of your mind, let it stifle your curiosity. You can trade your life of miracles for a life of convenience to make it happy. It's your choice. I choose miracles.

Building Unstoppable Success Momentum

Peter A. Anglin – London, England

Peter is the Director and Founder of Magnificent Momentum – a Digital Marketing consultancy and coaching business. His goal over the next 5 years is to enable 100,000 people in the UK to see, believe, and realise their inherent success potential.

Defining Success

How do you define success? Is there a single, ubiquitous definition that everyone tends to agree on? Does it even really matter whether there is or isn't?

Hmmm? – it's a discussion that can and does seem to roll on and on!

But you know what? One can discuss all one wants. Ultimately, where the rubber meets the road is in *achieving* success, not talking about it. And how to achieve success in a repeatable, proven, and systematic way is exactly what you're going to discover once you've read and taken action on the information within this chapter!

You're going to get the same system I used in my life to start and run my own business www.magnificentmomentum.com and its spinoff business www.knowingtheledge.com, totally from scratch.

51

You see, for a long time I was not fully happy at work and wanted to create a new path for myself – can you relate?

What I wanted to do was start helping individuals improve their quality of life via some kind of direct action, and also help small businesses (mainly in the complementary and alternative health sectors) improve their website performance so *they* could reach and help more people – an indirect action.

Ultimately, I wanted to make more of a positive difference in the lives of more people around the world!

Initially, I wasn't sure on the details of helping individuals directly, but I knew I'd figure that out.

I had the Digital Marketing skills because I specialised in Search Engine Optimisation (SEO), so helping businesses improve online would be straightforward; that was my day job already. I just needed to figure out how to kick off my business and get clients.

Some of the coaching skills were already there too - a Diploma in Performance Coaching and a nearly completed Life Coaching diploma, but I needed something more. I wasn't quite sure what, but I knew the answer would reveal itself.

I held my intention to find that answer whilst I was working on the business aspect of my goal, and the answer did indeed arrive. It came in not 1, but 2 different ways, and both from unexpected emails!

As a result of taking action on those emails, I'm now directly working with individuals through my Accelerated Learning coaching role with the SuperHuman Academy, and as an Energy Codes Certified Facilitator with the Morter Institute (the Energy Codes is a 7-step system I teach to individuals to help them heal imbalances, reconnect with their spirituality, and awaken to their true magnificence).

Plus, I'm helping individuals indirectly as a Business Growth Mentor and Digital Marketing consultant via my company Magnificent Momentum.

I set out to achieve a specific set of goals over 2 years, and I have done just that. My plan was to:

✓ Change jobs and become a department head at a new company to get more commercial experience

✓ Create a concept for and develop a main business, website, and client-getting plan.

✓ Figure out a great way to help individuals directly and then train and get qualified in that method.

So, if you're ready to receive the same ground-breaking blueprint I used for achieving my goals, then read on my friend, read on…

Whatever business or personal growth goals you want to achieve in the future, you're going to need an effective plan to deliver that success. And the execution of that plan will see you starting to generate momentum as a result.

However, unless you know how to generate the right *type* of momentum, you'll likely find yourself falling short of achieving your goals and missing your targets.

It's important, then, to make sure you are…

Planning for Growth Correctly and Creating Success Momentum Along the Way

First, let's start by looking at the definition of "momentum":

Momentum

/mə'mɛntəm/

noun

1. PHYSICS
   The quantity of motion of a moving body, measured as a product of its mass and velocity.
2. The impetus gained by a moving object.

From the definition, you may have noticed momentum indeed relates to Newton's 1st Law of Motion (yes, that's right – Sir Isaac Newton; he of the alleged apple-on-head fame!)

That law states…

"Every object will remain in a state of rest or uniform motion unless acted upon by an external force ".

"Errrm – excuse me?"

Ok – translating that into layman's terms in our context means this:

Every situation (object) you are currently facing will stay the same (remain in a state of uniform motion) unless you execute a plan (external force) against it to make it change.

By way of a simple business example…

Imagine your online business is currently and consistently generating £X per month, and you want that to increase to £2X per month within the next three months.

Unless you create and implement a plan to make that happen, save a sudden and unexpected upturn in your industry, in 3 months, you'll more than likely still be generating the same rate of £X per month.

"Yes – not a particularly earth-shattering revelation," you may say – and I agree; it's pretty damn obvious.

But here's the thing…

Though simple and obvious it may seem, it's not easy to do – because if it were, there would not have been so many books on success achievement already written, and people wouldn't still be buying them!

The question to ask, then, is: "where within this simple equation is the difficulty in creating these successful outcomes?"

Wherein are those pesky trap doors concealed?

The answer is…

Your Future Goal Failures Lie Dormant and Buried Inside the Structure and Execution of Your Plans

You see, there are certain aspects of a success plan that many people often neglect to include and address. And it's these omissions that cause them to fail.

Although you end up taking "massive action," you still fall short of the target.

Irrespective of whether the plan is there to achieve goals for your business, professional, or personal life, the work you put in will often lead to disappointing results.

The reason?…

Because you failed to build the right kind of momentum from the actions you took – the type of momentum that is critical in helping lead you to the success you are striving for.

You need to generate success momentum, and there are four specific aspects your growth plan needs to include for that to happen…

1. **Discern your starting position before you begin the goal-setting process.**
2. **Set your SMART goals and define any characteristics you feel will be needed to attain them.**
3. **Take constant and focused action only in the direction of your goals.**
4. **Be accountable and take full ownership of the results and outcomes generated in step 3.**

Now you've been introduced to the 4, critical, building blocks of successful planning that lead to a generation of success momentum, let's take an in-depth look at each element in turn.

Introducing the 4-step goal achievement method…

How to Create a Solid and Strategic Goal Plan That Delivers You Success

Before we get into each step, note this method was designed as a flexible and universal process to apply anywhere. Use it as-is, in part, or as a foil for other approaches you already employ – adapt it as you see fit!

OK – let's begin!

Step 1. Discern your starting position before you begin the goal-setting process

Knowing where you are right now before you start planning is critical!

Why?

Because building success requires you to plot a course towards your destination that starts from a reference point. Without that reference, you have no context for where you are going.

Here's a quick analogy for you...

Imagine driving to your best friend's new house deep in the countryside, when you suddenly realize you're lost. You pull over on a deserted country lane to check your mobile – "Damn!" – you've just run out of battery, and you threw out the old A to Z roadmap last month. "Doh!". You can see no signposts, and there's nobody else around for miles. Thankfully, you spy a phonebox in the distance and call your friend...

"Hey Stephen, it's Jennifer – I'm totally lost. Can you give me directions to your house please?"

"Sure Jen," replies Stephen. "Where are you right now? – I'll figure out the best route from there".

"Errrmmm?".

To be continued...

In this situation, it's obvious you need to know your starting point; however, this is not the case when it comes to goal setting. If it were, there wouldn't be so many people always overlooking it!

To avoid falling into this goal-setting trap yourself, make sure you measure the relevant baseline parameters, core metrics, and key performance indicators (KPIs) before you begin:

- Current revenue
- Existing numbers of sales
- Average website traffic per month
- How much you weigh
- Constituents of your typical daily meals
- How many times you tend to contribute to the discussion at company meetings
- How far you run per week

Etc.

(For business-related metrics, use averages from the past 6-12 months whenever possible/reasonable.)

In the case of my changing jobs, I first needed clarity on all the key things I knew related to my current role. I listed these out, which led to an immediate identification of what I didn't know or needed to develop regarding my next position. I prioritized that list and made a plan to fill in my primary knowledge and skill gaps.

When you have these measured, they give you your "what" – a quantitative "situational analysis" of your current position.

With your "what" established, move to identify the factors that most likely contributed to your current performance. You need to determine what things happened historically that led to "why" you are where you are today – these provide you with a qualitative benchmark and make it easier to identify what needs to change.

Ask yourself: What have you done that has led to your company making the revenue it does each month? What was it your team did to get the number of sales they're getting each week? What did you do or not do that resulted in you weighing what you weigh? Etc.

To be clear, this is not an exercise in beating yourself up, it's an exercise in identifying most likely contributors and causes that you can then work to transform to create a new set of results.

Because once you've established the "what" and the "why" of your current scenario, your "what next" and "where to next" questions immediately become easier to plan for.

Again, applying this to my job situation, I found the biggest "why's" were due to:

- Company structure
- The fact I was the sole person in my rôle

- Sales generated for the work I was doing not coming from me but from other departments I had no control over

The whole operational framework I was in did not lend itself to me progressing in the way I wanted to, so I had to find a new framework elsewhere. Getting clear on that helped me to know exactly what to look for.

Step 2. Set your SMART goals and define any characteristics you need to attain them

With your situational analysis completed, it's time to set your goals and plot a course towards your new success destination.

Setting goals is an exciting time for any business or individual. It's the point at which we turn our eyes skyward and imagine our future.

SMART goals will continue to be referenced throughout the book, so for those of you not already familiar with them, here's a little breakdown…

SMART is an acronym that stands for: **Specific**, **Measurable**, **Achievable**, **Relevant**, and **Timed**.

The SMART goal-setting framework is one of the most widely used success achievement methods today (certainly in the Western world) and is generally accepted to have been created by George T. Doran in November 1981 in Spokane, Washington.

Doran was a consultant and former Corporate Planning Director for the Washington Waterpower Company and published a document that was entitled "**There's a S.M.A.R.T. Way to Write Management's Goals and Objectives**"[6]. This was the first time the SMART goal method was introduced to the world – and the rest, as they say, is history!

Here's how it works...

S in SMART stands for Specific

The most crucial part of setting any goal is going to town on the details. This is no time to skip over the particulars and create a goal that is nothing more than a fuzzy fantasy – dive deep and craft your desired outcome!

Your goals need to be crystal clear and full of specifics, so you know exactly what you are aiming for. Because goals composed of laser-focused details are the mother of successful endeavors.

Taking the time to be detailed with your goals helps you more effectively prioritize your time and the actions required of you while in their pursuance. This high level of specificity regarding what is to be done will create unswerving focus – it serves as a beacon that you'll use to project your daily attention. In turn, these create a guiding channel through which your intention travels and attaches to the desired outcome, much like a master archer sighting the target and letting her arrow fly forth.

Ask yourself a series of questions once you've created your goal to check if you've been specific enough:

- Have I described exactly what achievement of the goal will look like?
- Did I make it clear in terms of who or what will be involved?
- Is there any reference to where I will be once it's attained?
- Do I need more clarification outlining what will have changed?

Etc.

M in SMART stands for Measurable

There needs to be solid tangibility when working with goals – you need to be able to measure your progression in concrete terms on some kind of scale:

- Revenue increase year-on-year in percentage or actual terms.
- Rise in average customer spend in percentage or actual terms.
- Number of email addresses acquired.
- Number of lbs gained or lost.

- The number of new contacts or acquaintances you've gained (as in trying to build your social circle).
- How many steps you've reached with your pedometer.

Setting goals based on sentiment or subjective interpretation such as:

- Make our customers "happier"
- Increase our growth "potential"
- Feel "better" about myself

...are not targets that can be easily measured, if they can be at all!

So make your goals measurable so you can compare where you are going to be with where you are now.

A in SMART stands for Attainable (*or sometimes Achievable*)

Setting realistic goals is the key to success – goal failure often happens because the scale of what you've set is simply not feasible.

You know the kind of goals I mean – the ones where, in the front of your mind, you're pleased and are metaphorically patting yourself on the back for how visionary you are, while in the back of your mind a quiet voice can be heard saying, "Yeah right – you know that ain't ever gonna happen!".

Yes! Those "goals"!

Of course, your goals need to stretch you and push you outside your comfort zone - otherwise, you'll never grow - but you need to be honest with yourself, review the current lay of the land, and ask yourself, "Is what I'm trying to achieve here practically possible given where I am now and the resources I have or could obtain?"

If the answer is "No!", that's fine – simply ease off a little, lessen the goal, and create an overall plan that consists of multiple, smaller goals that collectively represent a workable, yet still challenging path of progression.

Life delivers enough growth-inhibiting challenges without us compounding that by setting objectives we know we'll never reach!

So, work in ways that allow you to create leverage and momentum that pushes you forward and not backward – be, SMART about what you do (see what I did there?).

R in SMART stands for Relevant (*or sometimes Realistic***)**
Why are you setting this goal? How does it fit and support the bigger picture of your life? Will it reinforce or conflict with your values? What is the relevance to where you are now?

If the goals you are setting yourself seem misaligned in some way or are outliers that just don't fit where you are, what you're doing, or where you're going, you may want to reconsider setting them.

Because while none of us knows what's around the corner in business or life in general, we can get more of a feel for what's likely to come next based on what we've done historically and are planning to do in the future.

Therefore, try and leverage your time pursuing goals that make sense and will keep you on a trajectory towards outcomes you want.

Your life and your input into the lives of others are extremely valuable – don't spend it chasing worthless and irrelevant goals!

Make what you do count!

T in SMART stands for Timed (or Time-Based)

You may have noticed we tend to stretch or compact how long it takes to do what we do, to fit the time we've been given to do it – this is known as Parkinson's Law[7].

For example, how often have you been given a deadline to complete something that is an ample time window, say two weeks, only to find yourself cramming to get it all done in the last 2-3 days?

Or are you having to deliver a massive piece of work with impossible speed?

It happens all the time!

I remember scoping out a client project that was to take three months to complete. I was not happy when I only had 17 working days to deliver it due to the client messing about with the signoff and not changing the required-by date! But I had to suck it up because it was worth £260,000 and I had told my CEO I would do it.

I was literally working 15 hours days and getting to the office at 5:30 am to get through the work. But I did it, and I delivered all 740 pages of information with about 3 minutes to spare on the final deadline day!

And you know what?

It was the best project I had ever delivered!

Our ability to work, then, is elastic – it can stretch or compact relative to the allocated time.

If you know you're able to get a lot done in a short time when you put your mind to it, you can leverage this by setting tighter deadlines (but not as tight as the one I had – that was downright madness!).

Conversely, goals set with ridiculously long or no time limits at all will fail!

Enlist the help of an accountability partner to add another layer of pressure to your tight deadline. Being accountable to somebody during the process will focus you more, and you will not want to look bad in the eyes of somebody else – try this; it works!

Now that you know how to use the SMART framework, go ahead and plan out your goals. Once you have finished, review them and write them out in full and clear detail so you can easily reference them every day.

With that said, let's touch on the most common reasons people fall short of success and fail to hit their goals so you can avoid the same traps! You don't want to spend valuable time planning and getting your enthusiasm pumping, only to trip over and sabotage yourself unnecessarily.

So what if I told you I knew how to create a guaranteed successful future for you that takes all the things you've previously done wrong and shows you how to avoid repeating them - would you like to see that?

Of course, you would!

Well, you're in luck.

I've looked ahead six months, and here are…

The 11 barriers blocking your path to success and how you can obliterate them with ease.

1. You did not write down your goals

Your goals were never transferred from your imagination to the real world.

Solution: Write your goals out in full detail then put them somewhere you can see easily every day. Buy a hardback notepad and make that your goal diary. This helps keep your goals in front of your mind and also reinforces your in subconscious what it is you are aiming to achieve.

2. You waited to feel fully ready before starting

There will always be some reason why you are not adequately prepared which provides an excuse not to start.

Solution: Just get your best (not perfect) plan together and start – you can adjust and fine-tune as necessary along the way.

3. You didn't really believe you could achieve what you set out to do

If you do not fully buy into what you intend to do, you will not have the courage of your convictions, and the actions you take will lack the necessary force and focus to yield success.

Solution: Re-analyse your goal, identify what part of it caused you to lose your faith, and re-work or scale down that part until it feels achievable

4. You set unrealistic goals

You were overly optimistic and did not adequately consider how your goals might be impacted or derailed by various factors – too much blue-sky thinking with little appreciation of the related practicalities.

Solution: Re-scale your goals into multiple, smaller units that still comprise your original goal, and then map out the necessary considerations and implications of each smaller unit.

5. You tried to achieve somebody else's goals and not your own

What you tried to accomplish is not coming from your heart – it is the dreams of others that you are trying to follow and not your own.

Solution: Stop and be honest with yourself. Ask yourself the question, "what do I really want and why?"

6. Your enthusiasm and belief diminished due to setbacks or failures

You misunderstood what the nature of "failure" truly is.

Solution: Always reframe so-called failures as invaluable, guiding feedback. Through this feedback, you are being shown exactly what not to do to succeed.

7. Your efforts were inconsistent

Often linked to a lack of belief, you turned your efforts on and off like a tap causing regular interruptions to any momentum you had started to build-up.

Solution: Create an action plan that breaks down everything you need to do to make the goal a reality. Start at the goal completion point and work back through all the things you'd need to do and by when, and calendarize each one starting where you are today. This is starting with the end in mind.

8. You gave up before seeing results

Impatience caused you to expect things to happen much sooner than their natural completion cycle required.

Solution: Regularly analyze key results and use it to create a likely timeline of success based on how you're tracking in reality as opposed to how you imagined you'd be tracking. Depending on the size of the goal, adjust your data analysis periodicity accordingly. For example, there is no point looking at data every hour for a goal you initially thought would take six months to achieve – every other day or weekly makes more sense. And if the data shows that adjustments are needed in your approach, then be agile and make the necessary changes as you go.

9. You had a hidden fear of failure

Often without being consciously aware, you allowed fear to stop you doing the things you knew you needed to do.

Solution: Drill into the fear and ask yourself what you might be trying to protect yourself from – past experiences can be a valuable place to start. Also, applying the "what's the worst that can happen?" approach is good because you soon realize there is virtually nothing in life that you'd never be able to recover from.

10. You had a hidden fear of success

This may seem to defy logic, but it's strikingly common. The process of reaching your goals will change who you are, and change can be frightening. The prospect of living outside your current comfort zone can be a daunting and scary prospect and thus becomes one to avoid.

Solution: Ask yourself what you are more afraid of: the process of transforming into a better version of yourself? Or never believing in yourself enough to try?

11. Your goals were too loosely defined

There is a major lack of clarity and granularity in terms of what you are trying to achieve.

Solution: Re-work your goals according to the SMART principle.

I'm telling you, if you apply these 11 solutions to each goal you set, you will achieve that goal successfully – period!

OK – with the potential pitfalls of failure and solutions covered, it's important to remember that for the goals you have set, each should...

- **Stretch you**
- **Inspire you**
- **Make you grow as a person or your business evolve as an entity**

Make sure they meet the 3 criteria mentioned above before moving on.

Looking at the final of the 3 criteria in particular – to ensure your goals make you grow as a person or your business evolve as an entity, this is achieved by having a...

Focus on the transformational journey as well as the goal destination!

Because here's the thing...

The traditional goal-setting mindset focuses solely on what you will have once you've achieved your goal.

Whereas...

The progressive or growth mindset focuses on who you will have become once you've achieved your goal.

That word "become" means those of a progressive mindset is a world away in their thinking compared to those of a traditional mindset.

For the traditionalist, failure to observe the transformation occurring as they pursue their goals means successes tend to be one-dimensional. For the progressive, however, this observance illuminates how they are adapting, evolving, and transforming, such that their successes will always be multi-dimensional and profound.

One approach is akin to simply running and winning a race, whereas the other is more of a caterpillar-into-butterfly transformation.

Yes – the attainment of things and statuses are all elements you want and strive for because that's part of our human condition. However, for those with eyes to see, it becomes evident that the goals you strive for and achieve are the by-products of a deeper process that is going on – the process of unfoldment and becoming.

That said, the method by which you focus on the transformational goal journey is to consider the characteristics needed to hit the goals. When you do this, you are identifying future attributes you need to make manifest; you are making it clear in your mind what type of person or company you would expect to achieve these goals.

Let's quickly clarify what we mean by way of an example...

You set a SMART personal goal of dropping down from a size 36-inch to size 34-inch trouser waist in 1 month – here are your "I" statements as someone with a transformation focus:

1. I am going to lose 10 lbs in body weight so I can move down one trouser waist size and I will be doing this by purchasing and following the Belly Buster DVD exercise regime – I will start on February 1st.
2. I have all the space and equipment I need to be able to do the workouts and will be exercising three times a week for 20 minutes first thing in the morning for the next month.
3. I will weigh myself once per week on my bathroom scale.
4. I know this is possible because I constantly see professional sportspeople losing significantly more weight in way less time to make the cut for competitions – within days, not weeks!
5. By February 28th, I will be able to slide effortlessly into the pair of 34-inch jeans I bought last year during a shopping trip where I was clearly in denial (yep, we've all been there!).

With your SMART goal laid out, you now think about the characteristics of someone who has gone through such a regime and succeeded. They...

- Are happy to spend some time researching things online (hence they were able to find the Belly Buster program).
- Get at least 6-8 hours solid sleep a night (they take steps to facilitate the things they want to achieve the following day).
- Rise early and immediately once their alarm goes off – no snoozing (they create enough time so they can work out first thing in the morning).
- Use simple tracking aides like tick charts to provide constant visual feedback of the things that have been completed (they realize that reminders of past successes spur them on to do more, so they find simple ways to leverage this).
- Investigate what foods and supplements constitute a healthy diet and what harmful foods should be cut back on (through researching they've learned that diet not only impacts your physical health and vitality but also your psychology in so many ways).
- Tend to use significantly more positive words than negative (through experience, they've learned that positivity leads to more success).
- Watch and read inspiring videos and stories on a regular basis (this leads to regular contemplation of what else could be achieved in their life).

By doing this exercise, you mentally lay out the steppingstones that create the path of your future transformation (the same process is applicable for business goals).

Now that you have your list of characteristics, spend a few more minutes thinking about the type of life this ideal person is leading:

- What do they look like?
- How do they walk?
- What type of voice do they have?
- What clothes do they wear?
- How do they think?
- Who do they spend time with?

When you do this, you'll very quickly realize that what you're imagining is really a future you.

Currently, you are not the person you've described because that person has been imagined in line with a goal you are yet to achieve. However, once you embody those characteristics and broader attributes and take the necessary steps towards your goal as defined in part 3 – the next part of this process, you will have been transformed into that imagined person. That will be why you succeed.

Identify someone you know personally or know of (e.g., a famous person) who has already achieved your goal, and model that person. If for some reason you're struggling to think of anyone, then create an imaginary persona and give them all the attributes you want to develop and embody for yourself.

This is why this process is so powerful – it sets you up to understand the broader scope of who you will become and delivers much more than the goal itself. When you apply and focus on yourself in this way, your future successes start to become inevitable instead of dreams!

Step 3. Take constant and focused action only in the direction of your goal(s)

Having ascertained either your personal or your company's starting position, set your SMART goal(s) and define the necessary characteristics for their achievement. It's now time for you to execute the actions that will propel you towards the goal finish line.

The steps you take here are the most crucial of your entire goal-pursuit process because it is what you actually do that will generate the success momentum that ultimately will propel you to your goals.

Probably the most common error that occurs at this stage of the process is not being granular enough regarding the steps themselves – the key is to work backward from the goal and finish at the starting point. It's as if the future you left a trail of breadcrumbs outlining the exact steps you need to take.

As with the goals themselves, how you write them is nearly as important as writing them at all. They must be calendarized.

Many of us are still very lax with our calendars (if we use them at all – you know who you are!) – and the entries we make are often very general, e.g.

Sample calendar entry with vague business goal actions

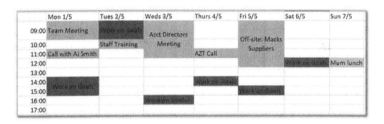

Yes, "work on goals" is *in* your diary and that's an important start – but let's be honest here, those entries are nothing more than placeholders; they're not telling you exactly *what* you need to do.

Remember, most online diaries allow you to schedule a time right down to the minute now, so use that function to get granular and lay out the specifics.

With that said, here is the method to help create your trail of breadcrumbs that reach back in time from your completed goal to the present day.

I'll walk you through the theory first, and then we'll go through an actual example from my life so you can see it in action.

1. If you know how much time you are going to need to spend working on your goal (either the exact or approximate number of hours), make a note of this number and proceed to part 2.
2. Take your goal timetable, i.e., how long you have set yourself to achieve it, and divide that numerical (measurable) goal value by the sum of the next biggest time units that make up that timetable.
3. If you set a goal for a year, the next biggest time unit is, therefore, a month, and there are 12 months in a year.
4. Dividing your yearly value by 12, then, means each month you will need to complete 1/12 of your goal value on average.

Repeat the process and break the values down by the next biggest unit. So, in the case of months, the next biggest unit is a week, and on average there are 4.33 weeks per month:

1. To calculate your weekly goal value, take your monthly goal value and divide that by 4.33
2. Repeat the process dividing your weekly value by 7 to get your average daily value.

This is the first part of the method completed, but there are some caveats to consider specifically in the case of business goals, namely:

- People invariably have some time off from work – most commonly the weekend or at least 1 day during the week, and generally at least 1-2 weeks holiday each year, rising to at least 3-4 with public holidays. Here in the UK, 3 weeks' holiday per year is probably the average with an additional 5 public holidays.
- Businesses exhibit some degree of seasonality, and certain times of the year are busier, and more profitable, than others.

As a result, you will need to account for these "off" periods and ensure certain weeks and months overperform when compared to your calculated averages, so you stay on track.

The next step is calculating what activities you need to get done per day to hit your monthly, weekly, and daily average values.

Let's work all this through by using the SMART goal I put in place when I was looking to change jobs.

In 3 months, I will learn and/or improve upon 8 areas of my business knowledge, such that I can either succinctly describe or easily demonstrate them (where practically possible) to any of my colleagues.

The first thing to do is use the calculation from part 1 to figure out how many hours of daily activity are needed to achieve my goals. There were 8 items I needed to get to grips in total for me to hit my goal, and I figured I'd need about 2 working days per item. There are 8 hours in a working day, so that means 8 x 2 = 16 hours per item, and there are 8 items: 16 x 8 = 128 hours in total.

- My overall timeline was 3 months and so the next biggest unit of time is weeks. This meant my weekly total was as follows :
  - o 3 (months) x 4.33 (average weeks per month) = 13 weeks
  - o 128 (number of total allocated hours) ÷ 13 (weeks) = 9.8 or rounding up, 10 hours per week
- I then needed to convert the weekly totals into daily total like this :
  - o 10 (hours per week) ÷ 7 (days) = 1.4 or rounding up, 1.5 hours per day

In the event I missed a day I would need to double up on another day to still be on track for my daily average.

From the situational analysis I ran before I set my goal, I realized that of the 8 areas I identified as needing work, I knew nothing about half of them.

As a result, I decided to focus on 5 aspects for each of the 8 developmental areas, i.e. 5 x 8 = 40 individual aspects in total. And to reiterate, my aim was to be able to succinctly describe each aspect to another person (e.g. a team member) and/or physically demonstrate it if that was practically possible. I figured that would give me enough competency and a strong enough base of understanding to move into a department head position.

I decided on the following aspects.

Excel	Departmental	Industry	Other Paid
Pivot Tables	Sales Forecasting	Networking Plan	Programmatic
VLookUp	Employee Costing	New Disruptive Players	Paid Social Overview
HLookUp	P&L Management	LinkedIn Rising Stars	Native Advertising
Macros	Hiring & Growth Planning	Awards Opportunities	Display Advertising
Advanced Chart Functions	Running Big Teams	Product/ Service Innovation Plans	Main Cost Models

SEO	Social	PPC	General Business
Log File Analysis	Tik Tok for Business	Novel SEO Integration Ideas	M&A
Basic JS Code Writing	Latest FB and Insta Game Changers	Latest Basics for Ad Creation	Balance Sheets
Inspect Element Core Functions	Gary V Year Ahead Predictions	Latest Ad Types	Business Plans
New Screaming Frog Features	New Players	Major Changes for Year Ahead	Strategy Principles
Familiarise JSON-LD	Latest Industry Top Stats	Google vs Bing Ads Top Line Stats	SWOT & PEST

I knew I had 16 hours to play with per item, so on average, I was looking at 3 hours for each of the 5 aspects per item (16 hours ÷ 5 aspects = 3.2 hours per aspect).

The final step was then to add these to my calendar daily and remember to double up on a day if one was ever missed, such as a weekend day.

Because I'm a morning person, I was comfortable kicking off a lot of my working days earlier with some additional learning time. I love to learn anything new, so I lapped up the opportunity as eagerly as a hungry cat given a saucer of milk!

Consequently, my calendar each week did not look like this…

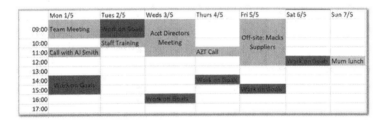

It looked more like this…

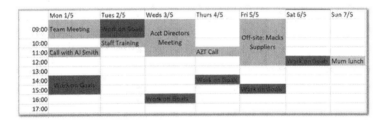

with subsequent weeks showing the remaining aspects I was focusing on.

There is a massive difference between the two as you can see!

I scheduled all of the 40 aspects across 13 weeks and got everything down, so I knew exactly what I had to do in advance.

An important point to note...

To make sure your goals stay on track during that initial time when starting your granular actions, you will need to be constantly reviewing how the performance is changing and taking notes on anything that may need to be tweaked or dropped for the next activity sprint. If something is not working and contributing to your goal outcomes, it's critical to identify it asap, rectify it, or replace it with something that works in your favor.

In my case, I was looking at how long it took to grasp one of the five new aspects to ensure I was not going to overrun on time. If it started to look too ambitious, I would have been agile and rescoped what remained asap by reducing the target to 4 or maybe even 3 new aspects per area to stay on track.

Step 4. Be accountable and take full ownership of the results and outcomes generated in step number 3.
You'll be pleased to know this last step is a short, albeit invaluable one!

The path to success requires you to own all the so-called failures as well as all the positives that occur on your path. Whether you are executing tasks yourself or briefing and delegating tasks for others – the outcomes and results are YOUR responsibility. You need to OWN them and be ACCOUNTABLE for them – ALL of them!

Because when things do not go as we planned, the all-too-often default position is to blame someone or something outside of ourselves.

How many of you have heard or given the following types of responses when things went wrong?

- "Well, if XYZ hadn't happened, then the project would have worked!"
- "If we had more budget to keep up with the competition, we'd have been able to generate greater market share and pull back the business we lost!".
- "The weather started to change and it was much colder and darker in the mornings, so exercising first thing was harder"
- "I simply didn't have the time to get everything done!"
- "We never get the support we need from the Marketing team so how were Sales supposed to deliver that increase in performance?"

- "There were a lot of social events happening, so there was no point trying to start losing weight just yet"

And the list goes on!

So, here's the bottom-line folks…

If you run a business – everything that happens in your business is <u>ultimately on YOU!</u>

If you run a department – everything that happens in your department is <u>ultimately on YOU!</u>

If you're an individual – everything that relates to your goals and choices is <u>ultimately on YOU!</u>

That may be a tough way of looking at life – but ask yourself this question – "If I had that approach to my life, what quality of life would I have compared to the quality of life I have now?"

Yes, of course, things go wrong in life – that's how we learn and grow. It's how we react to these challenges that maketh the person!

Use your "failures", setbacks, and challenges as beacons of light to illuminate opportunities to do these things better the next time. Own your mistakes – don't put them on somebody else. Admit your shortcomings – don't blame others for them.

See the things you missed the first time around – plan better for them next time so they don't happen again!

And that, my friends, is your 4-step goal achievement method – a proven, repeatable, and instantly usable formula you can take away and start to leverage and begin generating the levels of success you've previously only dreamt of!

I now am a Director of my own company that helps businesses to help others. I am also helping individuals to improve their memories, learn quicker, speed read, heal inner imbalances, and kickstart their journey to discover their spirituality and reveal their true magnificence. I've also been afforded the privilege of co-authoring this fantastic book!

My goal was to get out of the standard 9-5 rat race, because whilst in it, I felt unable to deliver the type of bespoke value I wanted to deliver to the world. I also wanted to become the change that I'd been looking for. This last part, in particular, is moving along very nicely and I have many more big plans to achieve in the next few years – I can't wait!

So, my friends…

Use this formula to start making *your* dreams a reality!

Love, peace, and appreciation,

Peter A. Anglin

The Power of Your Thoughts

"It's never too late to be what you might have been"

- Adelaide Proctor

Anastasia Kor – Athens, Greece

Anastasia is a Naval Scientist but continues to study in a wide array of fields including psychology, digital marketing, language learning, and life coaching. Her life mission is to help other develop the skills and confidence to fearlessly pursue their life and learning goals.

Introduction

At the age of 18, I was faced with the biggest challenge of my life. At least, this is how it felt back then. I had to take exams in order to enter college. 5 exams, 4 hours each. 20 hours that would determine which college I could enter, which would determine which profession I would follow. In other words, all my life was going to be determined by these outcomes.

The stress started when I was 16. At this age, you start building up your knowledge base for these final exams. You start preparing yourself mentally for what is to come. From that age, fear and feelings of not being good enough became my companions. Although I was a good student, taking exams always scared me. 80,000 students all over the country each took the same exams and only the ones

91

with top results got to choose which college to attend. The competition is high.

Reaching the final year, I was having all day lessons to get better prepared. As the exams grew closer, I was becoming even more stressed. I wasn't ready; I was going to fail; I was stupid. I remember reading a physics problem and having absolutely no clue what to do, just staring at the blank page and trying to find a solution. The exams grew closer and closer.

At some point, I felt that this could go on no more. No matter how much I studied, I felt that my knowledge was inadequate. I decided then to reach out to a brand-new tutor. Thankfully, I had the courage to try something new even in the last months. He believed in me and, slowly, I started believing in myself again. The negative thoughts and negative feelings faded away. Suddenly, the problems that had found me clueless before became simple. I no longer thought that I was stupid. In my final exams, I got one of my best grades in physics. This made me realise how much my internal dialogue affected my performance and how different my results could be if I managed my anxiety and negative feelings.

This event changed me as a person. But it also ignited the fire in me to continue to improve myself and explore my potential. I did not want to cloud my self-perception again. I wanted to control my internal dialogue. These were dark memories, but if I had not struggled so much back then, I would never have found the SuperLearning material. And of course, I would have never wanted to become a SuperLearner coach. But most of all, I wouldn't have recognized the critical role of my internal dialogue in my performance - the power of my thoughts.

Your words shape your reality

Oftentimes, we become victims to the circumstances we are facing and believe there is nothing we can do about it. We allow anxiety, anger, and depression a hold over us. We feel that we deserve to be sad and that we have every right to self-pity. This victim mentality is self-perpetuating. But it doesn't have to be.

You can control your thoughts, you are able to control your behaviour, and, as a result, you are able to choose the outcome you want.

We all have heard the quote: "Your words shape your reality", but what does this mean, practically speaking? This idea is just one piece of a bigger picture, a component of a larger system.

It begins with perception. Your brain processes 11 million bits of information per second, largely gathered by your senses.[8] 99.99% of this is processed by the subconscious mind, but what you experience is your conscious mind reacting to the juicy bits of this information - the stuff that is relevant to you. This conscious reaction, though observable, is still beneath the surface of what you normally consider a "thought"; it includes your biases and gut instincts. You then reflect on this reaction. It is only at this step that most people become finally aware of what they are thinking and feel that they are the originators of the thought. Based on this reflection, you respond, or take action. Every response causes a result.

Perception -> Reaction -> Reflection -> Response -> Result

If you are not seeing the results you want, this should disturb you slightly. How does your brain determine what information passes from the subconscious to the conscious mind? The information you ultimately act on.

The information filtering happens in the RAS, the Reticular Activating System. Since the brain cannot *consciously* process all this information, it filters it. So, how does the brain select which information is going to be pushed to the conscious mind? Our brain filters the information and shows us only what it deems to be most important to us based on our ingrained beliefs and immediate circumstances. My favorite illustration of this filtering process is when you are shopping for a new car. At some point, you decide on the model you want and anticipate the purchase. Then what happens? As if by magic, you start noticing this kind of car everywhere! Well, it's not magic. It is a change in your immediate circumstances. When your immediate circumstances are disrupted by some outside event - the need to purchase a new car - you suddenly start seeing new things!

But it doesn't end there. The pattern is not linear, but circular. The result becomes the perception and the resulting cycle looks like this:

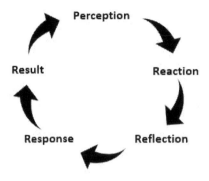

Perception

Reaction

Reflection

Response

Result

Thoughts come and go in your mind all day long. Without intentional intervention or significant external disruption, you end up thinking the same things on a loop. For example, if you do not like your work you may find yourself everyday waking up saying something like: "I hate mornings. I'm gonna have a rough day at work." and all day, your brain collects evidence to support this thought. Your coffee is too bitter. Your world is so boring. You made so many mistakes on the documents you delivered. You were so immersed in your thoughts you did not realize that you forgot to save the document you had been editing for the last two hours. You paid deliberate attention to all of these thoughts and you ignored the fact that your colleague complimented your new haircut. You completely erased the fact that your boss told you the previous week how grateful he is to have you on the team. Your brain loves to prove you right, no matter the consequences. This affects your performance, which affects your thoughts, which affects your performance...

So, if you keep thinking the same thoughts and you feel stuck in a rut, don't be surprised! If you take the same actions, you get the same results; if you get the same results, you think the same thoughts and take the same actions... You get stuck doing the same thing over and over again. This is why the quote: "what gets measured gets managed" is so powerful. You cannot change something that you are not aware of and humans are creatures of habits.

Habits have been part of human survival throughout history. By creating processes and habits, we save energy, physically and mentally. But this survival mode can sometimes trick us! The habits and processes we create are not always beneficial. When habits are developed, a neural pathway is created in the brain and you cannot simply delete it. You *can*, however, create another one to make the old one useless. Even if you have compiled some bad habits, ultimately, you hold the power.

Hacking your Reticular Activating System
Seeing your thoughts and actions in the context of this feedback loop might be discouraging; at first glance, it seems like we are all slaves to an endless cycle that can

only be broken by random life-altering events. Let's revisit the loop and take a closer look.

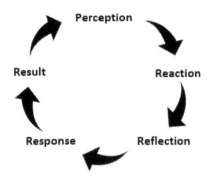

The Reticular Activating System controls the Perception piece of this loop, which strongly influences everything else. But remember how the RAS performs its filtering: beliefs and immediate circumstances. Do you see the key to taking control of the cycle?

As Ford once said, "Whether you believe you can or cannot do something you are right". When you believe that you will be able to find a better solution, you will eventually find it. You tell your brain to focus on finding solutions instead of focusing solely on the problem. When you are determined to find a solution, you can see the problem from a different perspective.

As soon as you take control of your beliefs, you take control of the whole system. You change your beliefs, you change your perception, you change your reaction, you change your reflection, you change your response, *you change your results.* And when you change your results, you gain at least partial control of the second criteria the RAS uses to determine your perception: your immediate circumstances.

"Every cell is eavesdropping on your internal dialogue."

- Deepak Chopra

Last but not least, the term "mind-body connection" is not pseudo-science. Neuroscientists have discovered that neurotransmitters are bathing every cell in our bodies and "eavesdropping on our internal dialogue.". Even in terms of your physical health, what you think is, at least to some extent, what you get. Your thoughts are not just extremely powerful when it comes to your mental well-being, but your bodily health as well.

Growth vs fixed mindset

"Nothing will ever be attempted if all possible objections must first be overcome."

- Samuel Johnson

People with a fixed mindset believe that to do something well, you must be talented. On the contrary, people with a growth mindset believe that everything is within reach if you put in the right amount of effort and are willing to fail and try again to learn.

Knowing that you can acquire any skill you want if you commit deliberate practice, you eliminate the idea of failure from your head. Instead, you see only feedback and you can become a more optimistic, self-forgiving person. How do you know you cannot achieve something if you have not given your 100%, and how can you give your 100% if you do not believe that you can do it?

That is why you should always try to see the bright side. This isn't living in a fantasy; it is actively creating a better world. Even though you cannot control every detail of your circumstances, you can effect real change through your beliefs. You can start seeing opportunities everywhere and exploit every difficulty you encounter. There is no point in thinking negatively about anything; it literally makes your world worse.

A person with a growth mindset accepts the mental preparation necessary to start something new. Fear will arise. Objections will arise. But in the end, there is no doubt that the goal will be achieved. And this certainty of success can be the driving force to propel you forward and overcome any difficulty that may come up. You may pivot many times, or discover something completely different from the original plan, but this is called evolution and is better than staying stagnant.

The Secret to Changing Your Beliefs

I have claimed that the key to changing your results is changing your beliefs. You might be thinking this is not so trivial as I made it sound. Can a negative person really change into an optimistic person within seconds?

You first need to understand that your head can never be truly emptied of thoughts. You cannot just say:" Stop thinking negatively". Your RAS doesn't listen to verbal commands when deciding how to filter." Don't think of a red elephant" - I bet you just thought of a red elephant. Replacing negative thinking is not a matter of merely turning all negativity off, it requires turning positivity on.

Besides, some of our beliefs are a part of our personality. That means that by changing them, we literally reshape ourselves. As creatures of habits, this is scary. It is scary to see how powerful we can be and there is fear, especially, when it comes to something that we are doing over and over again. But, if we take notice every time and are aware of how we are thinking, we can change.

How many times have you been afraid of things going "too well"? Are you suspicious on the good days? Limiting beliefs like this can really hinder our potential and inhibit change. Acknowledge your fears and suspicions; accept them and make a conscious decision to let them go. If you cannot, it is only because you believe you cannot. Make a plan and stick with it; ignore everything else. Focus on how well you are sticking to the process and detach yourself completely from the outcome.

Lastly, another powerful way to act the way you truly want is having a picture in your mind of who you want to be. What is the next version of you? When you want to give up, ask yourself: "Do I really want to become a person who......." For example: "Do I really want to become a person who gives up when hard times kick in? Am I a person who becomes a victim of the circumstances? Do I want to become a person who gets so affected by criticism?" If you find it difficult to do it this way, you can pick a role model and wonder how your role model would have reacted. In this way, you are putting yourself in the role of the observer and detach yourself from the outcomes; this is when you get your power back.

Your thoughts and your beliefs are so powerful, and learning to manage them will change your life. Take control of the cycle; take control of your results. Soon you will see opportunities where others find only problems.

Achieve the "Impossible" Through Visualization

Lorena Compean – Hong Kong, China

Lorena is an ultra-runner and Superhuman Academy Coach who believes we all have the potential to achieve the "impossible" with visualization, discipline, and a strong desire. She left her career as a business consultant in Mexico to obtain her MBA in Hong Kong where she has since worked for various financial institutions.

Outrunning Doubt

February 8th, 2020: It's 7am in Rotorua, New Zealand and I am about to start one of the most exciting adventures of my whole life. I'd had one single goal in mind for the last 6 months. I had completed my training plan and I was finally ready and finally here. It was even a beautiful blue-sky day – just as I was hoping for. The haka, a traditional ceremonial dance in the Maori culture and the annual prelude to this event was already underway.

The last few minutes before the race began seemed eternal. I could not stop thinking about the intense preparation I had completed to be here. Then I heard the starting gunshot. Time stopped and I started running. I smiled and ran with full determination to complete something I had once considered impossible. I felt more powerful, focused, happy, and strong than ever before.

103

With every step I took, I could feel the energy flowing through my veins. It was just as I had seen it all those times in my head: step by step, never stopping. The day's temperature started increasing and by noon had reached 25°C. Perfect!

Living in Hong Kong, I am used to training in temperatures over 30 degrees Celsius and high humidity. I told myself: "You got this. It is like a normal training weekend, just don't forget to pour enough water over yourself for the next few hours". The day continued, and I was focused on moving from one station to the next, pacing myself as I had practiced in my head and now knew how to do by heart: 14km, 31km, 40km, 48km. Suddenly, after 10 hours of jogging non-stop, I reached the 58km mark, where my crew was waiting for me with a beautiful smile and food for my body and my soul. My dedicated crew had flown all the way from Mexico to New Zealand purely to support me in my goal to complete this race and I felt incredibly grateful to have such amazing people in my life. After having something to eat and drink and getting a big hug, I continued on my way. I remember seeing other people struggling to retain food and liquids at their pit stop and many runners even had to stop as exhaustion took over their bodies.

But I was feeling completely empowered - it felt like I was flying through clouds without any pain. I kept using my breathing mantra and visualizing myself at the finish line until, 19 hours and 28 minutes after setting off, it actually happened. Just like that, I completed 102km of trail running and crossed the finish line of the Tarawera Ultramarathon (TUM) 2020. Unbelievably, I still had some energy left at the end for a picture of myself jumping in euphoric celebration. TUM is a world-class sporting event that pushes the human body to its limits and it was the best race I have ever done in my life.

Wait! You must be wondering how I made this happen?

Let's rewind.

Learning to See

You need to know that a few years earlier, I could not even run five kilometres without feeling I was going to faint. I was not particularly unhealthy, but I never thought I would be capable of running 100km. So, what changed, and how did I get to the finish line?

The answer is simple: visualizing and trying!

What would you say if I invited you to run with me on my next 100km race? Please take a few seconds to think about your answer.

I bet you are already thinking of a handful of reasons why you cannot do it, right?

STOP!!!

Yes, it is human to doubt. Our brains are rationalization machines, churning out every reason to stay in the comfort zone and avoid doing hard things. Sometimes these rational feelings are there to protect us from danger, but they will often also close the door to success.

For me, achieving the impossible started around five years ago, when a friend and I signed up for a 30km race, sponsored by our employer. It was not just the long-distance which made this a challenge, but also the 11 pm start-time which meant we would be completing the all-night event after a full day of work. My friend said: "are you up for this? We can have free beers at the end!" I said, "Sure, why not? "(I have to admit, I had no idea what I was actually getting into). That race was harrowing. We walked for 13 hours, one step at a time, going up and down hills throughout the entire night surrounded by the beautiful Lantau Island in Hong Kong. The race finished at dawn and we managed to be the very last ones to cross the finish line before the event concluded. Even though we were last, we were incredibly proud of our efforts. Even moreseo, we were relieved that the torture was over. When my friend and I were enjoying the promised beer, she said:

"Never again," but my response was
"What? I can't wait to do it again!".

During that race, at sunrise, exhausted and sleep-deprived with my body telling me to stop, I felt a superpower growing inside me and driving me to keep going. That superpower was the realization that I can do anything I set my mind to. I truly had that "aha" moment when I realized that my body will always tell me to stop, but ultimately, I have the power to keep it going through a positive mindset. That realization felt amazing, and I could not wait to feel that way again and again. After that 30km race, I signed up for my first 100km in Nepal. It would take three full days to complete so this race would be a challenge of another scale. So I decided to hire a coach. His objective: to help me to get physically and mentally fit enough to walk/jog 100km through the Himalayas in just 6 months.

One of the first lessons I learned from my coach was visualization. This technique required me to imagine the race and how I would feel when I had completed it. Over the following 6 months, I practiced visualization every day in addition to my physical training. I had never been to Nepal so I couldn't picture the exact location or finish line, but by looking at Google images of runners in similar races, I could imagine myself being there. Ten days before the race, I sprained my ankle, but I was so stubborn that I decided I would compete in the race anyway (I do not recommend that anyone else tries this!). My overwhelming desire to complete this race, combined with my excitement and my new-found powers of visualization, enabled me to become one of just six women who finished - and the only one to do so with an ankle sprain. So, though I was once again the last to cross the finish line, I was once again the happiest person to finish the race.

Why am I sharing all this?

Trail running has helped me learn more about myself than anything else in my life. Through it, I discovered what "doing hard things" really means. These experiences have given me so much confidence that I now know I can achieve anything I choose. After completing a 100km race, most daily tasks simply can't seem difficult anymore. Most of the challenges you face at work, or at home, suddenly become totally doable! You learn to listen to your body without letting your body or emotions define what goals you can reach. In a race, your body will always want to give up, but your ability to visualize yourself at the finish line will give you the strength to continue instead. This applies to any goal you have in life, even if right now, you are thinking that goal is "impossible".

The only way to know if you can accomplish something is by trying. So stop telling yourself, "I cannot run a marathon", "I cannot learn Chinese", "I cannot start a business..."

Have you given yourself a chance? Have you visualized yourself achieving it, and then... REALLY TRIED?

Let me ask you another question: Can hold your breath for 2 minutes?

You may think that's impossible, but guess what, it's not. It's something that anyone can learn, even you.

A few months back, my mother decided to become a healthier person and decided to start practicing the Wim Hof breathing method.[10] This method consists of mastering breathing techniques scientifically proven to improve your energy level, detox your body, reduce stress, and strengthen your immune system. She has been visualizing herself as a healthy person while practicing this technique every day. After only a couple months of daily practice, she was able to hold her breath for 2 minutes. It was not impossible at all. Because when you visualize and take action, the impossible suddenly becomes "possible".

So, what is visualization?
Visualization means creating a mental image of something we desire. Visualization in full, at least for me, is about imagining, in detail, how you will feel when you reach your goals. It's not just imagining how you will feel, but imagining what you will see, how it will smell, and taste, and sound at the finish line, as if you were already experiencing it. Imagining how you will keep walking and keep breathing will let you actually keep walking and keep breathing on the day.

According to Srini Pillay, CEO of NeuroBusiness Group and part-time professor at Harvard Medical School, and research by M. Jeannerod, imagining an action will stimulate the movement areas in the same regions of the brain as when physically performing that action.[11] (You will learn more incredible applications of this phenomenon in the chapter "Embodied Learning"!) This means that visualizing activates brain regions that can unconsciously map your path to success.

This technique can be used for everything in our lives. For instance, if you are going to take a test, imagine taking the test. The sensation of sitting on the chair, being calm, breathing slowly, feeling the pencil in your hand, submitting the final answer, and seeing the score or result you want. If you want success, visualize it; see yourself doing the activities you enjoy, having a boss and colleagues with the characteristics that make you feel positive in your work environment, as well as having the remuneration you would like. Feel it, imagine it in detail – this is the strategy that worked for me in my latest job.

For better results, I suggest being extremely specific. Once during a race (and before I felt comfortable using the "bush" toilet by going to the bathroom in the bushes), I was desperate to find a toilet and for an entire hour I told myself: "I will see a toilet, I will see a toilet" and then... I saw a toilet. An old piece of trash, a broken ceramic toilet was suddenly in front of me. It was not usable, but it was a toilet. At that moment, my friends laughed so much as they rightly said: "You wanted to see a toilet!". We all learn through experience, and this is how I learned the importance of being very specific when visualizing my wishes and needs.

You will see this principle of being specific re-emerge in various parts of the book in different contexts because it is so important - it cannot be restated too many times. If you want to reach your goals and dreams, you must see them clearly.

When I want to lose weight, I set up my personal goal like this: "I will weigh XX kg, and I will be strong and healthy by XX date, and I will put in extraordinary effort until I do, no matter what; there's no other option." And I don't just say it; I see it. I like to use the Daily affirmation template from Hal Elrod because it helps me set incredibly specific SMART goals (see "Building Unstoppable Success Momentum"), visualize them, and commit.

To visualize my goals, I always use two tools: a vision board and daily affirmations.

A vision board is a piece of paper, or poster board, that you can hang somewhere visible. It is covered with photos or a visual representation of what you want to have, do, or accomplish. Using images helps you to visualize your goals more easily. As they say, "a picture is worth a thousand words!". Make sure to place it where you can see it every day. So, if you want to travel to Antarctica (like I do), put up a photo of a penguin in Antarctica. If you want to cross the finish line of a race, put up a photo of the finish line and the gold medal for that race. Whatever you want to do, find a photo and put it somewhere you will see it daily. There are photos on the internet for everything, so there's no excuse - go get it! Go find those photos that will help you visualize your goals more clearly. Sounds like a great weekend project, right?

The second tool I use to complete my goals is affirmations, like those used by Hal Elrod. He affirms "I am committed to maintaining unwavering faith that I will reach my goal and putting forth extraordinary effort until I do, no matter what. There is no other option."[9]

Every day, I take two minutes in the morning to read aloud my affirmations (updated to contain all my goals). As I read them, I once again visualise what I am going to do and how I am going to feel, breathe, move, and talk in the moments I am achieving the goal. Reading my affirmations is always one of the first things I do when I wake up each day. It helps me massively. It is my daily reminder of all the dreams, goals, and wishes I have. This allows me to focus and to design each of my days so I tread the path to success.

Still sound impossible?

If so, then time to ask what exactly is impossible? Is it something you have always thought you cannot do? Have you thought about why you believe you cannot do it? Has somebody told you that you cannot do it? Have you told yourself you cannot? Why is it that, for a lot of things in our lives, our first reaction is to say we cannot do it, or that it is impossible, rather than thinking about how to achieve it?

So, let's think about an idea. How about deciding that you want to meet someone famous, that you want to do a handstand, that you want to cook a delicious fancy dish, that you want to climb Everest, that you want to learn Chinese, or that you want to build a successful business?. Instead of coming up with all the reasons you can't, how long have you spent thinking about why you CAN do it? Have you even tried? We thought about the "impossible" idea of coordinating authors from all over the world to write a book in two months, with no professional help; we gave it a go, and now you are reading it.

Most of the beliefs we have are exactly that: "beliefs." Something rooted so deep in our subconscious minds makes us believe they are the ultimate truth. However, they are not reality; they are "beliefs." Most of the time, the "impossible" is just a mental blocker, something we have consistently repeated to ourselves to the point that our brains have adopted it and have been reprogrammed to believe and act as if it were true. Other times, it is because our family or someone close to us has constantly reminded us how "bad" we are at doing something. I challenge you to think about something you have always wanted to do, but somebody else – perhaps your inner voice - has told you it is "impossible". I challenge you to try it now anyway. You can start by trying to cook something you saw on TV or learning a new skill (now you can learn pretty much anything by watching YouTube). I encourage you to take on a challenge you see as impossible.

Another amazing and unexpected outcome from doing something "impossible" is becoming an inspiration to others, which is a superpower. After I ran my first 100Km ultramarathon, two other friends who were afraid of long-distance running decided to try, and both are now way faster than me. I'm almost as proud of inspiring them as I am of completing those races.

The last technique I use to help me achieve "impossible" goals is public commitment. This strategy is simple, you just have to publicly announce your goal. You could tell your friends that you signed up for a marathon, tell your family you are cooking paella this weekend, share with your loved ones that you are going to lose ten kilograms in the next four months, and so on. In my experience, publicly committing to your goals gives you extra drive and means you'll have more skin in the game. Sharing your goal also generates excitement and happiness which helps you stay focused as you work toward it. Just think about the joy you feel when a close family member or friend graduates, finds a good job, achieves something incredible; by sharing your goals you can build these feelings as you move toward achieving them. Long story short, the goals that you share and commit to publicly are more likely to happen.

Conclusion

If you take away just one thing from this chapter, I want it to be the importance of visualization using all of your senses: see, feel, listen, taste, smell, touch, and imagine as clearly as possible and as if it were real. Imagine completing your goal as if it were happening right now. Do not underestimate the power of visualization to change your brain and unlock your untapped potential. Also, when you set a goal, remember to be specific and to commit to it publicly if it's a good fit for the goal. Vision boards and affirmations are also great tools to help you visualize in full and stay motivated to complete your super challenging or even "impossible" goals. So, start practicing today and make this year different. You will be amazed to discover you have your own superpowers, both to achieve what you want, and to inspire others to do the same.

The Sense Audit

Norman Chella – Kuala Lumpur, Malaysia

Norman is a serial podcaster, interviewer, digital marketer, and Superhuman Academy Coach. As the Podcast Rainmaker at ThatsTheNorm Media, he produces shows for clients, interviews guest and gives keynotes on podcasting. He uses SuperLearner® techniques to remember names, faces, conversations and interviews.

Know the Human

We are what we learn to be. Everything we learn starts with our senses. It's the only thing that stops us between where we are and where we want to be.

Before you can become superhuman, you need to know who you are right now:

What habits do you have?

What do you pay attention to?

What access to resources do you have?

What do you take into your body?

What do you consume?

etc.

This is who you are right now, a human. You must establish where you are before you can set the course for becoming a superhuman: the ideal version of yourself to strive for.

Intent attracts intent. Intentional inputs lead to intentional outputs. If you desire a certain output or a different future version of yourself, you must first know the inputs influencing you now. Only once you understand these inputs, where they come from, and how they affect you, can you begin to modify them with intention.

Awareness is a prerequisite for control. If you want to change yourself, you must know yourself, and to know yourself you must know your inputs.

In the following pages you will discover a framework for identifying and dissecting your inputs; the first step on the journey to becoming superhuman.

The Sense Audit
Get a piece of paper and something to write with.
With the paper horizontal, divide the paper into six vertical columns.
Label the first five with the following: Sight. Taste. Sound. Touch. Smell. These are the senses you use to understand the world around you. Leave the last column empty for now.
Write down your day-to-day experiences through those senses. These can be simple bullet points of 1-2 sentences each. Write as many as you can.

Sight: What do you see?

Do you spend most of the day on your phone? Looking at your news feeds? Checking out pretty pictures on

Instagram? Looking at dumb pictures on the internet? Netflix all day?

Are you reading books? Looking at people's body language? Staring back at them? Looking at the outside world, questioning everything?

What do you use your eyes for throughout the day? Why? For how long?

Write all your sights down.
Examples:
- *I spend time scrolling down my Twitter feed up to 2 hours each day.*
- *I stare out my window in between breaks working at my laptop. It calms me.*
- *I look at my dogs as I'm playing with them every morning.*

Sound: What do you listen to?

Do you listen to music all the time? Are your headphones in 24/7?

Do you always listen to the complaints of others? Do people share their burdens with you through your ears? Do their voices bring you down or up?

Write it down. Pen the melody. Note their moods. Write all their burdens down. Every single detail. These words go straight to your mind.

Examples:
- *I listen to meditative music at 8 AM every day to start my yoga.*
- *I have a playlist for Spotify for focusing on my work. It's 2 hours long.*
- *I hear complaints from friends over long calls.*

Taste: What do you eat and drink?

Do you eat fast food all the time? Drink soda, coffee, or alcohol? Are your meals balanced? Are you eating large portions? Does your body like it? Do you consider yourself healthy?

Write all your meals down. Note the unhealthy ones.
Examples:
- *I eat chocolate when taking a break. I feel good while eating it, but sick after.*
- *My meals aren't balanced. It's mostly meat, and there are few vegetables.*
- *I drink a beer with dinner every night. It helps me relax.*
- *I tend to eat ice cream every night.*
- *I eat nuts as a snack after working out at 2 PM.*

Smell: What do you smell?

What does your room smell like? How about your car or your workplace? How's your hygiene? What effect does that have on your confidence? What do you think of those who don't take care of their hygiene? Is it repulsive? Do you not mind?

Your nose acts like your second pair of eyes. Write everything that attracts you and repels you. Do you attract or repel?

Write it down.

Examples:

- *I smell lavender from my shampoo. It makes me feel more confident because I'm sensitive to body odour.*
- *The smell of coffee wakes me up in the morning.*
- *I have scented candles at night to help me sleep better.*

Touch: What do you feel?

What do you do in your spare time? Sports? A hobby? Art? Activities? What do you write about? Do you pull the blankets over your head and sleep in until midday? Do you hold up the remote with your left or right hand? Do you feel more comfortable holding your phone in your hand?

Examples:

- *I have my phone in my right hand all the time.*
- *I always make sure to wash my hands after every meal/trip to the bathroom.*
- *The feeling of my bed sheets is comforting.*
- *I go barefoot because I hate the feeling of socks.*
- *My keyboard is dusty, and it always gets on my fingers. I'm on my laptop all day working with this.*

Go as broad and as detailed as you can.

This is an audit of your daily life as told by your senses. You are holding 24 hours of your life in your hands right now.

All of these are inputs: data passed through your body to your mind. They drive the outputs. These inputs, and the resulting outputs, are what make you, YOU. If your life is a canvas, these are the colors you paint with. If you want a different picture, you need different colors.

Take a long, hard look at this paper and ask yourself:
Are you painting the right picture? Is this the life you want?
Are you happy eating unhealthy foods, procrastinating, making excuses, and not being the best version of yourself?
Are you happy with dreaming but not taking action?
Is this what it means to be superhuman?
With these questions in mind, write the title of the last column:

Thought: What do you think about yourself?

Be honest. Is this who you want to be?
What are your dreams? What do you aspire to be? Who do you idolize? Who are your heroes?
Write it all down. There's no right or wrong answer; just write it all down.
All of this is to answer the question: Why aren't you the hero yet?

When you're done, nine times out of ten: Your thoughts clash with the rest of your senses. Your desired outputs are not reflected in your inputs.

Let's put an end to that. Let's achieve.

Separate your Thought column from the others.

Throw the other five columns away. Rip them to pieces.

With your Thought column in hand, you now hold physical evidence of your struggles. This is the fuel that drives you forward.

This column is the foundation for the next step: write a goal. Plan. Do it within the year. Break it into monthly tasks. Weekly tasks. Daily tasks.

This newfound plan requires you to acquire a new set of sensory inputs designed to get you there.

Because superhumans are designed, not born. Intent attracts intent. Intentional inputs lead to intentional outputs.

Everything you plan to do must be followed by the right sensory inputs, instilled with the right habits, and the willingness to follow through on your thoughts. Your inputs must become subject to your thoughts, not the other way around. Everything you write from now on must lead you to that goal.

To be superhuman is to execute this plan you've built for yourself.

Execute, execute, execute. Your senses will shift for the better. You will achieve.

Your senses will thank you, and you will thank yourself.

Habit Building for the "Non-Habit Types"

"Let today be the day you give up who you've been for who you can become."

- Hal Elrod

Meg Zirger – Zaragoza, Spain

Meg is a coach and teacher for Superhuman Academy students and aspiring female entrepreneurs. She loves contemplating and exploring the science and spirituality behind human behavior, transformation and transcendence.

The Traveling Toothbrush

It was 6 pm on a Friday afternoon. I was at King Library in Oxford, Ohio slaving away as all my buddies were out enjoying cold drinks on the beautiful spring afternoon. How had this happened to me again?

After careful planning, I thought for once, just maybe, I'd be able to meet them. But, somehow, and for the millionth time, I couldn't make it. I was bitter.

I had a real knack for letting time get away from me. I'd start the day sure that I was going to get things done in a few hours time and have the afternoon to enjoy. But it never ended that way.

Never.

Eventually, my friends just assumed that even when I said "yes" I would never actually make it to the hangout. I'd work, get side-tracked, go back to work only to realize that yet another day had nearly passed me by and I wasn't finished with the ONE thing that needed done.

I was good at school. Well, I got good grades, at least.

Teachers and peers deemed me "smart", yet when it came to consistency, being aware of the habits that were running my life and managing my time and energy I was one lost kiddo.

I was so "non-habit-y" that the only thing that was consistent (besides my morning coffee) was my disastrous inability to focus and manage time. I knew I was chaotic and all over the place. But perhaps the day when I realized this was spilling over into everything I did (and didn't) was the day my sweet roommate Sarah asked me

"Do you realize that you never put your toothbrush in the same place?"
"Um, no." I laughed.

But this wasn't funny. I realized something had to change . . .

I had a habit of spacing out and doing things differently daily. Because there was very little automaticity in my life, everything took more time and brainpower.

I was tired of afternoons like this. The ones where I felt completely helpless, drowning in my to-dos. They were commonplace, and I was fed up. Why couldn't I be like my friends? Why couldn't I just get things done? Why couldn't I do things in a methodological way for once?

Or could I?

I'm sure you've noticed that some people have no trouble getting things done. They seem to have everything organized, together, and they never drop the ball; they make it look easy. On the other end of the spectrum, people are all over the place and drop every single ball they hold or that you hand them.

These apparent differences became a fixation for me because I so desperately wanted to be the girl that was organized, had all her stuff together, and have it been EASY. I remember envying my peers at university who seemed to be skating along with minimal effort, watching a whole season of a show during the week, and hanging out at bars with friends, while I slaved away at the library, drinking coffee and poring over books. They had the same amount of work as me, and I didn't think they were more intelligent, but they knew how to manage themselves so much better. I thought that I was among a minority of individuals who were doomed to be chaotic, unhabit-y, and always feeling like there wasn't enough time. I had no idea that my lack of ability to form habits (and awareness that I needed to) could be the underlying cause.

When I became a teacher, I realized I was not a minority. I noticed that there were plenty of people who struggled with disorganization and self-management, regardless of age.

This intrigued me. I knew I needed to understand it better, not only for my students, but also for myself. This led me to roll up my sleeves and do research in the space of behavioral sciences and personality psychology.

My findings confirmed the observation that a lot of people struggle to consciously select habits and keep them. Don't believe me? Type in "Habits" into Amazon books and see how many entries come up. You'll find pages and pages of books that are all about habits and how to build them. There is a huge market for this because it's a struggle for so many.

That being said, some people have quite a bit more difficulty than others. If we look at personality psychology, and The Big Five Model (the most widely accepted theory for approaching personality), there are a few traits that offer insight as to why some people are able to build and keep habits easier than others.

The Big Five Model, as the name suggests, looks at five different aspects of personality: conscientiousness, agreeableness, neuroticism, openness, and extraversion. If you are interested in learning more about it, and uncover your scores in each of these aspects, you can easily do so via the link on my resource page at www.superhumanplaybook.com.

While all of these factors may play a role in your ability to build and keep habits, there are two which have a greater impact. They are conscientiousness and neuroticism. Conscientiousness refers to one's tendency toward being responsible, organized, and adhering to rules and norms. Neuroticism, on the other hand, looks at the degree to which individuals are affected by emotions like anxiety, fear, anger, frustration, and may have trouble controlling urges and delaying gratification. So, it's no surprise that those who are more conscientious, and less neurotic are better at managing themselves and their impulses thus making habit building and keeping an easier task for them.

But before you look at your scores and panic, let me just say: no matter what the outcome, there is hope! All of my scores, including those in the conscientious and neurotic aspects, have changed over the years, and yours can too if you are willing to implement new habits which will shift your identity.

Had I taken a deep dive into this 20-year prior, it's likely that my findings would not have been so encouraging. It was once believed that personalities were fixed. Don't like the way you are? Tough cookies. Luckily, that's no longer the case. In fact, new research and longitudinal studies show evidence that personality can change greatly across a lifetime.

While the exact degree to which traits can be modified is not well established, there is now a great deal of anecdotal and scientific evidence that we can change many of our ways of being and doing. So, if it's given that we can change them, the question then becomes how.

How to build habits and keep them when you are SURE you're "the non-habit type"

Simply put: Our habits - our carefully selected behaviors, which ultimately become habits - are the key to rewiring our brain, becoming the person we want to be, and achieving the great goals we have for ourselves.

We all have this ability. Even if you have tried and failed in the past, you have what it takes.

One final note before we jump in. You will recognize a lot of the ideas presented in the following sections from previous chapters. I will reference goal setting, visualization, taking inventory of your sensory experiences and behaviors, etc. Resist the temptation to skim through. What you have read up to this point provides a solid foundation for the actions I am about to recommend. I will briefly review these ideas to contextualize them, but this chapter is all about how to make those strategies work for you, especially if you have failed in the past.

So, if you are ready to build some solid habits and shed the "non-habit type" identity you've been clinging onto for all these years, grab a pen and paper, and keep them on hand to complete the action steps laid out in the chapter. You will recognize these action steps by the symbol: ☐. When you see this symbol, it means that you are going to need to pause your reading and follow the specific action steps.

Speaking generally, desired behavior change has three steps. Throughout this chapter, we will be focusing on the first two. From there, you'll be ready to take action on the third step: implementation. Of course, this is a process that should be repeated over and over again as you choose new behaviors to implement and make adjustments as you move along.

1. **Awareness**: Bringing our subconscious behaviors to the consciousness
2. **Focused attention / design**: Looking at examples of when you are engaging in specific behaviors / careful design of new desired behaviors
3. **Deliberate practice**: Engaging with new desired behaviors and establishing new neural pathways.

We will start with becoming aware. The more awareness you have, the better your ability to find the tools to navigate situations with greater success.

In becoming aware, the first thing you'll need to do is look at your current habits. And by looking, I really mean looking. You need to see your habits written out. It's not enough to think about them. You need to write them out as exhaustively and specifically as possible. You may want to come back to this exercise many times as oftentimes we are not aware of our habits. Habits, by definition, are the automatic responses to specific cues and are housed in our subconscious. To differentiate, prior to a habit, you have behaviors. Behaviors are chosen responses, which come from the conscious mind. So, to select habits and stick to them you'll first need to take inventory of the ones you already engage in. If you are serious about this, you'll want to complete all the steps offered in this chapter. Don't worry, I'll be here to guide you through the process.

When creating your habit inventory, I advocate James Clear's approach (the author of the New York Times Bestseller *Atomic Habits*) which is to write down the habits you engage in, without a doubt, every single day:

- Get out of bed
- Go to the restroom
- Make coffee
- Make bed
- Close the fridge

Etc.

Followed by the things that happen around you or to you:

- The sun rises

- My alarm goes off
- The microwave beeps
- I get an email

Etc.[12]

☐ The easiest way to get things done is to break them down into little action steps and tick them off your list. So, rather than continue on and let the to-do's pile up and then never complete them you need to stop your reading right now, set a timer for twenty minutes and create these lists. You may have done something similar while reading "Putting off Procrastination"; revisit that list and see if you can add anything else to it. As I said before, as time passes, and you pay closer attention, you'll discover more and more hidden habits. But, for now, be as exhaustive as you can about the habits you know you engage in, and the things that happen around you. Set a timer to keep yourself on task and then come back to reading for your next steps when you finish. If you don't act on this right now, I'm afraid to say that you're already giving up on yourself and your quest to become the kind of person that builds and keeps habits.

Now that you've got these lists, put them aside. They will serve you when you are ready to work in new habits and anytime you'd like to add to your inventory. Before digging into that, however, there is a bit more work around awareness that needs done. It includes how you deal with rules and expectations. After all, habits start with a set of selected behaviors or "rules" that you impose on yourself. So, if you want to keep them and convert them into automatic responses, or habits, you'll want to understand how you deal with rules in the first place.

Having spent years in the teaching and coaching fields, I've come to observe that some students and clients do whatever you ask them to-do, others do whatever they think they need to do, and others . . . well, they do what they want when they want and don't when they don't. It's likely that in your work or study contexts you've observed the same. Yet, it wasn't until I stumbled upon the New York Times Bestseller *The Four Tendencies*, by Gretchen Rubin that I finally figured out how to fully help these very different styles to be successful.

The Four Tendencies expresses how people deal with expectations and rules differently. As you want to become the kind of person who is capable of crafting and keeping habits, you'll first need to understand how you respond to rules, or the imposed behaviors you'll be selecting for yourself.

A quick overview of the types as they relate to habits and percentages of the population they represent:

Obligers will be more likely to build and keep habits when they have **outside accountability**. (41%)

Questioners will be more likely to build and keep habits, which they believe to be **important, have evidence**

of **working**, are **efficient** to help them achieve their desires. (24%)

Upholders are likely to be very good at building habits. **Feeling fulfilled** and **upholding expectations** for both themselves and others is important. (19%)

Rebels will be more likely to build and keep habits that fit in with their **authentic selves**, or out of **love for others**. (17%)[13]

As you can see from their descriptions, the only tendency Gretchen suggests is quite capable of managing themselves and their habits, are the "Upholders". In other words, at least 81% of us likely struggle with it to some degree. As Gretchen offers that not everyone falls nicely in just one category, it's likely that some Upholders struggle to some degree as well. Either way, if you have interest in becoming the author of your identity and carrying out habits that you've selected for your life, you'll definitely want to uncover your tendency with Gretchen's framework as your next step.

☐Stop here and take 15 minutes to find out your tendency: Upholder, Questioner, Obliger, or Rebel. You can find the link to the quiz on my resource page at www.superhumanplaybook.com.

Once you know your type and how it works, you have one of the keys to constructing your environment in a way that enables you to uphold new rules and behaviors (which you'll later convert into habits). Save your tendency result as we will come back to this later.

As an aside, I would also highly recommend reading Gretchen's book *The Four Tendencies*, as this will not only help you in your habit journey, but also in understanding those around you better. When you know how someone deals with expectations, it's a lot easier to work with them successfully. So, if one of your aspirations is to become better in persuading people, this read would be a great inspiration to convert some behaviors into habits.

Once you've completed both of these steps, you should have two things: 1. a list of your current habits and environmental cues (the list of things that happen to you throughout the day) 2. Your tendency. Now it's time for my favorite step which is crafting your vision of where you want to go. That is, the answer to the questions: "Who is the person you want to see in the mirror in six months?" and "What are the specific things you want to achieve?". Farther down the road you will want to take the vision even further, say five or ten years. But, for now, six months is a great starting point and an exciting exercise!

☐ Stop reading and reflect on the vision you'd like to create for yourself. I recommend that you go to the most expansive and inspiring place you have nearby (a rooftop lounge, backyard looking off into the woods, etc.) By doing this, rather than writing this up in any old place, you greatly increase your capacity to see and feel possibilities for yourself. This may require you to plan in advance and isn't something that should be rushed. In fact, I recommend leaving at least half an hour for this on a first draft and to revisit and tweak it for a few days after. You'd be surprised how much you may add to your vision in subsequent days. This should be something that is a challenge, yet achievable. It also should inspire you, get you feeling excited. It might even scare you a little. The more specific and tangible you can make it, the easier it will be to spot the appropriate behaviors.

Now that you've identified the vision for your life six months down the road, it's time to design backwards. This means choosing your behaviors strategically based on who you want to be and what you want to achieve.

For this step, we will revisit Dr. BJ Fogg, PhD's, New York Times Bestseller: *Tiny Habits*.[3] We start with what Fogg calls the "Swarm of Behaviors Model". This consists of writing out as many behaviors as you can think of that you could implement in order to reach your desired outcome. This list could include behaviors that are frequently repeated or those which are done once.

For example, let's say you want to become healthier and you've given yourself a 6 month timeline to make it happen. Firstly, it would be important to decide what "healthier" in six months looks like to you. Maybe it's sleeping at least 7.5 hrs a night. Maybe it is losing 10 pounds. Write out the specifics you'd like to achieve and then take a look at possible behaviors that will get you there: buy blackout curtains, consume leafy greens five times a week, etc.

After brainstorming all of these behaviors, it's time to comb through them and decide which ones will be the best fit for you. In *Tiny Habits,* Dr. Fogg offers a couple of different ways to do this. The quickest way, is to pull out a highlighter and pen to select the behaviors that he refers to as "golden":

A "Golden Behavior is one that…

1. is effective in realizing your aspiration (impact),
2. you want to do (motivation), and
3. you can do [with relative ease] (ability).[3]

*for a more in-depth, systematic approach, review the "focus mapping" strategy laid out in *Tiny Habits.*

This framework works very well, especially when combined with Gretchen Rubin's four tendencies. So, when considering behaviors, you should also look at how you respond to rules and expectations. For example, let's say you are an Obliger and you want to up your reading from 200 wpm to 700 wpm in the next 3 months. You would benefit from an accountability partner who understands your goal and your tendencies. On the other hand, if you are a Questioner you may need a partner who is an expert in the material because in order to do what it takes to get good you'll need to understand why it's important. That said, when it comes to converting behaviors into strong habits, accountability can be a powerful tool for all types when approached correctly.

☐ So, now it's time to pause, brainstorm and find your "Golden Behaviors". You'll need a pen, paper and highlighter for this activity.

1. First, choose one thing that you want to achieve. This should be achievable in the next 6 months. Write it down.
2. Now, write out all the possible behaviors you can think of to achieve that outcome.
3. Lastly, highlight the behaviors that would be most effective in helping you and then star or circle those that you can do with relative ease and want to do.

* Remember your tendency and create behaviors that you are even more likely to consistently nail!

Something else to consider is what I like to call a "domino effect habits". Through my own habit building, I've found that there are certain habits that are not only highly effective, but also impact all of the others. A great example of this is improving your sleep. When you improve your sleep (and there are many habits to put in place to do so) it spills out into all other parts of your life:

You have more energy to: make good decisions, workout, respond well in relationships, learn and retain.

So, when looking at your possible behaviors you should not only consider the ones you can and want to do, rather, you should also look at the ones that will have the biggest overall impact. These are the behaviors which you will be able to sustain, wire in your brain to stay, and will get you where you want to go the quickest.

When you talk to experts in behavior change and habit building, they all talk about the importance of starting small. The mistake most people make is overestimating their ability to maintain their current motivation (which dwindles over time.)

So, whatever the habit you'd like to create, you should start with the smallest step. For example, if you want to begin every day with reading, you first need to make the start of that habit automatic and then increase from there. When I created this habit, it started with the simple behavior of picking up my kindle and turning it on while heating the water for my coffee. That is all I had to do. Once I was able to do that in an automatic way, I began to increase by reading a few pages. This slowly began to increase, and I now read for about 30 minutes. When starting out, however, it's so important not to overdo it. The goal is to make it as easy as possible and require the least amount of motivation when creating new habits.

☐ Stop here and write down your small behaviors for each one of your larger goal habits. In my case, my big goal was to read for 30 minutes every morning. My small habit that needed to be wired in prior to the desired behavior was taking the kindle to the kitchen in the morning and turning it on.

Now that you have defined the small behavior that you hope to grow into a habit you can carefully decide where you want to place it. If you don't have a specific cue (prompt) for it, it's destined to fail. In order to illustrate this, let's say you decide to meditate right after you make your bed. Your cue then is the moment when you finish putting the comforter in place, or the last cushion in its daytime place. Whatever the last action is that you complete is your suggestion as to your next action or behavior.

Most of the time, our environment is already filled with all kinds of habits (automatic behaviors we are often unaware of) and cues (triggers that spark these habits), which is why it's easier to wire a new habit in a new environment. Consider how you feel after a break-up. When you engage with the same environment that you did with your ex it's more likely you'll fall into old habits, ways of thinking, as well as memories. Your environment is a reminder to your subconscious. If you move to a new city, however, and thus open yourself up to a whole new set of environments, people and emotions you'll likely be able to set up and recover (or rewire your brain) much sooner.

This is no surprise when we look at the science of the brain. The brain is prompted by things that it sees. That's where the phrase "out of sight, out of mind" comes from. Your environment is key, whether that be your home, your desk, or even the people you surround yourself with. Your environment should make it easy for you to practice your habit or avoid those which you don't want to practice. As James Clear says, "If you want to make a habit a big part of your life, make the cue a big part of your environment." He suggests that every habit should have a home.[12] Context and specificity is key. When we don't design this well, we waste precious brainpower constantly reconstructing our cues and restarting our routines, increasing the overall effort in completing the behavior and decreasing the likelihood of consistently doing it.

☐ It's time for another pause. Now are going to define the when and where of your desired habits. It doesn't need to occur at a certain hour and minute, but it should fall in the same place within a progression. Here is my morning routine to illustrate this approach:

Habits:

1. Get out of bed
2. When my feet touch the floor, say "It's going to be a great day!" (The "Maui Habit" as coined and recommended by Dr. Fogg in *Tiny Habits*[3])
3. Grab Kindle

4. Walk to kitchen + Set Kindle on the counter
5. Start heating water
6. Use restroom
7. Wash hands + face
8. Put coffee in french press + stir
9. Turn on Kindle + begin reading (Here is where I celebrate)
10. Read a few pages
11. Press and pour coffee

Etc.

*Note: This morning routine isn't a written list now; it's ingrained in me. I just do it - out of habit.

Depending on your tendency from Gretchen Rubin's framework, you may want to get outside accountability (Obliger), define very clearly why it is important for you to follow through (Questioner), or identify how the new habits help others and align with your authentic self (Rebel).

Now that you have homes for your habits, it's time to add the good feelings. The brain loves to feel good. So, if we can attach positive feelings to our habit it will take root sooner and be easier to maintain. This is the key to rewiring the brain because it releases the neurotransmitter dopamine. Another thing to consider, as well, is that the brain doesn't have to necessarily engage in the behavior for dopamine to be released. Rather, it also does when you anticipate experiencing pleasure.[12] Surely you've experienced this and is why many of us have spent countless hours of our life imagining winning, being successful, etc. It feels good! In other words, we can even practice our habits outside of their place, create positive emotions to help us wire in our habits successfully.

However, if you are only imagining yourself completing the habits, you'll eventually become disappointed that you aren't actually doing them. So, it's obviously important to carry them out as well. As for creating positive feelings (rewards to encourage behavior) Clear and Dr. Fogg suggest different strategies.

I like to utilize both as I find each brings something to my habit game. Clear recommends doing a habit stack. In other words, putting a habit that you want to engage in after one that you need, or putting the one you need after one that you already do.[12] On the other hand, Dr. Fogg advocates for putting the new habit after a specific cue, which he refers to as a prompt, and then celebrating. He highlights the importance of celebrating *immediately* after the habit in an authentic way, at least until the habit is automatic.

☐ It's time to pause and create a plan to successfully transform your desired behaviors into long-standing habits. The only way to do that, apart from the careful design you've already engaged in, is feeling good about what you are doing. If doing a behavior doesn't make you feel good, you won't do it. I suggest celebrating authentically just like Dr. Fogg suggests in *Tiny Habits*.[3]

So, here you are going to brainstorm about possible celebrations that you will engage in. According to behavior science and Dr. Fogg, it's crucial that those good feelings which come about from celebrating occur immediately after.[3] This could include smiling, saying something positive to yourself in your head; it might be crossing something off a list. For more celebrations I suggest looking at moments you feel great or successful. What is it that you do in those moments? Once you've brainstormed about possible celebrations, you are ready to try them out to uncover which gets you feeling best.

If you've followed through with all the actions in this chapter, first I'd like to say "Congrats!" You are clearly committed to making a real shift in your current "non-habity" ways by becoming the conscious designer of your life and bringing constant improvement to it. This step-by-step process is a great start, but if you want to dive deeper, I'd recommend reading *Tiny Habits* and *Atomic Habits*. Both are gems, although I'm partial to *Tiny Habits* for its ease to implement in your life. I'd love to hear your experience with habits, whatever that may look like. You can find my contact information on the resource page for my chapter at www.superhumanplaybook.com.

Lastly, I invite you to consider the following. As James Clear says "success is not a goal to reach or a finish line to cross. It is a system to improve, an endless process to refine."[12] So, it's time to carefully build a system, start small, and scale from there. As you become "the habit type" you will begin to see your small habits grow, multiply and ultimately allow you to create the person you want to be. There is a reason why everyone talks about habits in the world of self-improvement. They are the way to better yourself and achieve success in every arena.

Performing in an "Agile" Way

"Achievement happens when we pursue and attain what we want. Success comes when we are in clear pursuit of why we want it."

- Simon Sinek

 Kevin Borrmann – Tuebingen, Germany
Kevin is an IT consultant, project management professional, and SuperLearner Certified coaches. In his "spare" time, utilizes all those skills and his beliefs for different kind of activities like martial arts, horse riding and learning piano.

The Journey

When you look back at your achievements in life, what comes to your mind? Maybe you think about your college diploma, maybe your first job or the promotion that came with a company car.

But how did you get there? Coincidence? Luck? Or did you pursue your dreams and your vision in life?

If you want to reach or repeat those achievements - let us take a little trip into your own mind. A trip that will help you find yourself and use modern project management frameworks for your own transformation journey.

1. Getting yourself a vision

When you think about visions, you think about the future. But what is your future? Where do you see yourself in a few years? These are the same questions over and over again. In order to answer them, you should know beforehand in which direction you really want to go.

Imagine staying in bed all day. Would you really do this, or is there something that gets you out of bed?

Many people have their own worldview, which motivates them to get up every day. The question is, how do you find such a vision?

2. Is what you do really what you want?

Reflect on the present. You have to ask yourself the question:

Is my current job what I really want?

The answer to this question determines whether you really want to change. Let us assume that the answer is clear: NO!

With this NO a big personal change process begins within your own thoughts, your own behaviour, and then further in your whole environment. With this NO, another question arises with little effort: What do I really want?

This question is now a much more difficult one because there is no universal answer. Answering this question is a very individual process for every single person, and a process that will take time. To craft your vision, you can look back on your life and talk to your friends. This look backwards in your life helps you identify what values you believe in, what is important, and what patterns of thought keep recurring in your life. The vision comes from your past and it will change your future.

For example, my vision is:

To create a safe environment of support and growth so that everyone around me can devote themselves to their work and goals with joy and passion.

This vision gets me out of bed every morning. And everyone who has a vision will agree that this is what drives their life.

3. Setting your Goal to fulfill your Vision

Once you have found your vision-statement - the idea of how you want to lead your life in the future - you need to define goals to reach it.

But how can you set goals to achieve this vision?

To do this, first of all, we take a look at whether we actually behave in a way that fits our newly found beliefs. What good is a vision, if we behave in completely opposite ways?

Imagine if I blamed all of my friends and family for every single one of my mistakes. Would this be in line

with my example? Should I not try to understand the reason for a mistake and think "How can I look at my mistakes, so that I can learn from it?". Would this not be much more in line with my example than blaming things on   others?
First of all, we have to start with ourselves.

It is only up to us whether we want to change, and only we can change ourselves.

This thought also means that we should put all our efforts into changing ourselves. Every action should further our cause. Our cause reflects our deepest drive and therefore the goal in our lives.

4. From Big to Small
Now that you have made your vision your innermost driver in life, you want to direct your actions towards this goal. However, one question still remains: How do you get closer to your vision?

Break down your vision into guiding topics, specific goals and tasks.

In order to get closer to your vision, the first step is to define goals that point in the direction of your own vision and that are also in harmony with it.

Not all goals need to be known immediately. They can change over time; they can expand whenever you broaden your knowledge about different topics. But they can also be affected by a change of scope, for example, when you realize a goal has become completely obsolete.

The first step for setting your specific goals is to develop guiding topics. These guiding topics describe all the subjects that need to be considered in order to reach your goal. There can be more than one level between the vision and a goal.

For my vision, these guiding topics can now look like this:

An identified guiding topic is the area "Accelerated Learning". From this guiding topic, one or more SMART goals are defined. They show you how to "conquer" this guiding topic and make it your own.

I want to read 600+ wpm with 80% comprehension within the next 12 weeks, so that I can read 2 books per month by the end of this year.

But now this goal is broken down even further, because a question arises: "What do I have to do to achieve this goal?"

These are then the specific tasks:

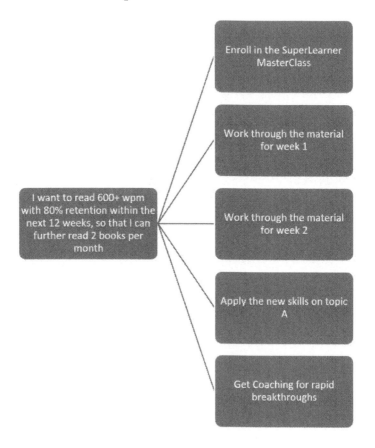

Now the individual tasks have been created from the simple vision. And every single task works for us. Completing those tasks of a guiding topic leads to our vision being fulfilled. The last step, of course, is to implement the individual tasks in your life and work them.

5. Outperform through Evaluation and Iteration

The task is done. The goal is reached. Now look at your next goal...and, wait a moment,

Now is the time to appreciate the underdog of all development processes: the "agile" approach. It does not matter if you talk about software development, project management or development of personal skills. This process is what makes or breaks everything we have reached so far:

Evaluation and iteration

Evaluation is key for every aspect in your life as a SuperLearner.

Imagine you have just started working towards a goal by completing the individual tasks. Things are going well; you can see progress. However, one hardly asks the most important question: Could I have done this more effectively?

In many cases, you can answer the question with YES. So, let us use a very simple technique:

take a step back.

Sit down for a moment and consider your path after reaching a certain "Milestone". Just look back to your starting point and reconstruct the way you chose to reach your milestone. And then, ask yourself: "How did I get there?"

The process followed to achieve a goal is just as important as achieving the goal.

To make this clear, let us look at our small task: "Working through the SuperLearner Masterclass course" in two different ways:

Way 1:

After 12 weeks I completed the course and got my certification. However, I only reach 600+ wpm with great difficulty. While working on the course materials, I also finished a couple series on Netflix and struggled to apply all the techniques I learned in the Masterclass in real life.

Way 2:

After 12 weeks I completed the course and got my certification. I have easily reached my goal of 600+ wpm with 80% retention because I was fully focused in every session.

The goal was achieved in both short scenarios, but it is clear which scenario has the better sustainability. This consideration helps you to turn your life into the life of a SuperLearner, because we have also found something that can be improved even further and in addition to our original goal. We have worked out the following statement:

I have to work to really focus on the task at hand.

This reflection now affects all goals and the processing of all tasks. It is not really a task at the moment, but a guideline for further improvement. And if this personal guideline is taken into account, this has an impact on the prioritization, the setting of goals, and the achievement of your unlimited personal potential.

And then comes the moment where *iteration* begins.

The term of iteration describes the repetition of a process. And performing the same process over and over again is the perfect way to turn it into a habit.

Once you have evaluated the process and refined your learning guidelines, the whole process starts again. We are defining our next goal, making sure it is in sync with our beliefs and our guiding topics. You can even prioritize your goals again and start working on those with your new guidelines in mind.

This is what you can call "agile" in a simple way.[14]

You can improve the way you learn, achieve your goals, and become the person you want to be, because you are learning to improve your complete approach based on evaluations and not just assumptions.

With this mindset, you can outperform yourself from day one.

Conclusion

In summary, it is important to find your own visions and to derive tasks from them in order to completely align your personal attitude with your goals in life. When we have done all of this, we only have to define our specific goals so that we can achieve our dreams.

And go even one step further and really invest the effort of reflecting your own approach on every task you tackle in the future. You will align all your behaviours with your vision and also be more self-aware. And further still: You will outperform yourself.

This is one of many techniques to achieve success in your life, but without evaluation and iteration, all other techniques are only as good as your first attempt.

Productivity is Social

"Dear George, remember no man is a failure who has friends."

- Angel Clarence, It's A Wonderful Life

Dahyu Patel – Washington D.C., USA

Dahyu is an Competitive Intelligence Professional, a Sales Velocity SME, a serial entrepreneur, a certified Unbeatable Mind, SuperLearner, and Time coach and much more. He has worked extensively with Special Forces teams, Intelligence Agencies, countless businesses, and entrepreneurs to maximize results through time-bending.

It's a Team Sport

Prosocial behavior is social behavior that "benefit[s] other people or society as a whole", such as helping, sharing, donating, co-operating, and volunteering.

Productivity is thought of as a solo sport. We hear the rules all the time - blueprints from so-called "life hackers" - but what you don't see is the critical role of community. We are leaving a lot on the table when we perform in solo mode: feeling alive and ahead, energy and flow, efficiency and effectiveness, and a host of powerful neurochemical benefits. The truth is, there is a counterintuitive way to reap all those benefits, and it's not the lone-wolf life hacks you've heard.

No Time for People

In my early teens, I experienced my first death in life. My cousin Chandra, living with us with her husband and young son, was the epitome of a walking angel. She lit up the room wherever she went and had such a grace about her that would melt any problems you had away. It was in the middle of the day that we received a call from the hospital. The house was loud and busy with visiting relatives, and yet an eerie silence passed over everyone. Time slowed. My aunt put down the phone, turned to the group, and, in a shallow voice, told us Chandra passed away while giving birth to her second child. Time stopped. I felt my body become light and empty inside. I thought of all the times I had chosen not to spend time with her because of schoolwork I procrastinated on, responsibilities deferred for the instant gratification of watching TV.

How many times had I foregone quality time with family and friends because of my relationship to time? I had constructed a mental pattern and neural connections around deferring responsibilities; it just became normal after a while. Then when time freed up - a snow day when I got to stay home - I said to myself, "I will use this time to catch up; this is what I needed"...but I continued to think time was infinite till it wasn't. This pattern of waiting for cancelations in my schedule to not only get caught up but to "get ahead" was the product of delusion, and I didn't grow out of it. I carried it with me even in my work for the Department of Homeland Security - picture Jack Bauer, but always running behind. Deferring responsibility always came at the cost of spending time with friends and family. Even when I did go out to parties or social gatherings, I wasn't fully present. I couldn't be! My head was full of these nagging thoughts, hovering and pulling me away from enjoying myself, reminding me of all the things I was putting off. Spending time with family and friends meant falling further behind, "catching up" - which never truly happened anyway - meant neglecting friends and family. Feeling constantly behind SUCKS, especially when it lasts decades.

The Covid-19 pandemic became the largest social experiment in recent history. What happens when you give a huge portion of a population of people who always feel behind unprecedented free time? Some began to complete the things they'd always wanted to do but didn't have the time for; most came face-to-face with the painful realization that time has never been the problem. It is not time, but our relationship to it that is the problem. Not time, but discipline. Not time, but mindset. More than ever, during worldwide shutdowns, we should have time to invest in our deepest relationships, and yet relationships continue to starve because most of us still feel like we are running behind. The ideas discussed in this chapter aren't just "hacks" to get more done, they are the key to unlocking a lifestyle of being fully present with the people you love and fully engaged in that which matters most.

Feeling Ahead

Feeling ahead is a nirvana-like state when your mind and thoughts zero in on the NOW and you are energized to take proactive action. When you start something that is due next week and get it done in 60 mins instead of 5 days, not only can you cross it off your list, you just recaptured all the mental energy you would have wasted thinking about it instead of taking action. When you own Parkinson's Law, instead of it owning you, you will achieve the ultimate productivity high: you will feel ahead. Feeling caught up is great; feeling ahead is infinitely better. When you feel behind, you are drowning. When you feel caught up, you come up for air... for a moment. Only when you feel ahead can you rise out of the flood, look around, and help others. This is true cost of feeling behind and feeling caught up, the cost of being there for others. How we relate to time determines how we relate to others. Your relationship to time affects not just you, it affects everyone around you and then it affects everyone around *them.* When you time-compress successfully, shortening the duration to complete a task, and you do so long before the deadline, there is an energized emotion that surfaces. So, when there is an "8-hour" project due in 2 weeks, and you immediately time compress and get half of it done in 2 hours, everyone you interact with afterwards benefits from an energizing ripple effect emanating from you. One who successfully time-compresses and feels ahead is **time affluent.**

Time Affluence and Poverty

Time affluence is the feeling that one has sufficient time to pursue activities that are personally meaningful, to reflect, and to engage in leisure. Time famine, or poverty, is the opposite, the feeling that one is constantly stressed, rushed, overworked, and behind.

So how can we have more of the former and less of the latter? The answer may surprise you.

Research performed at Harvard, Wharton, and Yale revealed a counterintuitive solution to the problem of time famine: give your time away.[15]

Doesn't make sense, right?

How can you give away what you don't have?

And that is exactly the point. When we give our time away, we tell our brains that we have an abundance. Give away enough time, and do so consistently, and the mind adopts a new perception of time. Time is no longer scarce, no longer fixed; it is elastic. This doesn't mean have to spend your days in the soup kitchen, but it does mean that if you want more affluence and less famine, you need to find opportunities to be generous with your time. There are infinite ways to do this, but this chapter isn't about those, it's just about one.

The Anatomy of Friendship

While building a tech start-up in 2007, I observed many other entrepreneurs building their companies alone. They were given the apt title of "solopreneurs". Even if you join a weekly or monthly mastermind group, it's incredibly challenging and lonely to build a company by yourself. So, I created and tested an accountability / accelerator framework for entrepreneurs to support one another and find new ways to test our relationship to time. I initially experimented with 150 solopreneurs to determine how long it would take strangers to become close friends - "3 AM-emergency-call" kind of friends who are always ready to support in times of trouble. A pattern emerged. On average, at 22 days into the relationship, something would change, something that proved to be the difference between strangers and close friends. What we uncovered was a conversational anatomy used unconsciously, and only, by loyal companions. After studying various entrepreneur organizations like EO and even successful Weight Watchers groups, we realized whether this conversational anatomy manifested or not came down to frequency of the human connection over a short duration of time in smaller groups (3-5 people per group). In an attempt to leverage this discovery, I invented PowerTribes™, in which 3-5 people would speak daily for 5-10 mins each to share 1-2 hard tasks for the day, reverse engineer them, and get feedback and strategies from the tribe to complete the tasks within a specific time frame. The PowerTribe would then reconvene when the tasks were completed to report success or face the SHAME of looking bad in front of the tribe... now, this was done with compassion and not true shaming or talking down to one other, but from the outside looking in, the distinction is difficult to appreciate. The art of supporting with firmness and calling out bullshit with love is not taught anywhere. It was through thousands of observations, hundreds of social experiments, and eventually, the formation of PowerTribes, that the ultimate secret to productivity and feeling ahead was uncovered: PowerUp calls.

PowerUp calls

PowerUp calls are exactly what they sound like, calls. If you are like most call-weary professionals, the prospect of being on the phone a single second longer than you have to may sound like a painful waste of time, and done poorly, it is! There are two critical components to PowerUp calls: The Who and the How. To illustrate the Who, consider the following.

The Who

In 2001, during a series of interviews, Tiger Woods attributed his rapid goal achievement to having daily morning calls with a group called "The Brothers." The Brothers consisted of himself, Michael Jordan, Charles Barkley, and Ahmad Rashad, and not a day went by that they did not speak on the phone, or at least correspond via email, to keep them connected, accountable, focused. They didn't wait for crises to strike to reach out with help and encouragement, they made time for each other proactively, building successful habits through a consistent, collaborative effort. How did Tiger create this unofficial PowerTribe for himself? It didn't just happen because he was famous; he waited patiently for Michael Jordan to shower, complete his postgame interviews, and sign the obligatory autographs at the United Center in Chicago. Tiger knew he needed help from people who understood the overwhelm of rising fame and constant pressure to perform at the highest level. To get the Who aspect right, follow Tiger's example. Seek out and connect with people that align with your values and beliefs and understand your circumstances. Create your own PowerTribe, like The Brothers, or just call someone you know will engage in intentional, mutual encouragement. As for the How, this brings us to the Timed Conversation.

The How: The Timed Conversation

Imagine you and your co-worker need to have a 30-minute conversation, and you start the conversation by saying, "I only have 5 minutes, so we are going to have to condense 30 minutes into 5." They are flustered, but you don't budge, and they realize they don't have an option.

Then something special happens: your co-worker shoots details at you in rapid-fire sequence, and, under pressure, their brain prioritizes and takes every shortcut it can find. We are told it is rude to speak too quickly, but something empowering happens when you do. You are literally thinking and speaking at the same time. Given the 5-minute challenge, your co-worker is energized, blood is pumping, and they are giving you valuable information without interjecting niceties or chit chat. This becomes a lean and productive 2 minutes. You tell them they have 3 minutes left, and somehow, they manage to get all the points across and answer all of the questions the conversation was meant to address.

You congratulate them. They have just given you 30 minutes' worth of content in 5 minutes, and now they can use the allocated 25 remaining minutes to do something else — they can go on a walk, call their kids, plan a date. Your co-worker will be energized because they have beaten the clock. They have become the magician, made more time in their day, and created space for something truly important to them.

Now think of 10 seconds. Yes, 10-whole-seconds. We all think we know what 10 seconds is — One Mississippi, Two Mississippi… but what a person can achieve in 10 seconds is quite miraculous. This is an exercise I often give to my students, and when I present it to them, they usually spend more than 10 seconds telling me it is impossible to do anything in such a brief amount of time. But it is the last 10 seconds on the timer when you truly push yourself beyond your self-perceived limits and bring everything together quickly and logically. We have to trust our brains and eliminate self-conscious thinking from the equation.

That said, in everyday conversations, the last 10 seconds means everything because it defines the experience of the meeting and it generates the energy that dictates the results. We normally end meetings with friendly banter and personal topics, so we finish on a soft note, but that covers up what really needs to be accomplished following the conversation. Use your final 10 seconds to say, "Great call. I'll send you the key action points now."

Right after you put down the phone, write up the five things that need to be done from your 5-minute call. Your colleagues will be so energized by your Be Ahead actions that it will speed them up too. You will create a culture of Feeling Ahead. Now everyone involved can enjoy their evening, be present with loved ones, and crave more collaborative results like this one. Because, in under 15 minutes, you have discussed a project and are moving it forward with key follow-up, time-sensitive points. YOU HAVE A PLAN. Why can't we make this type of behavior addictive and squash Parkinson's Law?

When we apply timers to conversations, we establish a commitment between all parties to get something done. There is a kind of accountability, a trust, a faith that everyone is making the most of a given timeframe. Anyone can add a timer to a social event, but what matters more than the actual timer is the context behind it, how we set things up before we start the timer and get everyone in sync with the mission and task at hand. Then we can break it down, think it through, and execute ferociously – like a bat out of hell.

Timed conversations are the way of the future. Used in the right context with the right intentions, it can change the polarity of your life and accelerate your results. I imagine a world where people make time for each other on a regular basis to push each other forward to be the best versions of ourselves, a world where people really energize people.

Forming Your PowerUp Network

1. Right now, put pen to paper - create a list of 5-7 people for the week to call and send them a note with some context to see if they want to opt-in. You can give them a time window and day you will call, but the fun part is: you get to pick the moment of the call. This format is based on a psychological concept called variable reinforcement. For many people there is a dopamine release and a corresponding rise in energy levels and focus when they know something is going to happen, but they don't know when. But be mindful that this is not the case for everyone. Some movers and shakers may require a heads up, so use discretion and experiment with what works best for you and your contacts.

2. Call one person a day and say, "I will help you reach your goal through a 10-minute timed phone call. (just pure help and we're OUT).

3. Let people know

   "There's only one catch: you won't see it coming. We're not going to schedule it.

You'll just get a call from me, and you either pick up the phone, or you won't.

Are you game? Let's see if we can both rapidly accelerate our execution time."

Guidelines for Power Up Calls

1. Call AFTER you have completed something hard off your to-do list – preferably using time compression – and set a timer for 10-15 mins. This action will generate energy that you can channel into the person on the other end of the call.

2. Clear emotional blocks by simply asking them to breathe.

3. Get clear on the sequence of tasks needed to complete the goal. Start at the end and work backwards. It's challenging to time compress a task if there are unknowns; if they do not know all the steps to get to the finish line, then one of the action items is to call 2 experts to learn the missing steps.

4. Get them to commit the time/space to do the tasks and text you the proof. There should be an established number of hours and minutes for this; don't be vague.

5. Announce when there are "5 mins left", "60 secs left", and "30 secs left". At 30 seconds left, start wrapping up, listing and agreeing on the steps to get the task completed within a certain time interval. During the last 10 seconds say bye and hangup…..if there is more to talk about, they can email you. It's very important to END ON TIME even if you feel there is more to discuss. If you don't respect your timelines, they are meaningless and will work against you.

Once they have completed their tasks, and become energized as a result, it's their turn to return the favor with a PowerUp call.

Besides the accountability, energy, and organization, PowerUp calls increase oxytocin – a hormone connected to a sense of happiness and fulfillment - which drastically increases your productivity. People tend to get sprint-like energy boosts similar to the stress boost related to a looming deadline, but the energy is connected to purpose than the deadline. The research shows that by helping someone for 45 mins, you can get back 75 minutes in terms of heightened creativity, enthusiasm, and clarity – not to mention reciprocity. You are building a savings account of human energy that you may need one day. What I have observed over the course of 150 social experiments is that when people energize people, everyone reaches their goals faster than from any other productivity system or hack.

Who are the people that energize and push you forward? You can be that friend. It starts with you. If you become an energizer through PowerUp Calls, then people will become energizers for you. Imagine receiving a call from a friend or colleague just to encourage you and help you reach your goals. How many energizers would you love to have in your day? This is what Navy Seal Teams do for each other on the battlefield and off. Be that for someone else and you will see unimaginable productivity gains, like achieving 2 years' worth of goals in 6 months. The results can be endless, and no productivity books or "guru" is talking about it. And remember what it is all about: You can't help others if you are drowning. You can't be present with the people you love, if you are always thinking about work. Get ahead, stay ahead, and PowerUp.

Repetition, Active Recall, and Reflection for Knowledge Integration and Creation

"Do yourself a favor and learn all you can; then remember what you learn and you will prosper."

- Proverbs 19:8 GNT

 Rahel Zeleke – Jonkoping, Sweden

Rahel is a Ph.D. candidate in Digitization and Automation in Construction Industry and a SuperLearner Certified Coach. She is passionate about learning and memory and inspiring people to achieve their big dreams!

The Pursuit of Prosperity

Human beings desire prosperity. There is nothing wrong with desiring prosperity. We are created to live in abundance and overflowing prosperity. The holistic meaning of prosperity can be put as the state of no lack. Even though material possession is one aspect of the manifestation of prosperity, the real essence goes well above and beyond that. Joy, happiness, victory, and freedom are some other aspects of real prosperity. A mind full of peace, emotional stability, undisturbed and untroubled well-being, a strong, fit, and healthy body. The list can go on and on.

A steppingstone to unleash all this abundance that is available to human beings includes using our brains optimally through learning and remembering. That might not sound very promising to you because maybe you have been learning your whole life and still you may not be able to prosper. The question is, though:

- Are you truly learning in such a way that you integrate the knowledge you are learning to the point where you can apply it and multiply it (creation of knowledge from the existing knowledge)?
- Are you maintaining what you have been learning until it becomes your second nature?
- Have you discovered the most fundamental subject of learning, which is studying and transforming yourself to the higher and prosperous self that fits the higher mission of life you've been called to as a living being?
- Are you able to release yourself from the regrets of the past and from the fear of the future?"

The subject of studying self is very fascinating because all we need for life is concealed in ourselves. All we need is to discover and release it. Discovering and developing ourselves creates abundance in our lives. The journey of studying self brings change in all aspects of our lives. It gives us the ability to do the creative best we can with our life. Even in the face of failure, we learn to rise up and continue our journey, knowing that we are not defined by our mistakes or by what is happening in our life. Learning, most importantly, accelerated learning, enables us to acquire this ability.

As said by the ancient, remarkably wise and exceedingly wealthy king of Israel, Solomon, "learn all you can and remember what you learn and you will prosper"! This is a sweet sound to my ear, especially knowing that I have the infrastructure and the techniques I need to learn all I can and remember all I learned in an accelerated manner. I am excited to share my experiences with you.

Knowledge Integration

Knowledge integration means combining externally acquired knowledge with knowledge already possessed by an individual to create new, innovative knowledge. One way of integrating your knowledge is to use Bloom's taxonomy. This framework has been used for several years by educators to help students learn effectively, and it can be used as a guide to start your process of organized learning (see Fig 1). The framework has six cognitive levels as a stairway to climb to a higher level of thought[18].

"Knowledge", "comprehension" and "application" are the lowest levels according to the old version of Bloom's taxonomy.[19] The new version uses verbs instead: "remembering", "understanding", and "applying"[19]. My focus in this chapter is the category that is labeled as "remembering," which constitutes the base of the pyramid. This shows that remembering is fundamental for the knowledge integration process. The fundamental level of learning primarily answers the question, "Can the student recall or remember the information?"[20]. "This taxonomy is hierarchical in that each level is subsumed by the higher levels. In other words, a student functioning at the 'applying' level has also mastered the material at the 'remembering and 'understanding' level"[18]. According to this statement, it is safe to say that mastering the "remembering" level is a pathway to whatever it is we want to achieve in life.

Figure 1: Bloom's Taxonomy[18,19]

The crucial question then becomes how we remember the knowledge we receive so that we can integrate it.

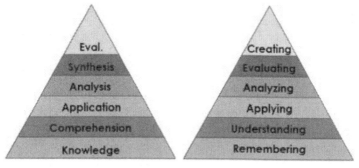

Old Version   New Version

Should we remember all information or only the information relevant to us?

1. The first important skill I developed on my path towards accelerated learning was to read and remember purposefully and to answer the question 'why'. Why am I reading this material? Why do I need this information? In other words, what information do I need to achieve my dream, to solve my problems, etc.?

2. Upon answering my why, my next task would be setting my learning SMART goals (SMART stands for specific, measurable, attainable, reasonable, and time-based). In my experience, having SMART goals increases the chances of achieving my goals.

3. The next step is deciding on and collecting the types of material (books or articles etc.) I want to read. Currently, we are bombarded with tons of information every day. Collecting and retrieving the most relevant and important literature is critical. It is, therefore, important to develop your skills of information literacy to be able to locate the right material you want to read. Information literacy is defined as "a set of abilities requiring individuals to recognize when information is needed and have the ability to locate, evaluate and use effectively the needed information"[21].

4. Once the right material is located, I will decide what learning approach I should use. The learning approach depends on the kind of material or subject I am learning. The majority of times, I only read the section of a book or article that answers my why and my purpose for which I am reading in the first place. The principle of purposeful and selective reading is important to gain knowledge in an accelerated manner. This does not exclude studying a subject in breadth and depth. But the idea is to understand and apply the selective

reading approach: "distinguishing key ideas from supportive evidence; major from minor points"[22]. All words, all phrases, all paragraphs in a book, scientific papers, or any material we are reading are not equally important. Skilled learners have the ability to locate the most important parts of their reading materials as they are led by their purpose and the learning goals they set beforehand. Applying the Pareto principle for reading, also known as the "80-20 rule", comes handy here as well. Eighty percent of the value in a book can be gleaned from twenty percent of its content[23]. Ultimately it is about gaining more with doing less.

5. Finally, I commit to memory all the relevant information I gathered through selective and purposeful reading. First, I will chunk the information into small and manageable pieces. Then I create markers for those chunks of information. Markers are visual images created in our minds by transforming a concept into memorable, exciting, and surprising images. Our brains can process and remember images faster than textual information. To speed up my marker creation process, I started developing my own marker dictionary. Most of the words I come across in my studies are technical and abstract. It usually takes some time to create brilliant and exciting markers for abstract concepts. To save time, I have created markers for frequently used keywords and key phrases. Then, whenever I review the

information, I review the markers to recall the original information. That accelerates my review time and makes my review interesting and fun. I highly recommend Jonathan's book, *The Only Skill That Matters*, for more information about marker creation.

Repetition

Repetition is an important tool to promote learning. Our brains need to encounter information several times before it decides to remember the information. One of the things that makes learning difficult is the fact that we forget information that is not exciting to our brains. This phenomenon is illustrated in the forgetting curve, which refers to the loss of information over time in the absence of reviews and repetitions (see Fig. 2). If it wasn't for the forgetting curve, we would learn once and for all. But our brain is always active in forgetting information that it thinks is not necessary. Our brain determines the importance of information by the frequent encounter of that information. Repeating information increases the strength of memory, and that eventually results in the information to be remembered long-term. However, the pattern of repetition should be spaced out. Kang mentions that "for durable learning, space out your review of the material over time: back-to-back repetitions are ineffective"[24]. Reviewing when we are just about to forget the information strengthens our memory, and furthermore, our brains pick up new details in the process. "Forgetting and learning are, in a counterintuitive twist, linked"[28].

Spaced repetition is a powerful learning technique usually done using flashcards we create for information we want to remember. It works in a pattern where newly created and difficult cards are reviewed in shorter intervals while old and less difficult cards reviewed in longer intervals.[27] "Spacing out the multiple review opportunities stimulates better learning and produces superior long-term learning, compared with repetitions that are massed together"[24].

Interesting points mentioned about spaced repetition include:

- The timing or arrangement of the review affects learning.
- Review is more effective when spaced out over time, instead of massed or grouped together.
- Spaced repetition enhances memory, problem-solving, and transfer of learning to new contexts.
- Spaced repetition offers great potential for improving students' educational outcomes.[23]

There are several spaced repetition software, including Anki, Brainspace, iDoRecall, etc. I use Anki software, and it helps me to review information periodically and efficiently by avoiding unnecessary reviews.

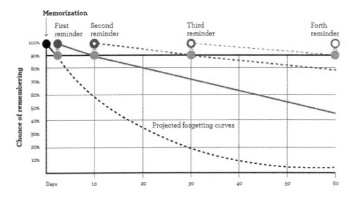

Figure 2: Forgetting Curve[28]

Active Recall

The most commonly used revision techniques include rereading, highlighting, and taking notes. In my own experience as a student, I found these techniques to be less effective in comparison with reviews that incorporate active recall. Active recall is the process of learning by retrieving information from memory. It is an efficient learning method that moves information from short-term to long-term memory, and it is an act of remembering facts without rereading or highlighting while reviewing. By rereading and highlighting, we are often lured to believe that the job is done. Of course, we need to review and understand the information before we start to actively recall the information without looking at our notes. However, a passive review without active recall will not

181

give us the ability to make inferences and logical reasoning from the information we learn. Understanding information without remembering it when we need it is of no use for us. Overall, understanding and remembering should always go hand in hand.

You might wonder how to do active recalling. While I am learning new information, I practice active recall by testing myself frequently through explaining what I just learned in my own words. I changed my habit of taking notes mindlessly to writing questions for the purpose of active recall during my reviews. I avoided rereading my notes and flashcards at all costs. If I fail to recall, I continue to review the information until I understand and recall the information. I learned to endure the pain of recalling from memory as a way to achieve learning goals faster. The good thing, though, is that it doesn't have to be painful. The SuperLearner technique of creating markers for each nugget of information I want to remember makes retrieving information from my brain super easy, fun, and less painful. I again highly recommend acquiring the techniques of creating markers for accelerated and efficient learning taught by Jonathan's Levi.

Reflection

Learning always requires reflection.[25] Reflection is a central element in the learning process and has a positive impact on innovativeness.[25,26] Engaging with both active recall and reflection after we learn something helps us to assimilate our learning, associate the new information with what we already know, synthesize the information to serve our purpose, and finally translate our learning into action. As we keep reflecting, we develop our ability to be creative and think critically.

Looking forward and reflecting on our dreams – the reasons why we are learning – as if they are already here is also a very powerful tool to keep our learning journey enjoyable.

I also use reflection as a tool to break out of mental stagnation, to come up with creative ideas, and to generate emotional energy. With reflection, I create and develop a personal and experiential relationship with my visions - the purpose behind my learning. As much as I reflect together with friends, I also developed a habit of conversing with myself about the things I have learned. In general, reflection in any form increases my capacity for imagination, and I found it to be a key to gain new insights and perspectives – a gateway to "knowledge creation" and innovation. Remember, we can only have what we have first imagined! Be encouraged to include repetition, active recall, reflection, and imagination in your learning recipe.

Summary
To summarize the steps I follow for effective learning:

1. Define the purpose of the new learning project and set learning goals.

2. Locate relevant material.
3. Based on the learning subject, choose your learning approach.
4. Apply selective and purposeful reading.
5. Memorize the relevant information.
6. Space out your reviews and use active recall.
7. Reflect and use your imagination.

Embodied Learning

"We categorize as we do because we have the brains and bodies we have and because we interact in the world as we do."

- George Lakoff, Philosophy in the Flesh: The Embodied Mind and its Challenge to Western Thought

Erica Appelros – Lund, Sweden
Erica is an associate professor in philosophy of religion at Lund University, Sweden, and loves teaching and learning. She also offers her services as a coach for students taking the SuperLearner MasterClass and is a published author in the fields of philosophy, theology, and literary fiction.

Not Just for the Mind

Learning is not just for the mind. For many years, I believed that studying meant sitting down at a desk, reading, and taking notes, hour after hour. I did this and got good grades and a lousy body. Then, study guides began to suggest doing some exercise in between study sessions to keep the body fit and better able to supply the brain with oxygen. I followed this advice and could instantly see that I had more energy to sit still and study for prolonged periods of time. Half a lifetime later, I am still looking for ways to optimize my learning, as taking on challenges is for me a huge factor in what makes life meaningful. Researching dance and embodied cognition, I began to reconsider the body's role in learning. Maybe my body could be put to better use than merely keeping me upright on the chair, holding books and pens, and bringing nutrients and oxygen to my brain? In this chapter, I share my discoveries and the revolutionary implications they have for the way we learn.

Proprioception and mirror neurons

We learn through our senses. The more senses we use, the more easily we remember what we learn. Associating a word or a name with a certain smell or image brings the concept back to mind more easily. But did you know that besides the well-known five senses of smell, sight, hearing, touch, and taste, you also have a sixth sense? The proprioceptive sense keeps track of where your different body parts are located in three-dimensional space in relation to each other and in relation to the surroundings. Located at the ligaments are sensory bodies that report their spatial coordinates to the brain. This is what enables you to make your thumbs meet (or not), even with your eyes closed. You use this sense when walking in a dark room. Dancers rely on their sense of proprioception to coordinate their movements.

As with all senses, you can fine-tune your proprioceptive sense. The fact that a potter can feel how thick the wall is on a vase she is working on just by holding her fingers on each side is not magic; it is a well-trained perception. Blind people often have a highly developed sense of proprioception.

The body sends signals to the brain about its location in space; this is the first clue to how to embody your learning experience and optimize your learning strategies. The second clue has to do with the functioning of so-called "mirror neurons". The discovery of mirror neurons in the early 1990s has revolutionized our understanding of ourselves. We now know that even abstract concepts are linked to, and can be recalled by, bodily movements.

Watching or imagining a bodily action activates almost the same neurons in your brain as if you had performed the action with your own body. Thanks to the mirror neurons, we are able to experience bodily movements that we merely perceive as if we were performing the movements ourselves.

Ever since researchers in the early 1990s accidentally discovered how the brain of a macaque activated neurons for hand movements, even though its own hand did not move -- the macaque was watching someone else reaching for a banana -- research on human mirror neurons has been intense and debated. In cognitive embodiment theory, mirror neurons have been linked to the higher functions of humans, such as empathy, language, and awareness of other minds (theory of mind), and researchers have endeavoured to show how motor activity underlies these functions.

According to cognitive embodiment theories, action and simulation of action share the same brain substrate. That is, when we simulate an action (witness it, read about it, remember it, fantasize about it), the brain partially reactivates the same areas that were activated in the original action along with the associated thoughts and feelings. Abstract concepts emerge from our bodily experiences and constitute embodied abstraction. Therefore, we can understand and remember abstract concepts both through our own experiences and through simulation.

As an example, let us take the cluster of abstract concepts encompassing forgiveness, guilt, and purity. These abstract concepts are captured in the experiences of becoming physically unclean and then cleaning the body from impurity. Both the everyday act of being cleansed of dirt and the more abstract concept of being purified, forgiven, or cleansed of one's guilt are embodied in concrete acts and rituals such as washing, rinsing off, erasing, baptizing, undergoing ritual baths, or immersing oneself in the river Ganges.

A scientific study has shown how the physical act of washing one's hands reduces the feeling of guilt more than watching a video of someone else washing their hands, which in turn reduces the feeling of guilt more than watching a video of someone who types on a keyboard.[29] Washing one's own hands is a bottom-up process, where sensory and motor experiences activate the abstract notions of purity and forgiveness. Seeing someone else wash their hands, on the other hand, is a top-down process where the brain, through its mirror neurons, simulates comparable sensory and motor experiences. In both cases, the feelings of guilt are reduced, but in the latter case, as the brain relives or simulates the experience of washing the hands, not all of the neurons activated in the original experience are reactivated, so the effect is lower. This study is one of many that reveal how humans embody even the most abstract concepts.

This study illustrates the theory of how abstract concepts can be linked to embodiment, which provides the theoretical basis for recommending incorporating bodily practices in your learning skill toolbox.

Rituals as embodied cognition

When you see the word ritual, perhaps it brings religion to your mind. But rituals are everywhere. You probably have a morning ritual that may include taking a shower and having a cup of coffee, or if you have children, they have a bedtime ritual that you need to follow strictly for them to feel safe and fall asleep easily.

Rituals, that is, actions happening in the same order, occurring at the same intervals and having the same purpose and meaning, make us feel secure and comfortable. Everyday rituals allow us to save mental energy by doing things routinely without having to think about what to do next. I don't have to spend time and energy in the evening to make up my mind whether I should brush my teeth before going to bed or not; I just do it.

However, rituals can also be very focused and anything but routine. If your morning ritual includes time for meditation, you could develop a ritual that helps you concentrate and focus your mind rather than letting it wander aimlessly. A mindful ritual can serve as a means to prepare your mind for a study period, a meeting, a creative writing session, or whatever you want to do next, by getting your mind in the right mode for the activity in question. A brain in a diffused mode would be the best for creative, inventive activities; a brain in a focused mode would be the best for a study session. Research has shown that the brain can be in one or the other of these states, but not both at the same time. In the focused mode, the brain is active in a specific area pertaining to the subject matter on which you are focusing. The neural pathways are tightly knit and established, as if the brain lights up a small area with a flashlight, leaving the rest in the dark. However, on other occasions, the brain is in its default mode, which is also called its diffused mode. When you are tired and unfocused, the brain "lights up" a wider area, but with a more diffused light. New neural connections may now be made between otherwise unrelated topics as the neurons fire away at a tangent, and thus new innovative ideas or solutions may pop up in your mind.

If you wish to create a ritual for a certain purpose, say for initiating a study session, the more vivid and embodied you can make the ritual, the better. If you then make it a habit of performing the ritual every time you are about to start a learning session, this will prime your brain and tell it that a learning session is coming up. You will then be able to embark on your session with a more focused and receptive mind than if you had rushed into it with no preliminaries.

When I wrote my thesis — a lonely work which I mostly had to carry out in the solitude of my bedroom — I had a very simple ritual to get me started every day. Each morning after having switched on my computer, I played one online card game. No more and no less. Then I would open my dissertation file and start working on it. The desire to complete another game made me want to turn on my computer. Rituals are addictive. With the computer already up and running and me sitting in front of it, the step to begin the day's real work on my dissertation had been reduced to a manageable size. I am certain that had I not had that morning ritual, the step would have seemed more like a giant leap to me, and procrastination would have been all too easy.

My dissertation ritual did its job, and I am grateful for that. But today, as I am older and hopefully slightly wiser, I have higher standards for my rituals.

Firstly, I want the ritual to be valuable in itself, not only lure me into something of value. The intrinsic value of a ritual may be that it is beneficial to your physical health, that it contributes to your mental or psychological well-being, that it enhances the quality of your relations, that it furthers your spiritual path, or that it benefits the wider community or the world.

Secondly, I want the ritual to be optimally effective, not just enough to do the trick. For a ritual to be optimally effective, it should draw on as many senses as possible and involve a multitude of bodily motions. The more embodied the ritual is, the more neural pathways it will activate, and thus the easier it will be to associate it with other things, and the more tailored it can be made to your needs.

Taken all together, a well-designed ritual is one that

1. has a low entry threshold and is easy to perform even if you are tired or not in the mood,
2. has an addictive aspect in that it gives you satisfaction,
3. is recognizable and repeatable,
4. has intrinsic value, and
5. involves several senses and the whole body in motion.

Such a ritual will provide the trigger you need to get going when you otherwise might have tended to tarry and procrastinate. Once in place, a well-designed ritual can additionally function as the foundation on which to stack other good habits.

What kinds of rituals involve the whole body in motion? Practices such as yoga, dance, the Japanese tea ritual, and many religious rituals (kneeling, prostrating, lifting hands) are prototypical. Elements from practices such as these can provide valuable components for designing your own rituals. For more than a year, I used the following morning ritual: First thing out of bed, I danced to the music "What a wonderful world" to stretch and awaken my body and get my mind in a positive and relaxed state. I then did my yin-yoga program and continued with sitting meditation. Finally, I put on the kettle to brew a cup of tea and curled up cross-legged in my favourite easy chair with my diary to record my reflections, plan the day, and decide on my focus. Rituals can change according to your needs and your life-situation, so it is a good idea to review them from time to time to see if they still fill their purpose for you.

What kind of rituals would benefit your life?
Take some time to design a ritual for a specific purpose!

Dancing as embodied cognition
When you dance, you involve the whole body in coordinated synchronized movements, either spontaneous or choreographed, to the rhythm and tunes of music.

Dance is the ultimate embodied experience, and as a learner, you can take advantage of this.

Dance is the source and goal of human life, culture, religion, and philosophical thinking. According to the philosopher and dancer Kimerer L. LaMothe, dance is any movement or activity that meets the following criteria:

1. it contributes to our bodily ego,
2. it shifts our sensory experiences, and
3. it is performed with conscious attention to what we with our movements create and become.

"What I am calling 'dance' happens when we consciously engage our sensory awareness as a guide to participating in the rhythm of bodily becoming."[30]

This makes dance a goldmine for dedicated SuperLearners seeking to optimize their learning.

Humans have been dancing for as long as there have been humans around. Some anthropologists go as far as to claim that religion and culture, as such, once originated through dance. The small groups of hunters and gatherers danced together to embody their group's values and to provide security and identity. In the dance, the dancers bonded with each other, and bodily expressed their feelings of wonder and fear of nature, life, death, birth, etc. Curiosity itself was originally danced long before any existential questions were formulated. Eventually, the dancing evolved into other types of rituals and cultural expressions to codify the group's values and belief systems.

Have you ever struggled to find the right words to express your feelings or to explain something you know well, only to find that you cannot formulate it -- yet you know what you mean? Then you know all about 'habitus'. The sociologist Pierre Bourdieu coined this concept for such cultural knowledge that is generally understood and presumed, but never argued for or explained. In your own culture, you know what comprises polite behaviour, you know how using words with seemingly the same meaning but with different connotations will affect the conversation, and you know a good joke from a bad one. But can you explain why? Some things cannot be easily put into words, but, luckily, meaning can be unlocked through movement.

When you participate in dancing, you gain entry and insight into a foreign culture in a more profound and bodily way than just by reading about the culture. When you interact with the other dancers during the course of the dance, you pick up the appropriate way to make eye contact, how to approach another person, the emotive significance of gestures and moves, and all sorts of other useful knowledge. Your body will pick up this learning, and the next time you interact socially, your body will know what to do to make you come across as "one of us".

Since dances encode and embody the culture, you can gain a cultural and linguistic understanding, that is in no other way available, by dancing its dances.

Embodied learning for SuperLearners

Do you like the idea of engaging your whole body in your learning, but not sure how to start? The remainder of the chapter will provide you with some suggestions.

When studying

You might want to consider learning a specific dance or dancing to a specific tune each time you begin to study a certain subject and end the study period by dancing to the same piece. This will associate the subject area you are studying with the dance in question and provide an anchor to what you have learned.

1. In the dance before the study session, you should focus on dancing your aims, questions, your desires, and your frustration, that is, your feelings, emotions and urges that drive you to study. Get it all out in the open so that when you sit down to study, your body is relaxed and your emotions have been released.

2. In the dance after the study session, you should try to embody the gist of what you have learned/studied. If you do free, spontaneous dancing, use the full potential of your body to mimic key concepts and images that have stood out for you during your reading. Make the post-study dance into a recall and revise the session in itself. If you use the Pomodoro method, dance is

the perfect activity for the long break that you get after a few Pomodoros. The Pomodoro method is simply that you set a timer to 25 minutes and study focused during that time, then take a 5 min break, followed by another 25 min of studying. Each of these periods is called a Pomodoro.

3. When you switch to another study subject, you should also switch the dance and/or music. Try to pick something that resonates with what you are studying in its energy, emotional load, and pace.

An additional benefit from using dance to enhance your learning is that in this way, you get some well-needed exercise amidst all the sitting down.

When reviewing

At a later stage, when you review your studied material, dancing can also help improve your retention.

1. Put on the specific music tunes that you have associated with the subject that you are about to review.
2. While you let your body move freely to the music, let your mind relax and recall what you have learned in your mind.
3. Maybe you will notice that when you forget something and have to pause in your mind to find the correct term or explanation, you have a tendency to freeze your body and pause dancing as

well. This is how closely connected your body is to your thinking activities. Resist this tendency and do not cease dancing.

4. Try to carry on dancing and let elusive answers come to you in the movement. If the answer still does not appear, then, in your next study session, go back, and review the correct answer.

The neural connections already made when you first memorized and learned the material will be strengthened, and each time you dance, the neural pathways will be reinforced by the auditory and propriosensory signals with which the music and the dancing provide your brain.

I remember when I wrote a paperback in graduate school; it was about the ancient history of Israel. Each time I sat down with my typewriter to write up the summaries of the literature I was covering, I put on a tape with Chinese flute music. The music started slow and then went faster and faster. I would end up typing away at a frenetic speed, and when the music came to an end, I was panting, and only then would I realize that I had increased my typing speed along with the music. Even to this day, I cannot hear this kind of Chinese music without feeling myself transported back thousands of years to the sandy origins of the Israelites in the Middle East.

When learning a new language

Learning a new language includes learning how to think in different ways from what you are used to. Perhaps there are grammatical or conceptual categories that allow you to have a more (or less) fine-tuned categorization of time, relations, morals, or snow. Perhaps every action has to be expressed as either being completed or as being ongoing, with separate verb forms for the two aspects.

Language embodies the habitus of culture in much the same way as dances do, as we covered earlier in this chapter. So, by dancing the dances of a culture, one may also become a better language learner.

Suggesting that you dance your way through your language course may seem like a stretch, but I want you to imagine the speaking body as engaged in a kind of constant continuous linguistic dance. How people move when they are arguing is quite different from when they are courting, or comforting a child, or trying to persuade someone, or confiding a secret. Even before you can understand any of the words of a foreign language, you can probably understand what kind of language dance the speakers are engaged in. Mimic these linguistic dances and let the words come later. This will give you the rhythm, the energy, the feel of the language, and will make you appear more natural.

The more you engage your whole body in speaking and practising the language you are learning, the faster and more accurately you will learn the language. Mimic what you understand as typical gestures and body language. Do whatever people habitually do: shrug your shoulders, throw your neck backwards, or tilt it, or bow it, gesture with arms and hands, observe the distance that people are comfortable with in conversations and adapt to it. Mimic facial expressions: Pout with your lips, or straighten them, or wrinkle your nose, or smack with your tongue, or whatever else you find that people speaking the language have a tendency to do. In short, do whatever you can to behave like a native speaker of the language, no matter if it makes you feel self-conscious, ridiculous, or unnatural. With a bit of practice, mimicking bodily postures, motions, and gestures is exactly what will make you seem natural and not at all ridiculous to the native speakers. You will become a proficient dance partner in the linguistic dance.

Be bold and engage in some proper dancing as well! Besides being fun, it will make you a better language learner by allowing you bodily access to those subtle subconscious nuances of language that are so difficult to grasp.

In the SuperLearner MasterClass, where I, as a coach, work together with students to help them achieve their learning goals, we practice a variety of accelerated learning skills, such as specific memory, pre-reading, and speed-reading skills. If you are not familiar with the SuperLearner method, please beware that in the following suggestions, I presume some knowledge of these skills.

When reading
While we should try to avoid moving our lips when reading so as not to subvocalize, other movements might

enhance the reading experience. You might want to try out some of the following suggestions.

1. Rocking to and fro in the rhythm of the text's emotional load.
2. Walk or dance while reading (if you can manage), and try to embody and reflect the quality of the text in your walking style. When an argument is defeated you may slump and hang your head and slower your pace; when there is something you don't understand or are surprised by, you may stop dead and shrug your shoulders or tear at your hair; when the text excites you, maybe you quicken your pace or take a leap.
3. If you cannot walk and read at the same time, you can apply the same principle standing up or even sitting down and tapping your feet and make the most of whatever bodily movements you are capable of performing.

All of this may make you feel silly, and I don't recommend using this technique while studying in a public library, but try it out, and you will be surprised at the vibrant detail your reading, understanding, and recall will take on.

When using memory palaces

The more than 2000-year-old use of so-called "memory palaces", where you store what you want to remember in an imagined physical building, is having a renaissance today. You can make the technique even more powerful by embodying the experience.

1. Physically walk your memory palaces and reach with your hands towards the places where you have located your items.
2. Do it with closed eyes so as not to be confused about what actually is around you.
3. Make sure you have some open space to move in, and no valuables to knock over.
4. Your steps and movements do not have to be full length. The important thing is that you face and move in the correct directions and stretch your hands towards the correct point and level. That is, if you have placed an item on the floor in your memory palace, you should bend down and reach towards the floor; if you have placed another item inside the microwave oven, you should mimic opening the door to the microwave and reaching for its inside.

Physically engaging with your memory palace will provide your brain with an additional layer of memory-enhancing support. Retrieval of the items will come easier by your bodily movements, which will trigger the right concept as the nerve signals from the muscles and ligaments signal not only the position of the body(-part) but also the associated concepts, feelings, and memories. With practice, it will be enough that you indicate the beginning of the relevant movement, which will then send the appropriate signals to the brain.

When pre-reading/skimming a text:

The purpose of pre-reading is to prime your brain for the actual reading by arousing the brain's curiosity and interest and to get the gist of the text. When you skim a text, to make it more embodied, I suggest that you:

Ask yourself what qualities of motion come naturally to you as you take in the key concepts and the gist of the text as a whole. (slow, abrupt, minute, large, featherlight, heavy, clumsy, petite, precise, bulky, funny, strained, laborious...).

Feel these qualities in your body while you pre-read. Through its postures and motions, you let your body signal these qualities to the brain, which will imprint them in the same neural networks that process the text and its conceptual content.

When you later read the text, you will have a thicker, broader net of neural connections to help you be an engaged reader and with more ease recall your pre-reading questions and what drew your interest and sparked your curiosity. You will feel the curiosity in your body while reading if you enacted it clearly enough when you first encountered it at the pre-reading, especially if you exaggerated your bodily expressions.

203

When making visual markers/mental representations

Encoding information in visual images and mental representations makes it easier to recall what you have learned, as your brain loves images. The more senses you involve, the better, and the sense of proprioception is no exception.

Try once in a while, combining the visual marker with a gesture.

Learning sign language may be doubly beneficial for you. Not only will you gain a means of communicating with people with impaired hearing, but you will also gain a totally new set of gestures already pre-encoded with meaning that you can use when creating markers.

Note that I am not suggesting that you translate the text you are reading into gestures or sign language. That would not speed things up, nor would it necessarily help you with the retention of the material. Using gestures or sign language is merely a complement to the otherwise mainly visually conceptualized markers that you create in order to store them in your long-term memory. A picture tells more than a thousand words, which is why the sense of vision is so important for remembering things. A moving picture is even more memorable, and maybe you create markers of that kind too, encoding your material as movies. I suggest adding hand gestures to your markers not to supplement the visuality of the marker nor its motion qualities; the gestures originating from your own body will do the specific job of embodying the marker and thus providing your brain with yet another hold on the memory, yet another hook by which to retrieve the memory.

The two foundations of the chapter

Everything in this chapter rests on two foundations: The first is our sense of proprioception, by which we perceive where in three-dimensional space each part of our body is located. The second foundation is the function of our mirror neurons, by which we achieve almost the same neural firings from simulating an action as from performing it physically and which explains how language and abstract concepts are truly embodied.

Tips for embodied learning

The tricks and tools that I have suggested that you might try out and add to your learning skills' toolbox do not comprise an exhaustive list but are purely examples of how to implement embodiment in learning. I encourage you to find other creative ways to incorporate your body in motion in your learning experience so as to become a truly embodied learner. I would love for you to tell me about your experiences, and if you come up with a tool or an application to a specific field of learning, I would be happy to share it on my website. You can reach me at appelroscoaching@gmail.com, or through my website: http://appelroscoaching.com/.

From Theory to Practise: Overcoming Perfectionism and Building up Skills

Elanor Kloester – Melbourne, Australia

Elanor is a Systems Engineer and Superhuman Academy Coach who is passionate about problem solving. She is people-driven and loves helping others explore their own boundaries, unlock their potential and ultimately find freedom and create the life they want.

Failure to Fluency

I clutched my bag closer and repeated the line to myself in my head again, feeling nervous but confident all at once. This would be my first time using the language I had been studying for three years in a real-life, non-classroom setting.

"Entschuldigung, wo ist der Hauptbahnhoff?", I asked (excuse me, where is the train station?)

"&%$#@^*)&%," they responded.

I had absolutely no idea what was said back to me.

After three years of studying German at University, after passing numerous tests, after flying all the way to Berlin, it was perfectly apparent that I could neither speak nor understand a single sentence of basic German when tasked in real-time. It turns out that for all of my diligent

207

studying and memorising; I had missed a critical component – live practice.

I had planned to go on exchange before I even got to university and had even deliberately picked a new language in which I could start again from scratch so that this time - unlike during the six years of learning French at school - I could learn it properly and become fluent. The plan had worked so far, and I was now standing in the centre of Berlin on the first day of my 6-month exchange. I had received good marks throughout my diploma (good enough to even get me a small exchange scholarship), and I thought I knew the language to a reasonable level. And I did in theory. But in theory alone.

Throughout my diploma, I had managed to sidestep the messy, imperfect step of practical learning. When put on the spot, I would always freeze like a deer in headlights. I got through my spoken assessments by pre-writing and memorising, and I was just plain lucky that most of the aural assessments were multiple-choice tests.

Looking back now, I realise that this was a symptom of my hang-ups around perfectionism. If I wasn't sure I would be right, I wouldn't even attempt it. Speaking half-sentences with wrong articles and missing nouns was unbearable and felt crushingly embarrassing, even in a classroom environment. This made learning basic conversation next to impossible, as you need to be able to speak imperfectly before you can ever expect to speak perfectly. If your main concern is working out whether you are "failing the conversation," you are not likely to listen.

Perfectionism and building theory-only expertise are repeat themes across my many attempts to learn new skills. Even today, they still hold me back (despite being more conscious of these habits now).

When I started high school, I switched from learning piano to saxophone, and my greatest dream was to improvise like a boss within Stage Band. I learned for six years and, to my credit, by Year 12 I was decent at playing the saxophone – but from sheet music only. To this day (nearly 20 years later), I still dream of being able to freely and fluently play along and riff against the jazz and swing tracks that I love so much.

Since leaving school, I have tried playing again and have also tried different paths to the same goal by attempting to learn piano again and ukulele. I have purchased 5-10 different online courses promising to teach me to play freely across numerous instruments. To this day, I still can't improvise... But I can still speak German fluently.

My fundamental goal for learning each of these skills was exactly the same – to achieve fluency and be able to express myself freely using my chosen medium (speaking German or playing sax). My approach to learning was pretty much the same in both cases too: attend the classes; study the information in front of me; practise in private where no one would hear my mistakes; and skip any practise that required me to "let go" and freely make mistakes to progress (i.e., improvisation, conversation or listening). Despite approaching both skills in the same way, I now have totally different skill levels for each.

Today, despite many years of trying, I cannot fluently improvise music on any instrument; however, nearly ten years since returning from Germany, I remain a confident German speaker. I know my vocab has rusted, but my fundamental skills and overall understanding of the language have not faded. I would be extremely happy to have a chance to riff with someone in German again tomorrow if the opportunity arose. So what was the big difference?

The way I practised.

To become fluent in any new skill, it's vital to practise. And by practise, I don't just mean recalling the relevant information as though you were asked about it on a test. I mean going one step further and finding some way to put that information to use. To really learn a skill, you can't just recall it. You have to *use* it.

In Germany, I found myself surrounded by good people who appeared genuinely pleased by my clumsy attempts to join-in in their native tongue. Had they decided it was in their best interests to speak English instead (as can happen in many European countries), I'm certain I would not have broken through my own barriers and self-conscious feelings and insisted on speaking messy, incorrect German with them until I improved.

When you can find fun in practice, it suddenly becomes easy. For an extrovert like me, it was enormously fun to find myself able to understand more and join in. It became a virtuous cycle, so the more I spoke, the better I got, and the better I got, the more I wanted to speak. Once you can communicate at a basic level, it becomes very useful to be able to speak with people in their native tongue. German language moved from being a thing I theoretically knew about to something I used daily. This was the key to my fluency. This is the key to all fluency.

What does this mean for you? How does this story relate to your journey?

It's meant as both a cautionary tale and one of inspiration. Any skill is learnable if you take the time not only to understand it but, more importantly, to use it. For SuperLearning, that means finding meaningful ways to apply the theory to your life. It means allowing yourself to let go, to not worry about whether a marker is good enough or if there are too many or too few.

By applying the skills to your own life, these questions will be answered for you, by you. You will have occasions where your visual-marker was too abstract, or your linkages were not strong enough. No matter, these experiences will teach you how much detail to add, or what sort of links are strong for you. You will also have positive experiences where you remember a colleague's name, and it makes you smile twice as hard because you're happy you remembered it, and you have a hilarious or odd marker that reminded you of it. Both the "correct" and the "incorrect" uses of the skill are valuable steps in your path to fluency.

This doesn't mean that there is no value in learning the theory. On the contrary, I am a firm believer that learning the theory and understanding a topic conceptually are hugely valuable components when learning anything new. BUT do not get trapped being content with the theory alone. If your wish is to be able to apply the skills and not just know them, then you absolutely must start to apply the skills before you know them perfectly.

I like to think of the theory and concepts as the skeleton, the facts that are immutable and solid. You can stand them up and point to them. You can use them to demonstrate how the thing looks and maybe even how it moves. But the skeleton alone will never have the detail, definition, or impact of the body. To learn something well, you need to have more than just a solid understanding of the structure and bones. You need to "flesh it out" through doing. You cannot get to a detailed understanding without first applying and testing your theory in real scenarios. Fluency comes through practical application and live feedback. Not through getting a high score on a written test.

If you are someone who relates to these stories, then your biggest challenge will likely be your ongoing resistance to using the skills while feeling that you're not skillful. For me, it took travelling halfway around the world to force me to apply my knowledge of German and to become good at using it. Even with this self-awareness, I find I am still strongly resistant to using my knowledge on the fly, and today still find myself spending too much time trying to perfect my theoretical understanding rather than the practical use (for example I have developed 2-3 different Person-Action-Object lists because I was unhappy with the images I first picked, but I have not yet practiced any version enough to make it useful). So how can we overcome these barriers? To help with that, here are a few key things to remember and try when working to move from theory to practice:

1. Be kind to yourself and forgiving of errors
2. Pick a practical application in which to practise the skill
3. Set-up one or more "forcing functions" (this is key)

Sounds simple? Sure does! But each of these steps is often easier said than done. So it's worth looking at each one in more detail.

1. Be kind to yourself and forgiving of errors.

This is easily the most important, the simplest to understand, and the hardest advice to carry out. I have been repeating this advice to myself for years and am still frequently told by friends and family to "stop being so hard on yourself." While this small piece of advice represents an ongoing challenge for many of us, here are some small, tangible strategies that can be used during the tough times when confidence seeps away and is instead replaced by disdain for oneself and one's efforts.

A) Review the real consequences

Okay, so you couldn't remember the answer even though you revised it twice last night. That doesn't actually mean you qualify as the world's stupidest person, and let's face it; it was only a practice exam. Reviewing the outcome of your perceived mistake or following it through to its logical conclusion can often help bring a better perspective to the moment and shift your current mindset from "I'm too stupid to ever succeed" towards "no one gets it right all the time and no harm done."

Ask yourself, what was the real consequence of getting it wrong just now? Did someone get injured or die? Admittedly, there are some mistakes - like failing a subject at university - that does result in a real cost (though even these occasions generally do not result in life-changing losses), but most mistakes have little-to-no real outcomes which matter. Zoom out and bring a bigger picture view into focus next time you feel like you've made a mistake or "failed" at something. You might just see that there's nothing really stopping you from keeping going but yourself.

B) Adjust your time to success

The planning fallacy means most humans underestimate how long something will take by roughly 3x. So next time you are flagging in enthusiasm because you are not as far along as you thought, try tripling your expected timeframe to reach success. Remember that there are no awards for getting there faster. There is also no timer above your head that tells anyone how long it took you to learn something. No one else cares about this, so you don't need to either.

C) Stop comparing yourself to others.

It's irrelevant that Jill can dance almost as well as you can but has been learning a year less than you. Maybe she trained in dancing before or played a lot of sports growing up, so it is really coordinated. Maybe she's practising twice as often as you outside of class. You won't know all the circumstances, and there's nothing to be gained in speculating. There's even less in assuming that Jill is better because you are incompetent (see point 1).

D) Expect some backwards slides

As a certified jack-of-all-trades, I have a long litany of skills that (during times of mental fatigue) I will chalk up to having failed at, simply because I have worked on them sporadically over a long period of time and have reached only a moderate level at best. On a bad day, I'm a failed swing-dancer, saxophonist, pianist, boxer, martial artist, French-speaker, coder & even SuperLearner. In each of these examples, I have successfully gone from knowing nothing to having some moderate skill level, but I have often quit after deciding that I hadn't improved fast enough for the time spent.

Expecting to improve along a linear and upward trajectory only serves to shoot yourself in the foot. Perfection or endless improvement is unreasonable because it's simply not how the human brain works. If we're not using a skill, we're slowly losing it, and once you reach a reasonable level it takes more work than an hour a week to improve substantially. You will likely never become a piano master or a highly skilled athlete by putting in just one hour a week, no matter how many weeks you put in (caveat: you can reach a good and satisfying skill level from one hour a week over many years though). If you are feeling impatient, or like you should have mastered something by now, try revising your expectations and adjusting your timeframe for reaching "success."

E) Replace keywords or phrases in your self-talk

The number of times I've told myself that I'm "stupid" or "an idiot" when I've gotten something wrong is obscene and, if I'm honest, has in no way been helpful. Self-flagellation does not motivate one to learn more; in fact, it has the opposite effect, so finding ways to soften the language you use against yourself is a clear and simple way to be kinder to yourself. Replacing "stupid" with "silly" greatly dilutes the severity, and similarly, calling "mistakes," "attempts," or "failures" "interesting outcomes" can shift the mindset.

You can go from finding nothing of worth in your efforts, to seeing every attempt as offering valuable information from which you can learn and grow. Remembering that we actually learn faster from making mistakes than we do from getting it right the first time can help maintain motivation and a positive outlook when discovering you need multiple attempts to master something.

F) Keep it light-hearted and fun.

Ideally, learning is supposed to be fun. Learning as an adult is most often entirely voluntary, so if you're opting to learn something but you're not enjoying yourself, then you might want to approach it a little differently and make sure you're finding some fun in the process. If you're bored, then I recommend trying to find a different voice on your topic of choice. If you're stressing because you didn't hit a goal on time, then just revise your goal. If you're too wound up over your pace and progress to revise your goal, then change it completely to an "anti-goal."

An anti-goal is the opposite of a SMART (specific, measurable, attainable, reasonable, time-bound) goal. They deliberately ensure there is no timeframe and no end-point. So instead of "I will be able to play all my scales at 100 bpm by March 13th" (a good goal, but one that might result in feelings of "failure" if not met), try "I will enjoy playing piano 2-3 times a week". This shifts the focus to enjoying the activity regularly instead of trying to reach a specific point at a specific time, which may better reflect what you're really trying to achieve.

2.   Pick a practical application for practice

This is a practical suggestion which may be much simpler and easier to carry out than Suggestion 1. Usually the most difficult part (which is not that difficult) is selecting an appropriate application. You want the practice-activity to be something that you find interesting, but which also requires you to utilise the skills you want to develop. The easiest way to think of a good practical application is to use the 5-Whys technique.

It's a very simple technique that just requires you to keep asking "Why?". You start with "Why do I want to learn this skill?" Then you ask "why" again and again (can be up to 5 times!) until you eventually get to the true reason why you are learning something. Why do you want to improve your memory? Because I want to be able to remember people's names. Why do you want to remember people's names? To remember who I meet. Why? To build up my network and get a better job. So go meet people! Or practise memorising names on LinkedIn. But apply the skill to the area you actually want to use it in.

3. **Set-up one or more "forcing functions."**[30]
What is a "forcing function"?

It's something that forces you to practise or take action and therefore removes your will to do something from the equation. A forcing function turns your goals from something you want to do to something you have to do.

There are many different types of possible forcing functions (for more details on this topic check out Benjamin Hardy's book *Willpower Doesn't Work*) but here are some that I've found to work well:

Team effort: where you agree to reaching your goal with a friend or partner. The social pressure to show up for them will keep you going strong. If you don't have a friend who wants to work with you, check out Focusmate.com (where you commit to meet someone online and each spend an hour working on your own goals).

Wager: make a high stakes bet with someone that you will achieve your goal. If you don't have anyone you can wager with, the Beeminder app (where you enter your credit card details and get charged for not meeting your goals) can be used without any outside help. You'll be surprised just how effective the threat of losing money is at spurring you on to take action.

Competition: similar to Team Effort, but instead of working with someone, you are competing against them. You can add a wager into this for added pressure!

Public commitment: sign up to a competition or commit to performing at a friend's birthday. The fixed date and social pressure to perform will keep you showing up to your daily practice until then.

4. Practise, Practise, Practise

Now that we've got some clear strategies to help move us into practise mode, it might be useful to know some exercises to get you practising your SuperLearner skills specifically.

Here's a fun exercise to do with a SuperLearner buddy or coach:

- Close your eyes and have your friend read you a paragraph of a book (you can also use an audiobook if you don't have anyone for this exercise)
- While they are reading, aim to maintain silence within your mind and instead try to focus on

"seeing" any imagery that appears in your mind while they read (this is usually easiest with fiction but could be anything).

- The point here is not to try to create a marker but to see what visual translations your mind is coming up with "on its own."

- Share with your friend (or write down) what images you saw. Note whether the images that appeared had a clear link or connection to the spoken words, or if they seemed somewhat random or a large stretch of the imagination.

- There are no wrong answers, so this can be a good exercise to understand the sort of imagery your brian generates as your "go-to" for markers.

- As you improve at creating markers, revisit this exercise.You will enjoy seeing the movies-of-your-mind become more detailed and free-flowing as your ability to create markers grows

A key element of the above exercise is that the text is fed to you, removing the requirement for you to process it visually (read it), and instead allowing you to focus your visual mind entirely on the imagery that the text brings to mind. The other key element is that you have someone there asking for your feedback. The last part - trying to notice what sort of imagery appears most easily for you - can be quite surprising. For example, I've noticed that I rarely picture any detail within people's faces, and I prefer to visualise fictional characters over "real" people.

Another useful exercise for practising mnemonics is an "A-Z list." Imagine one object (it can be anything, but most commonly, it's something that starts with the same letter) to represent each letter of the alphabet. Give yourself a maximum of 2 minutes to complete this list of 26 images. This prevents you from overthinking your markers too much. You can go back and change them later if you like, but the first thing you think of is often the best option anyway.

So now, you know the dangers of being content with the concepts, and you have some practical tips and examples to start building your skills up for real. So what are you waiting for? Get practising!

Help! I'm Not a Native Speaker!

"To have a second language is to have a second soul"

- Charlemagne

Andrea Szabo - Budapest, Hungary

Andrea is a Medical Doctor with a background in a wide variety of fields from neuroscience and pharmacology to yoga and coaching. Raised speaking one of the most complicated and unique languages on Earth, Andrea developed strategies for tackling new subjects in any language.

Behind the Iron Curtain

I was born and raised in the third-largest city of Hungary, the country where I have lived my whole life. My native language is Hungarian, spoken by approximately 12 million people, and it is the last one on the list of the 100 most-spoken languages in the world.[32] Similarly to Japanese, the Hungarian language does not belong to any language families; it is unique. Polyglots love learning Hungarian for an extra challenge as Hungarian grammar is exceptionally complicated. This makes learning a second language difficult for a native Hungarian speaker.

The first time I had the opportunity to study English was in secondary school back in the '80s, behind the "iron curtain". We had no chance whatsoever to practice the

223

language and no opportunity to speak with native speakers. Back then, all movies were translated into Hungarian, it wasn't possible to access English speaking channels on T.V., and the internet was not yet available for public use.

Today, almost 35 years after my first encounter with the language, though I am fluent in English and speak it at work every day, I still struggle. My knowledge is still far from that of a native English speaker, and I must continuously develop my skills.

I believe in lifelong learning; however, virtually every course I am interested in is available only in English. There are very few in Hungarian.

This has been a great challenge for me - still, I know I can overcome the difficulties and unlock every door on the way to the desired knowledge. Rather than putting my learning on hold and waiting for Hungarian translations, I rose to the challenge. Through years of painstaking effort, I have developed frameworks for learning in foreign languages. These strategies and tactics that have enabled me to overcome the impossible, I now give to you.

In this chapter, I want to share my experience and my favorite tried and tested tips that have allowed me to learn new skills in my second language. No matter what language you want to learn in, these tips will be of help to you.

What level of language knowledge is necessary to learn a course in a foreign language?

A vocabulary of 4,000-10,000 words is considered quite advanced in most languages. In this range, you can operate in a professional setting, use more sophisticated words in regular conversations, and even do pretty well on language tests.

In English, a vocabulary of 8000-9000 words is sufficient to understand 95-98 % of novels, newspapers, articles, and courses.[33,34] You should expect extra challenges if your vocabulary is less than this, as it can have a considerable impact on reading speed and comprehension. Learning will then require more of your time, you will face more difficulties than you probably expected, and yes, it will be frustrating.

There are many ways to measure vocabulary size; I will share the most common and useful method here. I am using English as an example, but similar numbers apply to other languages. Vocabulary is often measured in lemmas, or forms of a word that appears as an entry in a dictionary. The average 20-year old American adult has an English vocabulary of approximately 42,000 lemmas. Within this word inventory a distinction is drawn between passive vocabulary (words understood when presented, but not known by heart), and active vocabulary (words known by heart), which is more limited and estimated to be less than half of the passive word knowledge on average.[33,34] To estimate the lemmas in your passive and active vocabulary, visit the vocabulary size tests on my resource page at www.superhumanplaybook.com.

Learning in your native language is easier and more accessible because you can understand all the lecturer's words and phrases, even if they speak faster or in a dialect. When deciding to take a course in a second language, more motivation and perseverance are needed depending on the course, your language skills, and your personality. Learning a new subject in a foreign language presents unique challenges that can overwhelm the best of students.

Instead of getting permanently stuck on the mental block of believing that "I will always be worse than the native speaker students", I found another driving force: the will to prove turns the disadvantage into an advantage. I had three Polish groupmates at the Medical University. They each had an extra year prior to enrolling at the medical university to learn the Hungarian language. It was in the late 80's, so there were no online dictionaries. As mentioned above, Hungarian is quite difficult, and they had only one year to learn it from zero. I met them for the first time when we had started our first year of university. They were extremely dedicated. They were not shy and always asked if they had not understood something. And this is one of the keys: ask, ask, and ask. Two of them were in the top 10 % of the class. They had never given up despite difficulties. This is not a unique situation. Difficulty produces dedication and ingenuity.

Native speakers take their language proficiency for granted; they can procrastinate and still succeed. For non-native speakers, procrastination means failure. This weakness forces non-native speakers to be proactive, to take responsibility for their success, and to study smarter, not just harder. By reframing your language weakness in this way, you can turn your disadvantage into an advantage.

Your weakness is your strength. The extra effort you invest in learning will return to you with interest. You will gain more knowledge and experience than native speakers. Though you may progress slower, you will learn more and understand more deeply, all the while developing a "second soul," or another perspective, through which to learn and see the world. And do not be too hard on yourself! You need to be your greatest fan rather than your worst critic. Reward yourself for every step of progress. Focus on making daily incremental progress; investing 10-20 minutes per day is more fruitful than 60-90 minutes once per week.

Be proud of your patience, endurance, and results. Improve 1% each day, and you will not recognize yourself in a year. And last, but not least, don't compare yourself to native speakers except to appreciate your superior strategy and work ethic.

The Two Types of Courses
There are two primary types of courses.

Common: The curriculum can be easily mastered by watching videos or reading text. This is usually not a problem even if the language is not spoken perfectly.

Specialized: The curriculum is very technical or asks students to listen, read, and actively participate and solve tasks in the language of the course. The disproportionate use of active vocabulary and in-person application presents serious challenges to non-native speakers.

My tips to decrease your frustration
It is easy to understand that due to the language barrier, you can't expect the same results in the same amount of time as a native speaker; the competition is not "fair". You should not blame yourself. You are working much harder. You can't compare the result of the 400 meters run with the result of 400 meters hurdles.

How to approach a "Common" course:
1. Tutorial videos/recordings: decrease the playback speed if necessary. Several software are available that can modify the playback speed of a video even if the video itself does not have this setting (e.g., Video speed controller). This is a useful tool for slowing down the video/recording if you have difficulties understanding it. It works the other way as well. Especially when you are already familiar with its content, then it may help to speed it up to

1.2X or 1.5X depending on your comprehension level. It can save you a great deal of time.

2. Transcript of the video/recording: check if the video/recording has a written version, or if it is possible to add subtitles. This makes it much easier to identify unknown words and phrases. Even if no transcription is offered, there are many relatively inexpensive transcription services you can use to get your own.

3. Notes/mindmaps: a summary of the lesson in your native language or the language of the course will remind you of the keywords and concepts.

4. Translation into your native language: If you have difficulties understanding, most probably, you need to translate at least part of the course to your native language, but at the prospect of translating every detail causes many students to give up. Ultimately, increasing your vocabulary in the new language will always yield better results than relying on translation. Every new word you learn provides a recurring benefit that lasts a lifetime.

How to approach a "Specialized" course:

In addition to the previously listed tools, you might need to go a step further to overcome the challenges presented by the specialized vocabulary. Even a native speaker may not have prior knowledge of the jargon in a technical field. This levels the playing field a little bit and gives the non-native speaker the chance to keep pace with native speakers, at least in terms of learning the technical jargon. For example, the extensive special terminology in medical school will seem foreign even to a native speaker. A couple of advanced learning methods listed below are extremely useful for native and non-native speakers alike.

1. Spaced repetition software like ANKI. Intelligent, automated spaced repetition will drastically reduce the amount of time spent learning new vocabulary or reviewing concepts. Cramming will lead to burnout and worse results.
2. Memory palaces. This is an advanced memory technique. The fine details are outside the scope of this chapter, but every author of this book is well versed in this skill and Superhuman Academy offers many related resources.[36]
3. Major Method if you need to memorize numbers. The ability to remember numbers is often undervalued, but it can be extremely useful for mentally organizing information.[37]

You can find more in-depth resources for all of these tools at www.superhumanplaybook.com.

Reading

I was a smart kid. I had no problem learning anything; I have never had a problem understanding and recalling information. That said, there was one area which was a real struggle for me: reading. It wasn't comprehension that was difficult for me, rather my very slow reading speed. When I had to read aloud in elementary school, I would get nervous and make a lot of mistakes. This was not just a struggle of the past; it continues to be difficult for me. Something does not work properly in my head. My mind can read the text, but my mouth is not able to pronounce the words. It seems I have some kind of dyslexia, but it was never diagnosed because I compensated for this disability with good comprehension and fast learning skills. Most probably, my struggles came from the way I was taught to read. I guess the method is similar worldwide. The child is asked to pronounce the word aloud or with an inner voice, which means they need to involve additional organs in the reading. This connection works poorly in my case. Because of this, I hated reading, and as a consequence, my vocabulary developed much slower and still lags behind my other skills. Now, I am an avid learner with experience in a wide variety of disciplines. I love trying my hand at new hobbies and learning new skills that increase productivity and efficiency in all aspects of life. Every day, a new book or article arouses my interest. Keeping up with my constant curiosity and desire for knowledge is not easy, especially with my "dyslexia". It does not help that the majority of these resources are not in Hungarian.

I had to find a solution to overcome these difficulties and develop the reading and learning capacity to sustain my desire for knowledge.

Pre-reading and speed reading have dramatically increased the volume of the information I can read and learn. It was not an easy journey though. To my great surprise, I could kill two birds with one stone. I realized why I had read so slowly; it was because of subvocalization (or inner pronunciation of words), the biggest enemy to reading speed. The highest reading speed with full subvocalization (pronouncing every word) is between 200-250 words per minute. It is hard work to decrease subvocalization and read with only your eyes. Changing decades of reading habits requires perseverance, but it is worth it. You should remind your mind from time to time that you need to read in a new way.

During the learning process of speed reading, the language barrier steps in again. Reading in your native language and a foreign language is quite different. I was very disappointed when I realized my speed and comprehension in English was far behind my expectations. I started to learn the techniques in English. It was not a good idea. I was struggling, I gave up a couple of times, and I blamed myself. Suddenly, I had a realization: why am I trying to read in English? Why not in Hungarian? I knew the answer: I am reading in English because the books that I want to read are in English. Let's stop for a moment. Learning a new way of reading in a foreign language is very frustrating. I read better and faster in Hungarian - despite my dyslexia. I should learn the technique in Hungarian.

There are many elements to speed reading. You need to teach your eyes how to move efficiently, reduce subvocalization, and somehow still understand what you are reading. When I realized that I do not need to pronounce the words that I am reading, I could eliminate the part of the reading process that had caused all of my struggles! Changing your reading habit does not happen overnight. Learning the technique takes a lot of attention and energy and can be very stressful for many students. You need to be extremely determined not to give up. It is hard enough in your native language to begin with, so do not add extra difficulties by starting in a foreign language. Once you know the technique, practice a lot and you will reach a good reading speed and comprehension. After that, you can start reading in a foreign language, but the speed and comprehension will most likely not reach the same level as in your native language. The explanation is very simple. Naturally, you know your native language better, it will feel more natural and comfortable than the foreign language, so it is not a surprise that you can read faster. You should not blame yourself at all, just keep swimming!

Comprehension tests are commonly used in the course of learning speed reading. The majority of these tests are in English. Do not compare yourself to native English speakers. Do not be surprised if your results are well behind them. After all, they have spoken that language since they learned to speak. It is difficult to calculate your real result as it measures your language skill and not purely the comprehension. Do not take your results too seriously; be patient with yourself! You need to count on this extra difficulty and continue to practice.

Try to find comprehension tests in your language as it will measure your reading speed more accurately.

Learning a new language

There are many approaches to learning languages; unfortunately, the most widely practiced is also the least effective. I am speaking, of course, of translation. Using translation as the primary means to learn a new language creates a counterproductive dependency. Not only does it limit your vocabulary in the new language to your vocabulary in the old one, but it also causes you to understand the words in the context of the old language rather than the new one. There is a better way to bridge the gap, a universal language spoken by every nation on earth: images. This is how you learned your first language! The people around you put into words what you saw and what you experienced.[35]

The human brain remembers smells and tastes very well, but it is hard to convert concepts into smell and taste. Visual/spatial memory is the second strongest overall, and most useful for most learning applications. It is always easier to remember educational material or a new word (in your native or foreign language) if you transform it into images - vivid, colorful, funny images. I am creating images both in Hungarian and English, as I mix the languages. For example, when I needed to remember the name VAJPAYEE, who was a prime minister in India, I divided the name into two parts: VAJ (meaning butter in Hungarian) and PAYEE (in English). I could then visualize an Indian payee getting paid in butter, which is much easier to remember than a foreign name without meaning to me. In this case, learning in multiple languages becomes a definite advantage compared to those who only speak one!

Learning in a foreign language can be a struggle, but it can also be a great experience and fun. You can surpass the difficulties with perseverance and even end up having learned more than a native speaker. If you can understand novels, newspapers and articles in a second language, do not worry about starting learning as this means that you have sufficient language knowledge to complete a common course. If you can overcome the fear and doubt, you can turn your disadvantage into an advantage. The extra effort you invest in learning will return to you with interest as you will gain more knowledge and experience than native speakers.

Get started and enjoy your learning!

Break Free of Damming Liquid

"The day I became free of alcohol was the day that I fully understood and embraced the truth that I would not be giving anything up by not drinking."

- Liz Hemingway, "I Need to Stop Drinking!"

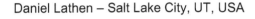 Daniel Lathen – Salt Lake City, UT, USA

Daniel is a Neuroscience Ph.D. candidate researching alcoholism, a SuperLearner Certified Coach, and an all-around brain-change and self-improvement specialist. When he's not enjoying time with his wife or daughter, he's often learning graphic design, bike mechanics, foreign languages, or breakdancing.

Misconceptions

How many times have you ever thought something to the effect of "I shouldn't have drunk last night," or "I shouldn't have had so *much* to drink last night"? Perhaps you've frequently heard other people express similar sentiments.

Now let's invert that. How many times have you or others ever said, "I *should* have drunk last night," or "I shouldn't have had so *little* to drink last night"?

Never? Me neither. It's such a rare sentiment that it sounds foreign and ridiculous. People often regret drinking, but they never seem to regret *not* drinking. And that observation is a huge red flag. It is a warning: how beneficial people *think* alcohol is to them is very different from how beneficial alcohol *actually* is to them. I'm not talking about the effects it has on your body; most people are aware that excessive drinking usually makes us feel terrible in the short term and often has catastrophic consequences on our long-term health, while the harms and benefits of small amounts are constantly under debate. We also won't dwell on the many societal harms caused in part by alcohol consumption, including family problems, damaged friendships, financial problems, lost productivity at work, drunk driving, violence, sexual assaults, and other crimes. Though far too common, most drinkers will never commit nor be directly affected by these dramatic consequences.

No, I'm referring to what most people rarely stop to consider: even if you never have any major problems, what are the effects of alcohol (*any* alcohol) on your own well-being and success?

If you're reading this, you're one of few people taking the first step toward a better life simply by considering that question. Read on and prepare to be challenged.

I'm sure you, like most people, have been told all your life that alcohol is a necessary part of life. These messages take many forms, both explicit and implicit. Maybe your boss tells you that you won't get a sale unless you get a drink with a prospective client. Maybe your friends tell you that you can't get a date if you don't drink. Or, more subtly, there are Superbowl commercials implying you can't enjoy American football if you're sober. There are phrases like "alcohol is a social lubricant" that imply that quality social connections require people to be disinhibited by getting drunk. There are endless stories and videos of people saying and doing hilarious things because they were drunk. There are practically no alcohol-free conferences, dates, restaurant gatherings, family reunions, or parties. After all, you *can't* have nearly as much fun or success if you're not drinking, right?

Right?

The myth: alcohol is helpful and even necessary for success and happiness, or even just for getting through life.

Spoiler: it's not.

In addition to being a Certified Coach for SuperHuman Academy, I'm also a Neuroscience Ph.D. candidate at the University of Utah. To be clear, I am not a medical doctor, but I've spent years researching alcoholism and how alcohol affects our brains and even longer studying how our brains work generally. So believe me when I tell you that alcohol is absolutely NOT helpful nor necessary for happiness and success.

In this chapter, you'll have a chance to ponder all the ways that alcohol just might be holding *you* back in life. You'll learn some scientific evidence supporting the idea that even when alcohol is not incredibly destructive, it lowers quality of life. Most importantly, you'll have the

239

chance to weigh the pros and cons and decide to continue using alcohol as you have been or reduce or eliminate your intake. If you choose to drink less, you'll learn how to do it. If you don't, that's fine, too. Ultimately, no matter what you think or decide, this chapter will 1) help you better understand the true role alcohol has played and currently plays in your life and 2) give you the power to make a deliberate choice about the role alcohol will play in your *future* life, a choice that you can be happy with.

The choice is yours.

My goal is to *ensure* that the choice is yours. Not mine. Not alcohol's. Not your craving brain's. Not the media's. Not your friends'. Not society's. Yours. Your soul's. Your deepest, truest self's.

Dam It.

To illustrate the role that alcohol may be playing in your life, please allow me to use a recent Disney movie as an example. In *Frozen 2* (spoilers ahead!), much of the plot centers around a dam that past leaders of the kingdom of Arendelle built as a supposed symbol of peace and alliance.[38] It was meant to help the tribes of people that lived beneath it, presumably by preventing floods and/or creating a water reservoir. At least, that was the story they told everyone. In reality, the dam was intended to do the exact opposite: it was meant to hurt the local tribes by drastically reducing their water supply, by revealing their numbers when they came out to celebrate, and by making them dependent on Arendelle, all of which would allow Arendelle to conquer and control them.

Alcohol is the dam. You were told it is beneficial, but it is actually harmful. You have been made to think that it is benefitting you, but it is actually holding you back and causing long-term harm. The verb *to dam* means to block up, hold back, and stop from progressing.

Alcohol is damming you.

Like the dam in *Frozen 2*, society has built a powerful façade around alcohol. To help conceptualize this, think of alcohol as, in Jonathan Levi's words, a "band-aid solution that only lasts for a few hours." If left on too long, it ironically prevents the wound from healing rather than helping. Alcohol is like cheating on a test, which has short-term benefits but long-term harm. It's like a crutch that you never stop using even after you don't need it, so your body gets weaker instead of stronger.

It's Fine, Except for the Bad Parts...

I need to clarify that alcohol is not 100% without benefits. If it didn't have some real advantages, humans probably would have stopped using it a long time ago. For instance, studies indicate that small amounts may have positive health benefits such as decreased risk of heart disease and type 2 diabetes, though these benefits can be gained better through healthier methods like improved diet and exercise.[39]

More relevant to this discussion, alcohol can be valuable as a way to loosen things up. Need an extra boost of bravery to approach an attractive man or woman, or to say something awkward to a loved one that needs to be said, or to sing karaoke in front of a crowd? Alcohol can give you that boost, to help you believe you can do something *that you have never done before.* It can prove to you that you really do have enough internal charm, boldness, humor, or whatever other quality you need to get the job done. But the catch is that if you *have* done it before, if you already believe in yourself enough to trust that you can do it, then continuing to rely on alcohol is only hurting you. It's preventing you from being able to access those charming, bold, or humorous parts of yourself unless alcohol is in your system. You cannot access them at will, which also means you cannot develop them. Alcohol owns them; you do not. If this idea is new or challenging to you, good. Later, we'll talk a lot more about the specific ways this tends to happen.

It's also important to acknowledge that for many people, alcohol never becomes a problematic habit. They never become addicted, never blow their rent money on booze, never miss important meetings or deadlines because of hangovers, never physically or sexually assault anyone, never cause an accident while DUI, never get arrested, never overdose or contract alcohol-related diseases, and maybe even never embarrass themselves saying or doing something dumb while under the influence. Only 21% of drinkers admit experiencing negative social consequences from their own use (limited to fights and harm to friendship, home-life, or job).[41] But that number depends on people being honest enough to admit problems and informed enough to recognize them. Most people are *not* educated on this topic, which is why this chapter is so important.

If the obvious, dramatic problems were the only problems alcohol ever caused, there would be no reason to write this chapter. No, for you, someone who wants to thrive in life rather than merely function and survive, we're going a step further. We're going to help you consider how consistent alcohol use, even seemingly harmless use, is practically guaranteed to be damaging your life and holding you back.

How Does Alcohol Dam *You*?

Referring back to the dam analogy, people often think the things holding them back are certain personal weaknesses or life problems. You might have good reason to think that your dam is poor charisma, health issues, weak memory, low confidence, or a million other problems. But what if there's a bottleneck that goes even deeper than all these issues, that blocks your ability to overcome them and move forward?

James Clear, the author of the life-changing book *Atomic Habits*, said that, "Time spent working hard is often better spent identifying where the bottleneck is located.

Working hard on the wrong thing leads to frustration, not progress."[12]

Or, as I like to put it, *a good solution to the wrong problem is a bad solution.*

Alcohol is the deeper dam that likely supports all of your other dams. Booze may not contribute to *every* problem in your life. But it probably contributes to *most* of them.

If you're serious about improving yourself, think about all the ways that you rely on alcohol. I've compiled a few ideas below. Put a check mark next to each statement that you agree with. At the end, you can sum up your check marks to get an overall sense of how much you rely on alcohol. Then we'll talk about how this dependence potentially *blocks* your growth.

~ ~ ~

_____ I use alcohol to "become myself".

_____ I use alcohol to pretend to *not* be myself and have an excuse for poor behavior.

_____ I use alcohol to be funny.

_____ I use alcohol to build relationships.

_____ I use alcohol to open up to people.

_____ I use alcohol to get *other* people to open up to me.

_____ I use alcohol to make social gatherings more exciting.

_____ I use alcohol to enjoy myself.

_____ I use alcohol as an activity around which to center social events.

_____ I use alcohol to speak and act in more interesting, exciting, expressive ways.

_____ I use alcohol to socialize.

_____ I use alcohol to combat social anxiety.

_____ I use alcohol to give me courage to talk to people.

_____ I use alcohol to give me temporary courage or confidence, generally.

_____ I use alcohol to risk trying new things.

_____ I use alcohol to enhance pleasure.

_____ I use alcohol to feel free in my body.

_____ I use alcohol to feel sexy.

_____ I use alcohol to increase sexual prowess.

_____ I use alcohol to increase sexual function.

_____ I use alcohol to soften people up to my physical advances.

_____ I use alcohol to drown out stress and other hard emotions.

_____ I use alcohol to allow myself to feel emotion.

_____ I use alcohol to numb physical pain.

_____ I use alcohol to enjoy something refreshing.

_____ I use alcohol to "warm up".

_____ I use alcohol to get creative.

_____ I use alcohol to think deep thoughts.

_____ I use alcohol to relax.

_____ I use alcohol to sleep.

My score: _____ / 30.

~ ~ ~

How did you fare? Before we talk about what a healthy range is, let's review each of the uses listed above to break down the deeper meaning behind them. Most of them are not inherently harmful. But consider the even *better* way of living that may be prevented by relying on alcohol. I've given some suggestions below, to get your mind going. Read these slowly. For each one, really think about it.

Ponder it. Feel it out. Is this (or something similar) true in your own life? They won't all be true for you, but some of them will be.

~ ~ ~

§ I use alcohol to "become myself" – when in fact I'm avoiding myself. I'm avoiding facing and dealing with all my limitations and imperfections.

"I'm not really the party person. I don't 'become myself' once I'm drunk. I don't use alcohol to be happy."

Jessie J

§ I use alcohol to pretend to *not* be myself and have an excuse for poor behavior – instead of learning to take responsibility for my actions and improve my behavior.

"Don't use alcohol for plausible deniability. Take extreme ownership."

Jonathan Levi

§ I use alcohol to be funny – instead of mastering good humor. Perhaps I'm just acting like a fool that people can laugh *at*, rather than laugh *with*.

Pause. If you're skimming, stop it. *Think* about these ideas. They may just change your life.

247

§ I use alcohol to build relationships – when in fact I'm not listening to nor remembering what others say, nor responding in a positive or even appropriate way.

§ I use alcohol to open up to people – instead of learning how to be vulnerable, assertive, and genuine with my own feelings, wants, and needs.

§ I use alcohol to get *other* people to open up to me – instead of learning how to create environments and relationships where people feel safe and willing to be vulnerable, leading them to open up naturally.

§ I use alcohol to make social gatherings more exciting – instead of learning how to make conversations and activities more interesting and fun.

§ I use alcohol to enjoy myself – instead of learning to appreciate the goodness of the people and events around me.

> *"I do like to have fun. I don't need alcohol to have fun."*
>
> *Rima Fakih*

§ I use alcohol as an activity around which to center social events – instead of developing the creativity to come up with special, enjoyable things to do.

§ I use alcohol to speak and act in more interesting, exciting, expressive ways – instead of learning how to be an engaging, entertaining person.

§ I use alcohol to socialize – instead of learning the arts of conversation and connection.

§ I use alcohol to combat social anxiety – instead of learning how to feel calm at social events.

§ I use alcohol to give myself courage to talk to people – instead of learning to overcome social awkwardness and my fears of judgment, public speaking, and socializing.

§ I use alcohol to give myself temporary courage or confidence, generally – instead of actually conquering my fears and accepting and believing in myself.

§ I use alcohol to risk trying new things – instead of developing a growth mindset and the courage to try hard things despite the risk of failure.

"When you quit drinking, you stop waiting."

Caroline Knapp, "Drinking: A Love Story"

§ I use alcohol to enhance pleasure – instead of learning how to notice, feel, and appreciate all the simple, wonderful things around me.

§ I use alcohol to feel free in my body – instead of developing the mindfulness to be present in my body and the self-acceptance to love my body and what it can do.

§ I use alcohol to feel sexy – instead of learning to discover, accept, and love my own sexuality.

§ I use alcohol to increase sexual prowess – instead of learning lovemaking skills.

§ I use alcohol to increase sexual function – even though it actually decreases it.[42]

§ I use alcohol to soften people up to my physical advances – instead of learning patience, and accepting and appreciating others' boundaries, true desires, and choices made when they are fully coherent.

§ I use alcohol to drown out stress and other hard emotions – instead of learning how to healthily manage, use, and master them

"That's all drugs and alcohol do, they cut off your emotions in the end."

Ringo Starr

§ I use alcohol to allow myself to feel emotion – instead of learning how to connect with and accept my own feelings.

§ I use alcohol to numb physical pain – instead of dealing with the problems causing pain, or eliminating physical pain in a more proactive and healthy way (stress reduction, dietary changes, exercise, hypnosis, etc.), or just simply getting stronger by toughing it out.

§ I use alcohol to enjoy something refreshing – instead of sleeping better, eating better, exercising more, and drinking more water so that my body can *actually* be refreshed.

§ I use alcohol to "warm up" – instead of meditating to prepare myself mentally for challenging events and instead of exercising or covering up to get physically warm. Alcohol actually cools you; the warmth is an illusion.

§ I use alcohol to get creative – instead of developing my ability to open up my mind and be creative whenever I want.

§ I use alcohol to think deep thoughts – instead of learning how to introspect and think deeply at will

"I don't need alcohol to see the world in its depths, I carry the sun in me."

Lamine Pearlheart

§ I use alcohol to relax – instead of learning how to let go of the things that stress me or resolving them.

§ I use alcohol to sleep – instead of learning to quiet my mind and practice good sleeping habits.

"There is more refreshment and stimulation in a nap, even of the briefest, than in all the alcohol ever distilled."

Ovid

251

~ ~ ~

Can you see why I said that alcohol is like a counterproductive band-aid, a cheat on a test, and a crutch? You might be able to think of even more ways that it holds you back and *causes* problems despite, ironically, being touted as a *solution* to so many problems.

It's also important to know that using alcohol as a shortcut to the many desired good outcomes above does *not* make you more capable of doing them – at least, not when you're *not* drunk. Learning is often state-dependent, meaning that things learned in one environment (such as with a drunk brain) are not as easily recalled or performed in other environments.[44-47] So if you *are* learning anything while drunk, you're only learning how to do it *while in a drunken state*. It won't carry over well to sobriety. This is a critical point because, as already mentioned, alcohol does appear to help you in many ways. But these benefits last only while you're under the influence. When you're sober, the pendulum tends to swing the opposite way, so that you're actually *more anxious*, get *worse* sleep, *more* overwhelmed with emotions, *less* confident, *less* sexy, and so on and so forth. And what's the net result? With drugs, it's almost always negative. You have your high and your low, your buzz and your hangover, but if you sum them all together you will always come out worse than if you would have just stayed at baseline.

This same idea applies to other ostensibly helpful substances like caffeine and sugar. Sure, coffee or energy drinks can wake you up well or get you through a long night finishing a project, but the subsequent crash will always be bigger than the high. Like alcohol, these drinks have both short-term and long-term negative health effects, including the potential for tolerance, withdrawal, and addiction. These drinks can also dam you if you rely on them to bolster your abilities instead of improving yourself. For optimum healthy lifestyle, these should also generally be avoided.

Remember that alcohol and caffeinated/sugary drinks overall don't inherently help you to perform well or feel good, but it can *seem* like they do because you've *trained* yourself to need them, or at least to feel like you do. Your brain has literally changed its structure and molecular composition so that it's unimaginable to go without the drink because you would actually be less functional than if you had never used it in the first place. You see, as you develop tolerance, you need more and more of the substance in order to experience the boosts of pleasure and ability you first enjoyed. Because your brain tries to compensate for the artificial spikes, your levels of sleep, energy, happiness, ability, etc. while sober all start to drop, until you need the drink just to feel *normal*. Forget exceptional.

So, despite the brief boosts, the net results are always negative. This same logic applies to many things consumed or done for the sake of self-help that are actually crutches holding you back. But the good news is that since your choices trained your brain in these ways, then your choices can untrain it, too. We'll get to that later.

Now that you have an idea of what your score really represents, how extreme is your dependence on alcohol? These are the rough interpretations:

1-5: Great! Alcohol isn't holding you back too much, but if you want to take the next step of self-improvement in your life, this could be it.

6-15: Not terrible, but many aspects of your self and your life are being held hostage by alcohol. You would probably be even more successful and happy without it.

16-30: Bad news. Alcohol has a stranglehold on your life. It's damming your personal progress until only a small trickle is left. Something needs to change.

Having read through those challenging ideas and seen the extent to which you depend on alcohol, this would be an excellent time to set the book down and rethink your relationship with alcohol. After all, knowledge without personal application is useless. Come back tomorrow if you need to.

***

Welcome back.

Make sure you have seriously considered the 30 points above, otherwise the rest of this chapter is probably useless. You may have pondered them and now feel disturbed by the realization that, like the dam, alcohol has been hurting you all along rather than helping you. That is a wonderful step to take. But don't dwell on any regrets you may have. After all, it's not your fault that society has taught you to value alcohol so highly. By the end of this chapter, I'll tell you how to break the dam in order to free yourself and your life from the limitations.

Two-face

Let's take a more critical look at the thing itself. The alcohol industry and most of its consumers try to put a good face on alcohol to hide the fact that underneath all the glamor and positive press, it is a toxic chemical. Scientifically, "alcohol" actually refers to an entire class of chemicals that can each have very different properties. The specific type you drink is ethanol (EtOH, for short). But "alcohol" sounds less like a scary toxic chemical, so that's the name they stick with.

You may recognize ethanol as a common flammable additive to gasoline. It's a chemical used as a solvent and preservative for varnishes and other substances. It's also used in many scientific experiments because of its ability to change the chemical states and structures of other substances. Importantly, it's ubiquitously applied as a disinfectant. Granted, the ethanol used for that purpose is more concentrated than the type people drink. Nonetheless, scientists like myself spray it on our gloves and equipment every day, because it's so good at *killing*

255

things. Yet people willingly drink this toxic chemical every day.

No wonder ethanol is naturally aversive. Animals like rodents and fruit flies are neutral to or repulsed by it.[48-50] People generally find their first experience with alcohol "unpleasant" when recalling the event years later, despite the fact that the initial intoxication would likely make the memory more pleasant overall. People also overwhelmingly describe the taste as "bitter," a taste sensation whose purpose is to warn and prevent us from eating toxic foods.[51]

The Proof is in the 80-proof
Earlier, we discussed ways that alcohol dams us, conceptually. But how exactly does this happen? What are the specific effects? Is there scientific evidence that alcohol can damage your life, beyond the well-known physical harms?

There is.

As you read this section, ask yourself this crucial question: in your life, is the short-term pleasure worth the drunken debilitation, the hangovers, and the long-term life impairment? Some people may consider the following evidence and decide that yes, it is worth it. That's ok. It's not my place to tell you how to live your life. My goal is simply to help you make an informed decision after thoroughly considering both sides of the argument, including the bad and ugly sides of alcohol, rather than only ever hearing the glorified good side of things from peers and the media.

Alcohol's acute effects are, of course, dramatic, and include both pleasant and unpleasant aspects. You may end up embarrassing yourself, having heated arguments, or puking all over the floor, but it will probably still feel good. The hangover the next day will not feel so good, as most of us are well aware, so let's not waste time reviewing these short-term consequences. The part that's often ignored is the chronic effects. These long-term consequences are less obvious and may show no clear connection to drinking, because they endure long after the buzz and the hangover have passed. Yet these problems are potentially the most serious.

You're probably aware that frequent alcohol use wreaks havoc on our bodies. Consistent use contributes to cancer, lung infections, liver disease, stroke, high blood pressure, digestion problems, fatigue, and infertility, to name a few. It weakens immune systems, leading to more sickness and less productivity. Plus, it can lead to miscarriages and fetal alcohol spectrum disorders. It also accelerates cellular aging and makes your skin look older.[52]

In contrast, you may have never heard of the many ways that alcohol harms the mind and general well-being, including day-to-day function, productivity, success, and happiness. Even weeks or months after your last drink, alcohol use is linked to…

- impaired learning and memory, including poor school performance and dementia.[16-18]
- diminished concentration and attention span, and confusion (i.e., "brain fog").[18]
- reduced quantity and quality of sleep.[56]
- decreased testosterone levels.[57]
- lower energy levels.[58]
- weight gain.[59] After all, alcohol contains many empty calories which your body treats as sugars, which are then stored as fat.
- inhibited athletic performance.[58]
- high expenses. The average American household spends about 1% of their gross annual income on booze, which equates to $565 a year or $22,600 in 40 years.[60] Other estimates find even higher spending: $484 a year *per person*.[61] Those statistics *include* the approximately 30% of Americans who never drink, so your total financial loss might be even larger. Also, that's only accounting for money spent on actual booze, *not* money spent on alcohol-related activities and indirect costs. Imagine how much your financial situation would improve if you kept all the money you'd otherwise be spending on booze, bar food, taxis or ride sharing (please, *please* don't drink and drive!), and any other random associated costs, like medication for headaches, reduced salary, hospital bills, and

inebriated shopping sprees (>$400 spent each time, on average).[63]
- job loss and low productivity.[53, 63-64]
- risky behavior and aggression.[65] The prefrontal cortex, the part of your brain responsible for good decision-making, loses mass, activity, and strength, leaving you less in control of yourself.
- bad moods and mental health issues, largely by depleting levels of serotonin and dopamine, neurotransmitters that contribute to good moods, pleasure, and motivation. Though the fact that alcohol is a "depressant" technically means that it reduces brain activity, "depressant" seems an apt name for something that contributes to mental health issues like anxiety, depression, bipolar disorder, self-harm, and suicide.[52,66] People who are dependent on alcohol are up to 120 times more likely to commit suicide than those who are not.[67] Also, the more you rely on alcohol for pleasure, the more you may experience anhedonia, which is an inability to feel pleasure because of the dopamine losses.
- slower healing from trauma and increased risk of trauma-related anxiety disorders.[68]
- lower happiness. It has (not surprisingly) been shown that in cases where alcohol use becomes excessive or a problem, people experience reduced feelings of wellbeing.[69-71] More interestingly, less

use is not linked to less happiness, which flies in the face of many people's fear that life cannot possibly be as good if they reduce (or eliminate) their alcohol use.[69] One way alcohol reduces happiness is by contributing to poor choices, which produce "moral hangovers" of shame, guilt, and regret.

- damaged relationships and harm to others. Alcohol often leads to near-sighted and selfish behavior. How many people have been directly harmed by others' alcohol use? At least 28%,[40] and this study's definition of sustaining harm is strictly limited to family problems, hurt sustained as passenger of a drunk driver, physical assaults, financial trouble, and vandalized property. That's over 2.1 billion people worldwide. How many people ruin relationships because of booze? People with alcohol use disorders are 60% more likely to go through divorce.[72] A colleague and friend of mine described how, even as a newlywed, her three years married to an alcoholic were absolute hell. They were by far the worst years of her life. Don't be the one causing that kind of pain. (If you're the one suffering, she hopes you know that "you are *not* alone." This friend, Gaelle, wants to help anyone that's in that kind of situation – if you need support, advice, resources, or a listening ear, please contact me at help@cortexevolution.com and I'll send you her information.)

Given all this damning evidence, it's not surprising that Jonathan Levi, despite not being against drugs generally, believes that "alcohol is a super shitty drug." It's not surprising that a scientist colleague of mine mentioned that "alcohol is probably the worst addiction you can have." What *is* surprising is how we as a society ever allowed alcohol to gain such a suffocating strangle-hold over us all.

Alcohol is *the* single most commonly abused drug, and alcohol misuse and abuse are leading causes of preventable death.[73-74] Alcohol directly contributes to about 6% of deaths around the world,[53] more than all other drugs combined. Alcohol abuse cost the U.S. *alone* $250 *billion* way back in 2010, mostly from lost workplace productivity, and that number has surely gone up.[38] 28% of people report being harmed by drinkers, as mentioned above.[3] In the U.S. *alone*, 18 million people (~7%) have some form of alcohol addiction.[73] These numbers are staggering. And they don't even include unquantifiable damage, like all the ways that alcohol holds us back and prevents us from living our best lives. How are we as a society okay with this?!

We need to break free.

But let's bring it back to you. What do you think? In your life, is the short-term pleasure worth the drunken debilitation, the hangovers, and the long-term life impairment?

Before you decide, let's think about one more important question: hypothetically, how might your life be different if you were to magically stop drinking now (or drink less)?

A Life Without Alcohol

To help answer this question, let's invert all the damaging aspects just discussed into positive life changes that should result from a less booze-centered life. Besides preventing or reversing the various diseases and physical ailments caused by drinking mentioned above, quitting or even just reducing alcohol intake can…

- enhance learning and memory.
- increase focus and cognitive abilities.
- improve quantity and quality of sleep.
- raise testosterone levels.
- increase physical and mental energy levels, probably because of better sleep, increased testosterone, and the fact that your body is not constantly fighting off toxic ethanol and its metabolic byproducts.
- contribute to substantial, healthy weight loss.
- improve athletic performance. My fellow SuperLearner Coach Lorena Compean doesn't drink for months before a trail-running race because abstinence decreases running cramps and increases energy, hydration, confidence, and focus.
- save you a *lot* of money.

- drastically increase your productivity and career success. To quote *The 28-Day Alcohol-Free Challenge*, "When you aren't nursing hangovers, chewing up 3-4 hours per night with friends, destroying your sleep with booze, — miracle of miracles — you get more done!"[76] Also, if you reveal your drunk escapades or drinking habits on any public platform, it's possible that your boss, potential employers, or clients put less confidence in you because of it. So, abstinence may just lead to your next job, promotion, or big sale. Outside of work, you'll also have more time for family, hobbies, and healthy self-care.
- reduce risky impulsivity and aggression as you regain mental control of your choices.
- improve mood and mental health, alleviating anxiety, depression, bipolar disorder, borderline personality disorders, self-harm, and suicidal thoughts. Motivation and the ability to feel pleasure will return.
- accelerate emotional, mental, and physical healing.
- increase overall happiness!
- mend and prevent damage to relationships. With a clear mind, you can make amends for past mistakes and avoid making new ones. You'll also build new and higher quality relationships. What's the point of heart-to-heart conversations with your pals at a bar if you can't hear, understand, and/or

remember what was said? There are more effective ways to create lasting connection and friendship. You'll also connect to higher and deeper purposes now that your life does not revolve around booze.

Perhaps most importantly, do you remember the 30 ways that alcohol secretly dams us? Imagine how your personal progress will take off if you abandon your alcohol crutch and *actually* master crucial personal skills like charisma, connection, emotional regulation, self-care, courage, and creative thinking.

So, one more time: in your life, is the short-term pleasure worth the drunken debilitation, the hangovers, and the long-term life impairment?

If you're one of the lucky minorities that honestly feels that alcohol has been and will continue to be a benefit to your life, I congratulate you and wish you well. You can stop reading now and go enjoy life. Please come back if your assessment of your situation ever starts to change. If you're still unsure if giving up alcohol could possibly be worth it, I recommend learning about *The 28-Day Alcohol-Free Challenge.* Despite their own misgivings and worries about the implications of quitting, the authors of this book / program tried one month alcohol-free for themselves and discovered that their lives improved in countless, surprising ways.[76] There are too many to discuss them all here.

For everyone else, for all of you that have come to the conclusion that alcohol is probably doing more harm than good in your life, it's time to change your life for the better.

The Experiment
My Challenge to you: try living ONE month alcohol-free

***Make sure to consult your physician first, especially if you think you might have any physical dependence on alcohol. In that case, abrupt abstinence can be life-threatening. You may need to work out a healthy way to wean yourself off.***

It seems like every company these days offers free or discounted trials. I've enjoyed free trials of Netflix, YouTube Music, and dozens of other products and services, including the SuperLearner Masterclass back in the day. One reason for this strategy is that companies are confident that if you'll just try their product for a week or a month, you'll love it. They're confident that you'll notice the positive difference it makes in your life and never want to go back. So that's how your new relationship with alcohol needs to start: a one-month trial to decide if it really is all it's hyped up to be and if you want to make any permanent life changes. This time frame is a long enough break for your body to largely reset from alcohol and for you to start noticing real life changes, but short enough to be manageable.

After the month is over, it's up to you: you can go right back to where you started, try to quit alcohol for a year or forever, or somewhere in between. You may decide to just reduce your intake or use alcohol with healthier habits and attitudes without any change in consumption. If you ultimately decide that just slight adjustments to your alcohol use are best for you, that's fine. That's great! Just remember that, at best, all alcohol can ever do is *borrow* happiness, energy, etc. from tomorrow; it's almost guaranteed to leave you with a net loss, so use it wisely.

Also, I must warn you that it's far easier to live 100% alcohol-free than 99% alcohol-free, or 50% alcohol-free. It's far too easy to drink three beers when you only wanted two, or two shots when you intended to just try one. After all, by drinking one, you're immediately reducing executive function in your brain's prefrontal cortex, which controls decision making. That means that every drink makes you much more likely to have another. For these reasons, recovering alcoholics strive to avoid *all* cues and *all* alcohol. Jonathan Levi chooses to completely abstain because he found that pressure from others and lack of support made it nearly impossible to have just one drink. Your peers are more likely to respect a decision to simply not drink. It's just easier to make the decision once and never have to decide again rather than having to muster your willpower and make tough decisions every single time alcohol is an option.

Regardless of your final decision, before you choose, you have to try life 100% alcohol-free; otherwise, you'll never know if you're missing out on an even better life.

Can it Really be Done? *Really*?

You're probably wondering, though, is giving up alcohol (or even just reducing) really possible? One study participant aptly said that, "[Drinking is] like a rule that you can't break."[77] Which is true – it is "like" that. But similar to the façade of how good it is for your life, the idea that you can't *not* drink is also a lie.

You may think you're too addicted. But I've spent years watching and helping people break free of addictions, plus years studying and researching the topic. I've personally guided people through this process of change, including people who seemed to have extremely small chances of changing. I can attest that, although it may take some time, experimentation, and persistence, it's *always* possible.

You may think everyone drinks, so you'd be a social outcast if you did not. But this is an example of pluralistic ignorance, which is a phenomenon where most people go along with an action because they *inaccurately* assume that most people support the action. In fact, the majority do *not* support it; they're just doing it because they *also* think the majority support it. This concept is illustrated in the classic tale of "The Emperor's New Clothes," where swindlers convince the emperor and his household that they are tailoring fine clothes for him that are invisible to stupid or incompetent people. In reality, they sew absolutely nothing, but no one wants to admit that they cannot see

267

anything because it would reflect badly on them, and they all assume everyone else can see it. As a result, the emperor struts around naked while everyone praises his clothing, which they cannot see simply because it doesn't actually exist. The public indecency only ends when a child is brave enough to go against the perceived public opinion and shout out that the emperor is not wearing any clothes, after which everyone admits that that is their opinion, too.

Relating this story to alcohol, most people do *not* want to drink alcohol as much as they feel obligated to, and many people in any given social situation would rather *not* drink,[76,78] but they go along with it to fit in because they assume drinking is the common consensus. Ironically, in these situations, by drinking you are actually going *against* what the majority of people want you to do. Besides helping your own life, you can help others by being the child from the story with the courage to speak your honest opinion, namely, that you would rather not drink. No preachy explanation necessary – just honestly state your preference. Don't be afraid to speak up first when the waiter comes around asking what you all want to drink.

You'll be surprised how many people share similar sentiments. Some will feel relieved that they're not the only one who'd rather not drink, giving them the opportunity to *also* be true to themselves by following your example. Remember, it's easier and better to be the one who *sets* the precedent than the one who has to go against it after it's already set, or worse, the one who gives in to it.

One could argue that even if you don't let alcohol become a crutch, you can't control the fact that other people might. Other people might be utterly incapable of having fun or connecting without the benefits of "social lubricant." Or, more likely, they merely *believe* that they're incapable. That's fine. It's not your place to criticize or shame them for letting themselves be held back. But you shouldn't join them, either. You know that it will be better for you to not drink, and it would be better for them to not drink, too. So kindly explain your choice and, if appropriate, encourage similar choices from them, but never think or treat less of people who have not made the same decision you have.

You may think you can't possibly have fun or relax or enjoy social gatherings or be accepted by your peers without it. But there are hundreds of millions of people around the world who enjoy plenty of pleasure, happiness, and comradery completely without booze.

You may think you can't succeed in your career without it. But Jonathan Levi, Benjamin Hardy, Tyra Banks, Brené Brown, David Beckham, Kim Kardashian, Shania Twain, Jim Carrey, and Tony Robbins don't drink, and they're all quite successful, don't you think?

Now, you may be thinking, "sure, you can have *some* fun, success, social life, etc. without alcohol, but not as much as you could *with* alcohol." And that's true. In the short term. Remember all the ways we discovered above about how alcohol is like a crutch? Well, in the short-term, an injured person trying to run without a crutch is going to have a much harder time than an injured person with a crutch, this is true. But in the long-term? Who's going to win a massive marathon, an injured person hobbling along with a crutch or someone who abandons the crutch and gradually builds up their own muscles until they can run powerfully again?

Life is the massive marathon. Don't let fear of the short-term struggles prevent you from experiencing the long-term gains.

Remember the quotation that we started this chapter with? "[You will] not be giving anything up by not drinking." [42] In fact, why not completely shift your mindset so that "alcohol is no longer something you're giving up, but a threat to your dreams and goals?" [39]

You can give it up for a month. And if you can give it up for a month, you can give it up for a year. And if you can give it up for a year, you can give it up forever, if it feels right.

It's time to break that so-called unbreakable drinking "rule." It's time to break your damn dam.

Once you do, you'll open yourself up to a flood of positive life changes. You'll save money. You'll enjoy more energy. You'll feel less tired. You'll lose weight. You'll suffer through less headaches (not even counting all the hangovers you'll avoid). You'll enjoy deeper, rejuvenating sleep. You'll have more passionate, enjoyable sex. You'll benefit from enhanced focus and memory. You'll endure less embarrassment and anxiety. You'll have more time to be productive and to spend on healthier ways of enjoying yourself. You'll form deeper, more genuine relationships. You'll enjoy more success at work. You'll know and accept yourself more deeply. You'll face and overcome weaknesses and challenges that you used to just avoid. You'll supercharge your personal growth and development. You'll change your life.

It's for all these reasons that I never drink. It's for these reasons that Jonathan Levi, Tony Robbins, and all the successful people mentioned above don't drink. It's for these reasons that many of my fellow SuperLearner Coaches and millions of other people rarely ever drink, while millions more never drink at all – not because of religious beliefs, fear, or health constraints, but because they've realized that abstinence is the best choice for their lives. I'm confident that it would also be the best choice for yours.

It can be hard to admit that something needs to change in your life. It might be even harder to admit to yourself that something that you've trusted, enjoyed, and depended on for so long has actually been hurting you all along and needs to go. But consider this: *the degree to which you are willing to admit and accept your ignorance and imperfections is the degree to which you can overcome them.*

So, are you willing?

Your Toolkit

For some people, quitting or reducing alcohol intake will be extremely easy. For others, it might be extremely difficult because addiction has already set in. For most, it will be somewhere in between. After all, you've endured a lifetime of societal influences telling you abandoning alcohol is not necessary, not worth it, or not possible. Those influences have changed your brain so that harmful beliefs and habits are wired into you, all totally out of your control. But fear not – your brain is literally changing every day. Everything you learn, say, do, choose, and experience changes your brain, no matter your age. If it didn't, you'd wake up every morning as the exact same person you were yesterday, essentially memory-wiped. That means that no matter your personal situation, there's hope.

Anything that can be wired into your brain can be wired out of it. And this time, *you* will be in control. Entire textbooks and self-help books have been written about how to quit alcohol. I won't attempt to make a thorough, copycat version here, but here is a very brief description of tools usually required to quit or reduce alcohol (not necessarily in order of importance). You can find links and more information on this book's resource page.

-   A guide to quitting. Addicted or not, if your attempt to drink less is not as easy as you hoped, I highly recommend you find a well-proven resource to guide you through the process. (Note: I am not affiliated with the following resources in any way. I simply trust and believe in their ability to help you change.) I suggest starting with *The 28-Day Alcohol-Free Challenge*, which takes you through a step-by-step daily process of changing your beliefs and habits surrounding alcohol.[76] It also covers the challenges that people face when they try to quit alcohol, and provides excellent resources, tips, and strategies for dealing with them. You could also consider the well-acclaimed 12-Step program from Alcoholics Anonymous or similar approaches; they are powerful ways to change behavior even if you don't consider yourself an alcoholic. For more general methods of habit-change, check out books like *Atomic Habits* by James Clear and *The Power of Habit* by Charles Duhigg, or research strategies like mindfulness-based relapse prevention and cognitive behavioral therapy.

- Professional help. Remember that addiction is a brain disease, and no one can be blamed for the wiring of their brains that has built up over the years. So, there's no shame in turning to professionals to help make this life change, even if you're not addicted. Whether it be a therapist, coach, or habit and addiction specialist, if you need the extra help, please get it. The investment in yourself will be worth it.

- Motivation. You need to define your "why", so that when the going gets tough, you have something to fall back on that will keep moving you forward. Dig deep. What's the "why" behind the "why"? If you're reducing your drinking to have more energy, why? If the energy would let you have more quality time with your kids, or get more done at work, why does that matter? And so on. Usually, our deepest motivations ultimately come down to how something will make us *feel*. Yes, even for things that seem selfless and altruistic, like stopping drinking so you'll be more present for your significant other or so you can serve your community better. If you haven't found a feeling yet, you need to dig deeper.

- Alternate routines. According to Charles Duhigg's book, *The Power of Habit*, and substantial psychological research, habits consist of four primary elements.[43] First, something about your environment acts as a *cue* to remind your brain that if you engage in a given behavior again, it will feel good again, like it always does. These cues can be the time of day, the location you're in, other people (or lack thereof), your immediately preceding action, or your emotional state, to name a few. Because of these cues, you engage in the *routine* (i.e., the good or bad habit). As a result, you obtain the *reward*, which with alcohol can be numb feelings, enjoyable socializing, a mental break, yummy flavors, a sugar rush, or many other things that feel good and/or stop you from feeling bad. Or even a combination of things. After these three steps, your brain's reward system recognizes that if you do that routine when that cue happens, you'll get that reward! And that feels good. So, you'll be more likely to do the routine next time the cue happens. Hence, the last element of habits is *craving*, which is your brain pushing you to complete this "habit loop" over and over and over again.

The key to habit change is generally *not* to eliminate the habit loop. We can't simply make the harmful habit circuits in our brain disappear. They can fade away simply by disuse, but that is a long and difficult road because our brains are so darn good at remembering things. Instead, we must *alter* the loop. Ideally, you'll eliminate a bad habit and simultaneously create a good habit (like exercise!) to take its place.

To do so, the first step is to acknowledge the harmful routine. Then, do some introspection and experiment with slight tweaks to your routine until you identify the reward that is driving the behavior. Next, observe and identify the cues that lead you to start craving that reward. Simply avoid the cues if at all possible, including bars, a stocked fridge, beer commercials, the liquor aisle, or people that are a negative influence on you. To whatever extent that's not possible, find an *alternative* routine that you can do when the cue strikes that will provide the *same* (or nearly the same) reward. That alternative routine could be positive, neutral, or just less negative than the original.

For instance, if your desired reward is a refreshing liquid and an energizing sugar boost, why not try non-alcoholic beer? Or a soda? Or, since those are both excessively sugary, why not some ice water and some fruit? The important thing is that you can easily do the alternative routine when you feel cravings prompted by the cue, and the new routine will bring you a reward similar to the original routine. Whether your cue is arriving home from work or friends offering to buy you a drink at a bar, it's critical to have a plan for avoiding or dealing with these situations and to mentally rehearse (visualize) responding to the cues and executing your plan in the ways you want. There's a more complete description of these strategies in

The Power of Habit, and plenty of information online.

Remember, according to the famed neurologist and psychiatrist Viktor Frankl, "Between stimulus [the cue] and response there is a space. In that space is our power to choose our response. In our response lies our growth and our freedom."

-   Faith / belief. In addition to identifying the elements of the habit loops described above, Charles Duhigg points out that changing routines requires a *belief* that change is possible.[80] Without that, you will eventually, inevitably, slip up (i.e., temporarily give up) when faced with tough situations. Like Henry Ford said, "Whether you think you can, or you think you can't – you're right." That's one reason why many people find that the best tool to encourage change is a support system, where you can be inspired by others' examples and successes. Alcoholics Anonymous is successful largely because newer members see people that used to think, as they might think now, that change was impossible. They couldn't imagine going a week without booze, let alone years. But yet they did it.

To help with finding belief, it will help if you recognize that, despite appearances, most of the people around you are *not* fully comfortable or happy with everything about our alcohol culture. Remember pluralistic ignorance, with our example of the naked emperor? If you're open about your convictions, you'll find that many people will appreciate, support, and follow you. You will inspire each other.

- A support system. Life change is so much easier if you have people around you to encourage you, empathize with difficulties, keep you accountable, and help you to change your environment and attitudes to increase the chances of success. Find those kinds of people, and ask them to help in the specific ways you need. Your support system could be an organized group like Alcoholics Anonymous, online communities, an unorganized group of like-minded friends or strangers, a couple close friends or family members, or even just your partner. The more the better, and ideally they will share your conviction, but they certainly don't have to. I also invite you to share your commitment, find support, share successes, and find accountability partner(s) through public platforms dedicated to helping people quit. To find other people trying to improve themselves, you can also try the SuperLearner Facebook page, or you can contact me for help.

Using these powerful tools, you can do this. As a certified learning and memory coach, I firmly believe that the only thing you can't learn is the thing you don't *try* to learn. And the only thing you can't change is the thing you don't *try* to change. Time to try.

The Happy Ending.

Largely thanks to encouragement from *The 28-Day Alcohol-Free Challenge* and similar initiatives, millions of people have made the leap of faith to live without alcohol for a time. They discovered, as you will, that that one crucial choice set them free and improved their lives in many wonderful ways, some completely unexpected. It can be done, and when it is done, the positive effects are real and so life-changing that many people never go back.

Referring back to *Frozen 2*, one of the protagonists appears to magically freeze and die because the crime of her grandfather building the deceptive dam had gone unpunished. However, when the dam is broken, she is brought back to life just in time to save the day. She becomes the magical hero and leader she was always meant to be so that she can protect, serve, and unite the people. In other words, breaking the dam unfreezes her, allows her to accomplish amazing things, and unleashes her full potential. Her higher self was always within her, but it could not be found and freed until the dam was broken.

So it is with you.

What will happen after you break *your* dam? What good will *you* accomplish? What better version of yourself will *you* become?

If you don't break it, you'll never know.

Get Fit at Home – Even if You Have No Idea Where to Begin: A Crash Course in Calisthenics for Strength and Fitness

Dylan Peterson – Minong, WI, USA

Dylan is an IT Technician, SuperLearner© Certified Coach, father of four, entrepreneur, wrestling coach, and active member of his local community. A strong brain needs a strong, healthy body - and that is what he is hoping to bring to you in this book.

Weighed Down
"Oh, no...not this again..."

I walk up to the bar set up in the school gymnasium, what feels like thousands of eyes on me, and make what I know is a futile attempt to do a pullup. I already know I can't - most 230 pound 15-year-old boys would struggle here - but I have to at least try or I'll get an "F" in Gym class. Who gets an "F" in Gym?

Trembling, I step up to the bar and reach my hands up to get a grip on it. As my feet leave the floor, I can barely hold myself up. The bar might as well be 100 feet above me as I pull with everything I have.

Defeated and thoroughly embarrassed, I finally give up and drop back to the floor. "Genetically cursed". "Unathletic". "At least he's a smart kid…".

But there has to be something I can do. Some way to fix this. I mean, I've never seen a newborn do a pullup, so there has to be some measure of "skill" involved, right? It can't all be about "genetics" or "natural athleticism". Anyone can learn this stuff; it can't just be "uncontrollable"…

Thus began my years-long series of experiments, studies, trials, and eventual successes in calisthenics training. I grabbed every resource I could find on exercise, did pushups until I felt like my arms would fall off (which didn't take long in the beginning), experimented with various diets, and even went so far as to run multiple miles wrapped in garbage bags to "sweat it out".

Eventually, I found ways that worked. I lost over 40 pounds in the span of a year; I entered my Freshman year of high school around 230 lbs and was below 190 by the beginning of the next. This was the beginning of my lifelong relationship with calisthenics and bodyweight exercise.

I've learned a lot since then. I can get up from my desk right now and do 20 pullups. I'm consistently at or below 15% bodyfat. I'm more comfortable shirtless at 32 then I ever was as a teen.

I'm not a fitness professional. I have three kids and another on the way and I spend most of my day fixing computers. I'm not in the gym 6 hours per day - heck, I'm not in the gym at all. Far from it.

My purpose for writing this chapter is to distill years of struggle, trial, effort, failure, and success into an actionable, digestible guide that anyone can follow. Can't do a pullup yet? Cool, no problem. 25% body fat? No judgement, I was there once too. I took action and changed it - and so can you.

I also strongly feel that no discussion of how to optimize your mind for learning would be complete without addressing the optimization of the body - get your workouts in and your brain will thank you for it!

Fitness doesn't have to be complicated. It doesn't have to involve commutes back-and-forth to a noisy, crowded gym. In fact, it can be done pretty much anywhere you are - as long as you have the right tools and knowledge.

That's exactly what I want to give you in this chapter - a crash-course in how to get fit at home with very little equipment so you can create your very own, go-to, no-excuses workouts. Along the way, I will also direct you towards resources beyond this book that you can use to expand your learning and take the next steps.

I do want to preface with a few quick items to be sure bases are covered and expectations are clear:

I am not a physical fitness expert, nor am I a medical professional - please consult your doctor before following any of this advice. I am, however, a guy who has tried quite a few different approaches, consumed many hours of content, and used myself as a guinea pig for years. You can benefit from this by using the information that I have distilled over years of learning and experimenting to have a well-informed and no-nonsense approach to fitness without wasting your time chasing fads and "bro-science", wasting your money buying every new fitness gizmo, spending hours going to a conventional gym, or avoiding exercise entirely due to overwhelm. This is not meant to be some ultimate guide to health, but a way to get you started on the path to getting into great shape at home without the "magic" pills and complicated routines that can easily come along with trying to find your own way in the fitness world.

I have been practicing Calisthenics and bodyweight exercise for years now and have a regular practice to this day - despite a very busy lifestyle and no time to waste on hours-long workouts. You can do it, too!

This chapter is limited in length and scope, so I will often point to external resources for more in-depth information. I am not affiliated with these sources in any way beyond having successfully used them myself, and I will not point you towards anything I do not firmly believe in. These people have done some amazing work to provide and maintain these programs and all credit goes to them.

So, with that out of the way, read on and discover how a kid that couldn't do a pullup in high school learned to use his own body as a gym to propel himself towards fitness goals that he once considered impossible...

What is "Bodyweight Exercise", Anyway?
Bodyweight Exercise, or calisthenics, is a physical fitness method that uses your own body as resistance rather than relying on external "weight", as you would during traditional weightlifting and certain other forms of cardiovascular exercise.

Why Bodyweight Exercise?
There are a few major advantages to calisthenics and bodyweight over other forms of physical training. These include:

- *Convenience* - no gym membership needed, no noisy weightroom, no waiting for equipment. Just you, your tunes, and your body. All you need is a space on the floor big enough for you to lay down and a pullup bar.
- *Calisthenics encourages a healthy body composition* - let's be real, it's harder to do calisthenics when you're overweight. Your body will recognize this and, over time, adopt

proportions that make the movements easier. This is true of all forms of exercise, but when your body is your gym, your body composition shifts to support your specific build and optimize your movements, not just lift arbitrary external loads.

- *Improved mobility* - weight machines at the gym let you "cheat". Sitting down on a padded stool with your back against the padded bench isolating one muscle at a time does not push your body to develop new ranges of motion. Calisthenics progressions will challenge your body in positions it may not see very often, which will improve your flexibility and help prevent injuries.

- *Improved coordination and reflexes* - Calisthenics often uses full-body, compound movements that incorporate many muscle groups working in unison, which teaches your body to work as a unit rather than as individual parts.

- *Good for all ages and fitness levels* - want to work out with your kids? Your parents? Your buddy who considers walking to the fridge "cardio"? Calisthenics offers progressions suitable for any/all situations.

Mythbusting - Ignore the Haters

As with any exercise culture, bodyweight exercise is subject to its fair share of criticism. Let's look at some of the bigger myths and see if we can poke some holes in them:

- *You can't build muscle with calisthenics* - allow me to point to Tee Major, Hit Richards, Hannibal for King, Todd Kuslikis, Austin Dunham, the Kavadlo brothers, and Chris Heria (just to name a few from the top of my head). While it's true you probably won't be winning any pro bodybuilding contests without throwing some iron around, you can certainly achieve a very aesthetic physique with bodyweight work alone
- *You need "muscle confusion" to build muscle* - this term gets thrown around all the time as a reason to constantly vary up workout regimens. But frankly, no, you don't need to. Case study after case study of accomplished strength athletes in any field, not just bodyweight work, shows that principled practice following a few basic rules (covered below) will be enough to get you pretty far. Anyone telling you to over-complicate your workouts for the sake of "keeping your muscles guessing" is just trying to sell you a program.
- *Bodyweight workouts are only good for endurance* - this myth is driven by the many "1,000 pushups a day" style routines. If you stick to the same exercises and just keep cranking up the repetitions then yes, you'll enter the "endurance training" range (more on that in the sets/reps section)
- *Bodyweight workout only works for thin/small/light people* - while it is true that

287

shorter, lighter people will have an easier time achieving some of the more advanced feats, there are certainly taller athletes that have done so and it does not stop you from improving your fitness. Just remove the ego and realize that you're still improving.

- *Calisthenics is just endlessly increasing repetitions of a handful of exercises* - while this may be what you've been exposed to in the past, well-structured bodyweight exercise focuses on a concept called "progressive overload" (more on that below). In a nutshell, this means that once you reach certain goals within each exercise you'll move on to more difficult variations (progressions) for fewer reps. This keeps the strength gains coming and holds the super-long sets at bay. So, ironically, the opposite is true - as you increase your strength and mobility, the variability of the exercises will increase and the reps will often decrease in favor of other forms of progressive overload.

Essential Gear

So, how do you get started? What do you need to begin?

The equipment required is very minimal - the only things you'll need are a pullup bar, some rings, and some optional resistance bands.

Even if you can't quite do pull ups yet, you'll quickly be exposed to progressions meant to get you to your first one.

You can get a bar that simply hangs in a doorway at just about any store, or online, for ~$30. My favorite way to do rows (and many other exercises) indoors is to use gymnastic rings hung from a doorway pullup bar - this will allow you to easily adjust the height of the rings for different exercises and difficulties.

If you have the room, you can build a more permanent bar - search around for plans and ideas online, there are quite a few great designs. This can also be used to anchor your rings for a calisthenics "gym" - all with materials you can find for relatively cheap.

Some other basic equipment might include resistance bands for stretching, warm-ups, and to assist with some more difficult exercises, along with a Yoga mat.

You may see other equipment as you check out online videos but, for now, this simple setup will get you started. By the time you want to expand your equipment, you'll be knowledgeable enough to either know what you need and what you plan to use it for or you'll have resources to use to find these answers.

That's really about it. All you need is your body, an open piece of floor or ground, and a few simple pieces of gear. Now you're ready to get started!

Setting Yourself Up for Success

Like any discipline, Calisthenics and bodyweight fitness is all about FOCUS.

People start working out for a few common reasons:

1. They want to lose fat (not "weight", necessarily - more on that in a minute).
2. They want to get stronger.
3. They want to gain muscle mass.
4. They want to improve their athletic performance.

Now, you may see plenty of fitness programs out there claiming that you can "lose 25 pounds AND gain muscle mass AND add 50% to your bench press AND get your dream job/girl/car/etc." and, while this is possible for some rare genetic outliers with the help of certain "supplements", you will just get overwhelmed and frustrated if you try to chase everything simultaneously.

I know that fitness magazines and online articles are packed with the "do everything at once" workouts, but these sorts of results are only sustainable if you're also taking steroids. While steroids will certainly make your fitness goals easier in the short-term, the long-term dangers and side effects far outweigh the upside for the average person. If you still think that steroids are right for you, then the rest of this chapter isn't. If you want to get fit safely and naturally without selling your soul to the fitness industry, read on.

Pick a goal and stick to it for at least 4-6 weeks.

What goal do you start with? Well, what's the most motivating factor of the four goals I listed above?

If your goals are aesthetic (i.e. looking better naked), then you'll need to decide which to do first - lose fat or gain muscle mass. This choice can be made simpler by considering your current state and remembering that muscle mass doesn't show as well if your bodyfat percentage is too high. If you're carrying around some extra weight (no judgement - remember, I was a 230 pound 15-year-old at one point in my life) then your first priority will probably be to cut some excess body fat before focusing on adding mass.

If your goals are more performance-based, then take a look at what aspects of performance you want to improve. Strength? Power? Endurance? In a few pages we'll go through how to structure your exercise to target each of these goals - stay tuned!

Setting Fitness Goals

Without clear goals you run the risk of "program hopping" or jumping from this type of workout to that type of workout from day-to-day or week-to-week. Your progress will stall, you'll get frustrated, and eventually you'll give up this whole exercise thing altogether.

This is coming from personal experience - trust the guy who's already made that mistake far too often.

So, we're going to set some SMART goals to keep us focused and in-line with what we want to get out of our exercise program.

For a refresher on the SMART goal-setting process, refer to the chapter "Building Unstoppable Success Momentum by Peter Anglin earlier in the book.

Let's look at a few examples of how we can apply SMART goal setting to our fitness journey:

"I want to get stronger." Specific? Measurable? How much stronger? Stronger at what? What about "I want to be able to perform 10 pullups (specific, measurable, ambitious, and relevant to our goal of "getting stronger") in one set (measurable) in two months(time-based)"? That seems much more attainable - you know what you need to do, why you want to do it, how it relates to your overall goals, and how you'll know if you succeeded or not.

Why "Losing Weight" is a Terrible Goal

"I want to lose weight." Let me start by saying that "weight" is not the best measure of success when it comes to aesthetics. The "ideal weight" for a given person will be dependent on so many factors (existing muscle mass, height, body type, etc.) that it becomes very difficult to find accurate, workable measures. I prefer to use the term "body composition", as it really says what we're after - we don't want to "weigh less", we want to have healthier body fat levels, we want to be more athletic, and we want to look better naked. Besides, "weight" can change based on many factors - how much salt you've eaten recently, the time of day, hydration levels, and where you are in your natural hormonal cycle (yes, even for men) all play a part. If you're new to resistance training, then you will probably gain some muscle mass as well - this will cause your weight to fluctuate even if your bodyfat percentage does drop.

If you lose two pounds of fat and gain two pounds of muscle in a month, you'll still weigh the same. If we go by weight alone, then all your hard work was for nothing.

So, what should you focus on then?

If your goals are purely aesthetic, then measurements are simple - take weekly pictures of yourself and compare progress to previous weeks. Don't just look in the mirror, as it becomes very difficult to see incremental changes week to week without an objective measure (in this case, your pictures from previous weeks).

If your goals are more holistic, or the mirror test is frustrating or not showing results, you could do waistline measurements, body fat measurements with simple calipers at home, or the "do these pants fit better?" test. That way, you're measuring a real metric that doesn't constantly fluctuate based on a variety of factors and you can keep your sanity.

In terms of SMART goals, you could try to "get to 15% bodyfat (men) or 23% bodyfat (women) in three months" or "fit back into those pants I wore a few years ago by June 1st" or "lose two inches from my waist by summer".

Just be sure you measure at roughly the same time every time - every Monday morning right away in the morning, for example. Morning before you eat or drink anything is generally best. If you are tracking weight, do not weigh yourself multiple times per day - it will wreak havoc on your psyche to see that number fluctuate as you eat, use the bathroom, and drink, which can encourage bad habits like starving or dehydrating yourself just so you can see that number stay lower.

Try to avoid doing so after a night of eating poorly and/or drinking - the extra sodium and alcohol can play serious havoc on your body and throw off your measurements. If Saturdays tend to be a night when you eat out, Sunday mornings aren't the best time to measure.

Finally, remember that MOST of the work in weight management and body composition change comes in the kitchen - if you want to make significant improvements to body composition, stop eating loads of garbage! You simply cannot outwork poor eating habits; I can't stress this enough.

That being said, let's take a quick dive into some basic nutrition guidelines.

A Quick and Dirty Nutrition Guide
For the sake of brevity, I'm going to keep the Diet/Nutrition info light and very generalized here. For

more information, I will add some links to great articles on the resources page for this book and you can also see the next chapter called "The Quickstart Guide to Optimal Performance ".

If you are resistance training, you want to be sure you are consuming enough protein to maintain and feed your muscles. The word "enough" means many things to different people, depending on who you ask, but most of the science seems to settle on roughly 2 grams of protein per kilogram or .9 grams of protein per pound of bodyweight. This is true for both men and women, so get that protein in, ladies!

For example, I currently weigh around 170lbs (or ~77kg). 170 lbs x .9 = 153 grams of protein per day. If I eat three meals per day, that's roughly 51g per meal. You can check out the resources website for some great examples of foods that will boost your protein intake without adding a ton of empty calories to your diet.

Your nutrition will depend a lot on your goals, so I will try to keep it simple here. I'm not going to get into all of the different dietary philosophies - frankly, whatever diet you'll actually stick to is "the right one" for you so long as it follows the basic principles below.

First, stick to whole foods as much as possible. Eat plenty of vegetables (their caloric value is virtually negligible, so don't be shy), vary your food intake, and avoid overly-processed "food" from a box as much as possible.

If you want to gain muscle, you will need to eat more calories than you burn so that your body has the resources (protein and calories) it needs to produce muscle. You can't grow if you don't have enough calories. There may be exceptions to this rule (people who gain muscle on a caloric deficit), and this is much more prevalent in people new to resistance training (often referred to as "newbie gains"), but after you've gotten past the initial adaptations you'll need to pay more attention to this. Eating more calories than you burn also leads to fat gain, so keep it under control - a 10% increase is often enough to start and going higher than that often leads to disproportionate fat gains. Try to keep these extra calories "clean" - doughnuts are probably not the best choice. Focus on foods that have as few ingredients as possible, like vegetables, fruits, nuts, meats, etc., and avoid processed foods when you can.

If you want to lose fat, you'll need to burn more calories than you consume. Again, this does NOT mean a super calorie-restricted diet - in fact, doing so will jeopardize the muscle and strength gains you're hoping to make. A deficit of up to 25% of your daily calories, when strictly adhered to, will result in steady weight loss without burning up too much of your hard-earned muscle mass in the process. Protein remains important during fat loss, too - if your protein consumption is too low, you will start to burn off muscle to use as energy to replace the missing calories. Protein will also keep you feeling "full" longer, which can help keep cravings at bay.

Typically, the easiest way to remove unnecessary calories from your diet is to trim back on carbohydrates and sugars - drop the breads and noodles and avoid sugary or calorie-laden drinks.

If you want to get more specific, you can find links in the resource page to tools that can help you determine how many calories you burn on average in a day and you can adjust from there.

Keep it simple. Grab one of the calorie tracking apps linked in the resource page, set your goals, and let the software do the work. The app keeps tracking your food simple - you can enter food items by searching the built-in database or by scanning their barcodes and you can save meals for future use. The only caveat here is that you'll need to manually adjust the protein goals to match those listed above - it really isn't too hard to figure out, though, so play around with the percentages until you're close. If you need to increase your protein percentage to increase the grams per day goal, reduce your carbohydrate intake to keep it balanced.

I do suggest tracking your food for at least a few weeks, especially if you never have before. Doing so can grant some valuable insights as to your consumption habits, and can help to answer questions later (why can't I lose weight even though I'm dieting? why can't I gain weight even though I'm eating more?). After 2-3 weeks you can drop it if it drives you crazy, but if you start to have trouble reaching your goals checking your nutrition can be a good place to start.

Progressive Overload

In order to progress and get stronger, you need to apply a principle called "Progressive Overload".

Don't worry, it sounds more complicated than it is.

The short version is that we need to keep adjusting variables in our training to challenge us. If we do not, our progress stalls out quickly.

The entire idea behind strength training is that your body will adapt to the stimulus you place on it. Lift heavy stuff and your body grows muscle and gains strength so you can lift heavy stuff easier next time. Run a few miles and your body will shed weight and streamline your running mechanics so that you can run further/faster next time (so long as your diet is in check and you're getting enough sleep). This is referred to as the Specific Adaptation to Imposed Demand (SAID) principle.

Some exercises are complementary, i.e. squats strengthen your legs and make you a more explosive sprinter, but for the purposes of this chapter, we are going to consider specific movements, and their physiological impact, independently.

Like some of the myths we've mentioned above, this is where a lot of training programs can fall short. Doing 100 pushups a day does not follow the principle of Progressive Overload (at least, not without some conscious manipulation of the variables listed below), which is why some people try calisthenics for a short time only to declare that "it doesn't produce results".

So, what are some of these variables?

In order of importance:
1.   Amount of resistance
2.   Range of Motion (RoM)
3.   Number of reps per set
4.   Rest between sets
5.   Speed of each rep

Let's tackle them each a bit more in-depth.

1.   *Amount of resistance* - in weightlifting terms, this would simply be manipulated by adding or removing weight. Now, you may ask "but my body weighs roughly the same amount every day, how do I add or remove weight?". This is where the various exercise progressions come into play - we're not going to change your weight, but we are going to manipulate leverage and body mechanics to change the difficulty of each exercise.

For example, let's take the classic pushup. Want to make it harder? Put your hands closer together to put more stress on the smaller triceps muscles in your arms or raise your feet up higher to put more weight on your upper body.

What about making them easier? Put your hands on the back of your couch and do your pushups at a 45-degree angle to the floor ("incline pushups").

For a great example of this, check out some of the progressions and examples I will link to in the Resources page.

This concept can be applied to any exercise progression - if you have an exercise, there are ways to make it easier or harder depending on your needs.

2. *Range of Motion (RoM)* - doing an exercise with more RoM makes the movement more difficult, as well, while decreasing it will make the movement easier. Generally speaking, we want to work with the maximum RoM we are capable of for any given movement - but there will be some exceptions (especially in the "in-between" progressions from one major movement to another).

3. *Rest Between Sets* - this is another, more subtle way we can use progressive overload. When we structure our workout (more on that below), we will program in specific rest periods based on our goals. Increasing these rest times will decrease the difficulty of the workout, giving you more time to

recover between sets. Sometimes, as a way to make smaller changes to our workout (typically when moving to the next progression is just a little bit out of reach), we can simply decrease the rest time between our sets to boost the challenge and push for more.

4. *Number of reps per set* - another way we can alter the level of challenge is to perform more or less reps in each set. More reps means more work.

5. *Speed of each rep* - performing reps slower and with more control requires more control throughout the movement while speeding up the reps requires more power to perform. Different people are naturally inclined more towards one than the other, so experiment and see which camp you fit into. Once you know which is more "natural" for you, doing the opposite is a way you can increase the challenge.

Ok, let's use an example so we can see how this all works together.

Let's stick with the push up - when I do pushups, I start at three sets of eight reps with one minute of rest between each set. When I successfully complete that goal, I have to find a way to make the exercise harder.

I could…

1. add more reps and do three sets of nine reps next time,
2. decrease the rest time to 45 seconds between sets,
3. do each pushup a little bit slower,
4. put my feet up higher to change the leverage and put more "weight" on my upper body (in a pushup, your feet support some of your weight),
5. or focus on getting my chest all the way to the floor and having my arms completely straight at the top (increasing RoM)

If I couldn't complete my three sets of 8, I could make it easier by putting my hands higher (like on the back of my couch or up on a platform on the floor), resting longer between sets, doing fewer reps in each set, doing each rep slightly faster, or doing each rep with less RoM (though I should work to improve this RoM over time and not use it as an excuse to have poor form).

Warming Up

Warming up is ESSENTIAL to avoid injury and perform at your best during your workout. It is often skipped, much to the detriment of the trainee.

My favorite warm-up that I've ever used is from the Reddit Bodyweight Fitness subreddit (link on the Resources page) - it hits all the necessary components without being overly complicated, being a workout in itself, or taking up half your workout time.

Another warm-up that's a little bit lower impact is from StartBodyWeight (also on the Resources page). This might be a good place to start if the Reddit warm-up seems a little daunting. Either one is fine so long as it works for you, so don't stress it too much. Other methods exist, so feel free to poke around and find what works for you through experimentation.

The purpose is to literally get the body warm (warm muscles are less likely to be damaged by exercise) and to "wake up" muscles that might be sleepy from sitting or improper movement. When you're done, you should feel "ready to go", like you're ready for whatever your workout can throw at you, and you should probably be a little sweaty already. This is a good thing - it shows that you're warm and that your body is priming for exercise.

Establishing Baselines

When we first start resistance training, we need to establish our baselines - our current strength and fitness levels - so we have an objective way to measure our progress. We want to avoid subjective measures (how hard does this movement feel?) so that we know, for sure, if what we are doing is working.

One good way to do this is to simply pick a few exercises targeting different muscle groups and do one max-effort set (one set of as many repetitions as you possibly can) in each after warming up. So, for example, we can use pushups, pullups, and standard squats to gauge our strength.

If our goal is more sprinting speed, we might choose to measure our current 40-yard dash. If endurance is your goal, you might choose to measure your current one or two mile run times (if you're physically ready for such an attempt - don't jump in over your head yet!).

Find a movement or test that corresponds to your goals - you wouldn't test your 5k run time if you want to get stronger, and you wouldn't test your pushups if you wanted to improve your sprinting speed.

Once you've chosen your metrics, give it your all.

If you're choosing strength movements, give plenty of rest time (10 minutes or more) to make sure you are recovering fully between each exercise - maximum effort resistance work takes longer than you would think to recover from fully, and we want these to be the best sets we are currently capable of. This will be your workout for the day, so don't hold back.

Now that we have these baselines, we know where we are starting from. Do not beat yourself up over these if you don't score as high as you'd like - these scores will improve over time, that's why we are here! Remember these tests, write down your results and do this same test again in 4-6 weeks to gauge progress. If your performance improves, then you know what you're doing is working.

Next up, we'll talk about how to format our actual workout based on our goals.

Programming for Strength and/or Muscle

We're going to get into some of the geekier aspects of exercise here for a bit.

How you structure your strength workout will depend on your goals.

Here is a quick breakdown of the general principles:

Strength gains
- Reps: 4-8
- Sets: 3-5
- Rest: 2+ minutes

Muscle gains
- Reps: 8-12
- Sets: 3-5
- Rest: 90 seconds or less

Endurance gains
- Reps: 12+
- Sets: 3+
- Rest: Minimum

What does this all mean?

If your goals are purely strength related, you want to do fewer repetitions of harder exercises. For example, if my target exercise was pushups, I would shoot for 3-5 sets of 3-8 repetitions each with 3+ minutes of rest between each set. So, you would do 6 reps of pushups (one set), rest for 3 minutes, then do your next set. You would repeat this until all of your sets were complete.

If your goal is to build muscle mass, you would do a few more reps (8-12) of a slightly easier progression in each set and cut down the rest times to 60-90 seconds - you want to damage the muscles so they will heal bigger and stronger, so you want to find the balance between being able to perform the exercise and damaging the muscle fibers to provoke change.

For endurance training, you want exercises that are relatively easy to perform and you're going to do LOTS of repetitions with little rest between your sets. If I was doing pushups, again, I would move to a progression that allows me to perform at least 12 reps. Then I would perform as many reps as possible, rest for as little as possible so that I can perform my next full set.

These numbers are all very generalized, and different sources will give you different ranges. The optimal range for each person is dependent on quite a large number of variables that are beyond the scope of this chapter, so by all means experiment around and see what works for you.

So how do we put all of this information together?

Let's go back to our example of pushups. Let's say I can perform 4 pushups for three sets with two minutes of rest between sets, so I do that for my first workout.

On my next workout, I will increase the reps by one (total, not per set). So, my next pushup workout would be one set of five reps -> two minutes of rest -> one set of four pushups -> two minutes of rest -> and a final set of four pushups. If I complete that successfully, I will do five-five-four on my next workout, then five-five-five, and so on.

Once I hit the top of my target rep range (say 8 reps if I'm looking to target my strength), I would then move up to the next progression in pushups - I would either move my hands closer together for "close grip pushups" or put my feet up on a platform for "decline pushups" - and decrease my reps back to 4 to start working my way up again.

Calisthenics for Cardio
The most common way you'll see calisthenics used for a more cardiovascular workout is with High Intensity Interval Training (HIIT). This is usually done one of two ways.

The first method, which is simpler and easier for a beginner to start, is to pick an exercise that allows you to perform many reps (15+ at least). You'll then perform that exercise at maximum effort ("as hard as you can") for a set interval, then rest for a set interval, then repeat until done.

The intervals most often prescribed seem to follow a pattern: beginners are working at a 1:4 ratio (i.e. 15 seconds of work and 45 seconds of rest) and progress from there - work periods become longer and rest periods become shorter.

This allows you to choose a relatively simple exercise that works for you and repeat it with an easy structure. Just grab yourself an interval timer (you can use a standalone interval timer or an app on your mobile device), set up your desired intervals, and go to work.

Common exercises include:
- jumping jacks
- sprinting/jogging
- burpees
- shadowboxing
- jumping rope (or just mimicking the motion if you don't have one)
- or any other relatively light exercise

The second method is to train "circuit style", where you will choose a few exercises targeting different body parts and perform them with little rest in between.

For example, I would choose
1. a full-body exercise to get the heart rate up (burpees, jumping jacks, high-knees, shadowboxing),
2. an upper body pushing exercise (pushups, dips, handstand pushups, pike presses),
3. a lower-body exercise (squats, lunges, box/broad jumps),
4. an upper body pulling exercise (pullups, chinups, rows),

5. and a core exercise (planks, knee raises, hollow body holds, supermans)

Then repeat those 5 exercises again (or a different set of exercises that target the same goal), for a total of 10 exercises.

10 exercise examples:
1. Burpees
2. Pushups
3. Squats
4. Chin-ups
5. Planks
6. Jumping Jacks
7. Pike Presses
8. Lunges
9. Rows
10. Knee Raises

Set your timer, do each exercise for a set time (see the interval structure above), get your rest, and then move to the next exercise. Often, at the end of the circuit, there will be a longer rest period (1-2 minutes) followed by a repeat of the entire circuit. This is often done for a total of 3 circuits, though you can certainly do more if desired or less if pressed for time.

The ideal length for these workouts seems to be in the range of 20-30 total minutes, though you can get a pretty good workout in about seven minutes if you set your timer for 30 seconds of work and 15 seconds of rest and do one hard circuit of ten exercises. Don't use this as an excuse to "take it easy" though - if you're only doing one circuit, make it count!

The exercise selection for circuits also changes - you can do more "strength" exercises, since you'll have much more rest between them than with the first method. In the example I gave, I would have a few minutes between all of my sets of upper-body push exercises, so I can pick an exercise that challenges my muscles a bit more than if I was doing pushups for the full 30 minutes. This means I can get some extra benefits - I'm getting a good cardio workout in, and I'm getting some strength and muscle added on while I'm at it.

If you're pressed for time, focus on circuits. That's where you'll get the most "bang for your buck".

Exercise Progressions

Here, I will attempt to give you a few progressions for each exercise that can get you started. YouTube is your friend here - again, for the sake of brevity, including a long list of exercises with photos and tutorials would take up a lot of real estate and others have already done it better than I could anyway.

Here are some suggested starter progressions:

Upper-body push:

- incline pushups -> pushups -> close-grip or diamond pushups -> decline pushups -> uneven pushups -> archer pushups
- hands-elevated pike presses -> pike presses -> feet elevated pike presses -> handstand pushups against the wall

Upper body pull:

- incline bodyweight rows (the more upright you are the easier the exercise becomes) -> inverted rows -> chinup negatives -> chinups -> pullups -> typewriter pullups

DO NOT SKIP OUT ON PULLUPS AND ROWS! Pulling work like pullups and rows are essential exercises - without them, you can develop muscle imbalances and movement disorders. Your chest and front shoulders will get stronger while your back and rear shoulders do not, which creates posture problems and can lead to shoulder issues down the line. Often, if you look around at quick "at home" workouts, you'll see that they lack this pulling work - this is a major problem, and why it is a very good thing that you are taking the time to educate yourself by reading this chapter.

Lower body

- assisted squats -> squats -> lunges -> cossack squats -> split squats -> pistol squats

Core

- planks on your knees -> planks -> side planks -> planks with feet elevated
- tucked hollow body holds -> straddle hollow body holds -> full hollow body holds
- superman with only upper body -> superman -> superman rocks

If these seem strange to you, or you've never heard of these exercises before, check them out on YouTube or a similar site - the community has put together HOURS of video tutorials on just about any exercise you could think of from some very generous and talented athletes.

Great progressions that have been put together by others can be found on the Resources page for this book. These are not mine, I did not make them and take no credit for their existence, though I do want to tip my hat to the wonderful people who have put these free resources together.

Tracking your Workout

This is yet another instance where you can make it as complicated as you'd like.

I tend to track on a spreadsheet. This allows me to easily copy/paste workouts from one day to the next and track years' worth of workouts in a single file. This file gets kept "in the Cloud" (i.e. Google Drive or Evernote) so I can access it whenever/wherever I am for workouts on the go. You can use a spreadsheet, try by hand with paper and pencil, or whatever works best for you.

Tracking is another essential component - so don't skip out on it! All you really need are the basics - time and date, what exercises you're doing, your goal sets and reps for each exercise, and your actual performed sets and reps. You can also, if desired, track things like diet (when and what have I eaten recently), mood, physical condition (was I sick? was I tired? was I feeling awesome?), or anything else you can think of - more information may lead to interesting insights and patterns in your performance.

Conclusion

And that, as they say, is that. You are now ready to start your fitness journey - at home, with little equipment, following a pretty simple program (after some practice, of course). So no excuses - get out there and get a workout in! You cannot get the results if you do not do the work, so go try one today. Right now, if you have time. Don't put this off in the "someday" pile, or it won't happen.

As with any new skill or subject, go beyond this chapter and explore. Check out the provided resources below for more great information and some other programs. Explore YouTube and other sites to find tutorials or answers to specific questions. Experiment and see what works or doesn't work for you.

Most importantly, take action on what you've learned here as soon as possible and have fun with it. You are beginning a lifelong journey in a discipline that takes years to master. Don't rush it, don't expect it to be perfect every time, and don't beat yourself up if it is a little clumsy in the beginning.

Remember that when I started this type of exercise, I couldn't do a single pullup and the beginner levels of HIIT training were daunting. If I, the "genetically cursed", "unathletic", 230lb 15-year-old can learn it, so can you.

No excuses - get out there and start!

The Quickstart Guide to Ultimate Performance

Nguyen Tran – Irvine, CA, USA

Nguyen is a UCSD graduate with a B.S. in Physiology & Neuroscience and a Certified Transformational Nutrition Coach who works with overwhelmed professionals to upgrade their health. Nguyen believes that a healthy diet doesn't only consist of what you put into your mouth – it's about focusing on what feeds and nourishes you physically, mentally and spiritually.

The Struggle

When you take a step back, what exactly is it that you're trying so hard for?

And more importantly, is it worth it?

I found myself contemplating these same questions once I pressed "TURBO-MODE" during university. I crammed 4 years of classes into 3 years while finding jobs to do, and somehow stumbled into a neuroplasticity lab. I absolutely loved my time there, getting into the nitty-gritty of people's research and developing my own skills. And those were the glory days, up until it got soul-crushingly depressing. At that moment, I truly wished that there was some kind of blueprint or some sort of guide to life that really addressed everything I was going through.

But before we get into that, let's take a few hops backward to see how I got here.

I was a chunky kid growing up. The kid that always wore a hoodie because they felt naked and insecure about their body without one. I always thought that if I just exercised enough and ate a little less, I could eat whatever I wanted. Yet, no matter how much I exercised, I never seemed to get my weight down. I only gained 20 lbs each year until I ballooned into a 220 lb kid just starting high school, which was clinically diagnosed as obese.

One of my most significant interests throughout my high school and university years was getting into medical school and becoming a doctor. And of course, I was going to be a neurologist! There were so many things to learn about the human brain, its functions, and how it controls our bodies. What's not exciting about that? So, to reach that goal, I had to pack all my classes and study as hard as possible.

Each quarter, I tried to take the maximum number of classes, so I felt like I was ahead of the curve. I even found some time to knock on a neural plasticity lab, ask for a tour, and end up volunteering as a lab assistant the very next week! Everything immediately became fast-paced; there was absolutely no time to rest. It was this insane schedule of getting to the lab early, running to class for lectures, skipping lunch, analyzing data from the lab, taking the bus home, cramming homework in at midnight, waking up at 6 to make it to the bus, and repeat.

As the quarter went on, the workload just got worse and worse. I ended up ditching classes because I believed working countless hours in the lab was the golden ticket to enter medical school. It was one of the "resume builders" that was an unspoken requirement among premed students. My grades took a considerable beating, yet I still thought that working in a lab showed more grit than studying for class. I would be there almost every day, even weekends. And if I wasn't there, I'd be at home working on all the backed-up data analysis from last year for the entirety of my weekends. I skipped lunch and possibly even dinner sometimes. But hey, I was finally losing some of that stubborn weight!

Eventually, I started making little mistakes while working. The yelling I would get from my mentor was absolutely traumatizing. It was like I was living my childhood all over again. Each and every day, I had to come there, my body shook with dread and anxiety. I was afraid of making one little mistake. I didn't want to learn anything new for fear of breaking something. I had to come in later at night because it was cheaper to work after hours, but I was slow. So slow that I took almost three times as long as my mentor would on a single project. There were many nights where I'd get home at 2 A.M., get some sleep, and repeat it all again at 6 in the morning throughout the whole week.

And through the many sleepless, tear-filled nights in the lab, I said to myself over and over, "Just keep going for another year, it'll be worth it in the end." It's alright to skip another class, it'll be worth it. Don't worry if it takes until 2 A.M., your mentor will write you a killer letter of recommendation for you to get into medical school. Hey, it's just another year of this, that's it! How hard can it possibly be?

A new quarter rolls by, and I think I'm going to start setting boundaries so I can manage my grades and lab. I'll be studying for 5 different classes. However, I'll still be volunteering 30 hours in the lab, which I thought was generous enough. I set a strict schedule for my working hours in the lab and sent it to my mentor so she could take all those things into account.

In the first week, she had me work in a dark, underground microscopy room with no one around from 6 P.M. to 2 A.M., while she went home around 4:30 P.M.

I cried my entire time there, and in the end, I turned in my keys.

What exactly was I trying so hard for?... Was it worth it?

It wasn't worth it.

Throughout this entire time, there were either sprinkles or huge red flags of living a very dysfunctional lifestyle. I never bothered to take care of my body, I kept pushing myself to exhaustion, and I let everything affect me. But despite all that, were there some lessons that we could learn from here? Absolutely!

Let me tell you right now that this is absolutely no way to live. Yet this is how many of us operate in our modern society, believing that it'll be worth it. And so, throughout the next two years after I quit that lab, I decided that it was finally time to address all the pressing issues that were seriously holding me back from being my best self and living a fulfilling life.

It started with my curiosity about healthily losing weight, and not through endless stress and skipping meals. My interest then drove me towards my learning and exploring my emotions and how I presented myself to others in the world. Some of these things, you really have to wonder why they don't teach this in school. I've gone to therapists, coaches, doctors to really learn the ins and outs of what could truly make a difference in your life without costing an arm and a leg.

This chapter is the culmination of what I've learned and tested throughout those two years, condensed into a little step by step guide to help you optimize your health and your performance. By no means do you have to follow everything in this order, but it's written in this way for good reason. So, when you're ready, let's get started.

Step One: Addressing Your Kryptonite

Don't make the mistake of saving the task of addressing your kryptonite for another day. Work on finding out what these things are FIRST when it comes to your journey of optimal performance.

Superman is a figure most of us grew up with. He's the stunning, flying do-gooder we all wanted to be as a kid. But there was just one thing that could stop him from being the dazzling superhuman that could save the world, and that was kryptonite.

Kryptonite was Superman's exploitable weakness. And, while we can't fly and lift cars with our fingers, we all have our own versions of kryptonite that keep us from being our own definition of "Superman," and many of us have more than just one. Kryptonites are the distractions and bad habits we allow into our lives that hold us back from being the best versions of ourselves.

Living with these kryptonites for months, or years for some people, transforms us into monsters that can harm ourselves and possibly others. Kryptonites can range from small internal thoughts to negative physical treatment of oneself. What we don't realize is that these problems start small. It can be someone who spends *all* of their time working. That individual is constantly busy and will have little to no time for self-care. They don't make time to be with friends and end up isolating themselves to keep working. Their work supersedes themselves, and they prioritize the next project over their health. Eventually, this leads to an immense amount of stress. Then chronic illnesses settle in.

This is why the first step towards your optimal performance is to address your own kryptonite, not finding some new product or thing that'll make your life slightly better in the short-term. We want things that will consistently give us results in the long run. We want to be better people, physically and mentally, whether it's five years or ten years. We want to be and feel like our best selves. This is why it's essential to recognize and confront our kryptonite, because if we don't, we'll let things keep getting worse as time passes by.

Knowing what our kryptonites are can give us a sense of how we can take steps to tackle it, get it out of the way, and move forward in all the other aspects of our lives.

If you want a place to start, take a look at the common kryptonites down below and *circle the ones that resonate with you.* Yes, you read that correctly – get something to write with and CIRCLE them.

| Sleep Deprivation | Distractions | Living in Your Head |
| Fixed Mindset | Trauma | Overly Stressed |

Present Moment Resistance	Untrained Memory & Attention	Emotional Suppression
Busyness	Obsessions	Nutrient Imbalances
Isolation	Obesity	Unmet Emotional Needs
Poor Self-Care	Sedentary Lifestyle	Insulin Resistance
Addictions	Drugs	Toxic Relationships
Inner Critic	Poor Food Choices	Gut Imbalances
Alcohol	Toxic Work Environment	Poor/Lack of Boundaries
Allergies	Environmental Toxins	Sugar

If you circled any of these, know that this is the perfect steppingstone for you to start your self-development journey. You've passed the first step of acknowledging your kryptonite! This is a significant first step towards becoming your best self. Now, some great tactics you can do to combat your kryptonite are getting to know these issues a bit more deeply (think about how it impacts you and when it started), seeking help (from family, your friends, or a therapist), and finding a wonderful support group.

When beginning this journey, you'll need to know how to step off on the right foot. Most of the time, we'll be up in our heads caught up in thoughts about how terrible the past has been or how the future will be. What we need to do at this moment is to start pressing the brakes. Action and growth don't happen in the past, nor does it happen in the future. Where it all takes shape is when you start working in the present moment and centering yourself.

Step Two: Align with Presence

What's the number one thing that gets in the way of anyone's personal development? If left unchecked, this one thing could uproot a person's career, relationships, and entire life. But if you have this under control, you become unstoppable.

That number one thing is an *unhealthy, dysfunctional, human ego*. And the hallmark of this is blame and distraction. The ego is basically your self-image. Over the years, there will be many different identities and labels that you'll experience throughout your life, some of which you'll take on for yourself. If this isn't under control, we allow ourselves to get distracted when we're presented with something that could change us for good. What I ask of you, is that you give your full attention to these words you're reading. Everything in this book has profoundly changed at least one person in some way, and the next person to experience that change could be you.

So, if you're doing a whole bunch of other things as you're reading this, either stop doing those things and read this book or stop reading this book and do those other things. But keep your focus and give your whole-hearted attention to whatever it is that you're doing. As you go through this book, approach everything that comes your way with an open, interested, and curious attitude.

What you need to be doing is making use of the information given to you to make some kind of change in the way you're behaving, your thought patterns, your emotions, or the like. The last thing we want this to be is just another book that you've done nothing with. You can read or listen to all the insightful presentations, densely packed books, inspirational speeches, and so forth, but that by itself won't help you. It's ultimately about taking action. What matters is that you take something from this book, experiment with the different chapters, implement it into your life, discover new things about yourself, and change and evolve for the better.

So, first things first. At the core, everything you do and everything you will do should arise from *presence*. So now you're thinking, "what the heck is presence?" It is merely living in the present moment. Being mindful, aware, and fully immersed in what you're doing. Awareness is the key to presence.

The word "presence" has been tossed around a lot lately, and most of us inherently know we should live in the moment. But let's take a look at a hypothetical situation of someone not aligned with presence, and see how living with presence would be in comparison.

It's finally Friday, 8 P.M. John is commuting an hour back home after yet another overtime shift when he gets a text from his boss saying he needs to cover weekends as well. Shit. As he tries to read his texts while driving, he misses his exit, and it takes him an extra ten minutes to get back home, which is ten fewer minutes to eat dinner or get ready for bed. John gets home a quarter past nine, and his wife, visibly upset, is waiting for him. "You told me you'd be home around 6:30 P.M.! What happened to you?!" John, clearly not wanting to have another argument, says, "I'm really tired, I just want some food and sleep. Can we talk about this another time?"

"You ALWAYS do this, John. Why can't you get home on time? It's really late, and we haven't even talked about all the other times you were late!"

John, stone-faced, rummages through the fridge and eats whatever he can find. He doesn't want to deal with all this nagging anymore and decides to lie back and watch his shows on Netflix to calm down. He can't sleep, it's getting close to midnight, and he has to wake up at six in the morning just to have enough time to get ready and drive right back to work.

He ends up falling asleep around one in the morning, exhausted after looking at all the posts on Facebook.

Now, most of us can see there's a huge problem here. And not just one, but multiple problems. Did John notice that, underneath the nagging, his wife was deeply concerned about his health? No. Did he realize his wife's concern for their relationship, as they still haven't addressed their previous problems? No, he was too busy getting away.

John was in a reactionary state, letting his ego take charge, and unconsciously going through life. He let the environment control how he felt and how he lived. That's how most of us are living in this very moment. *We let others dictate how we feel and how we act in this world,* as opposed to living in the moment, being in control of our emotions, and consciously responding to whatever comes our way.

If you're living unconsciously or from the ego and it's somehow working for you, your relationships, and your personal betterment, then keep doing it. It's all about making it work for you. But if it's not, then at the very least consider the possibility that there's another way to live and be in this world that will work for you. That's what this book is all about: finding new possibilities and making it work for you.

So, how can you be present? If you're consciously thinking and making a considerable effort to be present and in the moment, you're not in presence. You're in your head, thinking about it. Being aware is just that – awareness. It's being aware of your left hand vs. thinking about your left hand. You are simply aware of it without conscious effort.

That being said, there are a few exercises out there that can help facilitate present moment awareness. The key with these isn't to go out and practice them for hours straight. The key is to practice one of these, consistently, over a long period of time in a way that works for you. So, if you're ready to learn, here are the two most helpful presencing exercises.

Centering

Centering is a popular technique in martial arts, used to access a calm, aware presence even amidst a fight. Centering practices bring you back from living from the reactionary, unconscious ego into present moment awareness and consciousness. When a coworker makes you upset, many stories often come up in your head, clouding you from making rational decisions. Any action taken from that point is an unconscious *re*action that came from your untrained ego, which will usually lead to further adverse situations.

Physiologically, feeling stressed makes your fight-or-flight system kick in. This leads to shorter breaths, faster heart rate, and increases in the stress hormone cortisol, which contributes to chronic health problems. Being able

327

to control your breath, lower your heart rate, and reset these systems makes centering a potent and liberating tool. You can use this centering exercise whenever you're feeling stressed, rushed, overwhelmed, uncertain, stuck, reactive, challenged, under pressure, distressed, confused, unfocused, angry, anxious, or fearful, or when you're stuck in procrastination or any unhelpful thought pattern.

How to center yourself:
1. While smiling, either on the inside or physically smiling, count down slowly and silently from five. As you count down, breathe into and soften your lower belly.
2. Notice what shifts physically, emotionally, and mentally.
3. You will know you are centered because your mind will be still yet alert.

The process of counting downshifts your emotionally driven reactivity (driven by your brain's amygdala) into calm, considered responsiveness (driven by the prefrontal cortex). Focusing on your belly drops you out of your head into your natural biological center of gravity.

Living from conscious awareness and being fully present in what you do requires you to get out of the unhelpful stories you've created, move away from negative thoughts, and center yourself. Practice this centering exercise as often as needed to find presence, whether that means ten, twenty, thirty, or even fifty times a day. It will get easier as you do it more. The more you practice, the more you strengthen the related neural pathways in your brain, thus making this into a routine.

If you notice yourself thinking, "This exercise is too difficult. How can I possibly use this throughout the day?" or "I can't get into presence, I must be doing this wrong," that's the perfect moment to just smile, take a deep breath in, and count backward from five, focusing on your lower belly. Notice what happens when you do that. That's all it takes.

Mindfulness

Mindfulness meditation: an excellent, entry-level, practice for getting into presence. The more you let go of the seeking-control aspect of your life, the more you focus on the attention aspect of your mind. The simplest way to do this is through meditation, on which there are many tutorials.

Mindfulness meditation trains your attention and focus. As our modern lives attempt to grab our attention at every turn, through social media and other means, it becomes difficult to sit still on one thing. A lot of people have trouble concentrating on a single task and their attention wanders every which way.

To be focused on the work at hand and not following every thought that comes up is one of the best ways to become productive and master your emotions. The core of mindfulness meditation is simply noticing when your attention wanders, and, without judgment, bringing it back to what you were focused on.

Here's one simple way you can practice mindfulness meditation:

1. Sit on a chair, or wherever makes you comfortable. Straighten your posture and allow your spine to support your body naturally.
2. If it's safe to do so, relax your gaze and close your eyes.
3. Focus on your breath. Pay attention to the in-breath, the pause, and the out-breath.
4. You will inevitably have thoughts come up (negative, neutral, or positive). Once you notice them, gently bring yourself back to focusing on your breath.
5. Continue for as little as 5 minutes to as long as an hour.

Generally speaking, 15 minutes is a great starting time to practice this. Some may even want to start with 2 minutes and slowly move up to 45 minutes. 45 minutes is when you start to experience the most benefits, but it's fine to practice only 15 minutes a day.

As an alternative to doing mindfulness meditations while sitting still, they can be practiced in almost any situation – brushing your teeth, driving, walking, eating, working.

Negative and distracting thoughts will arise. It takes a calm, curious, and open attitude to skillfully move your attention back. Look at your thought without judgment, and accept that this is a thought, like any other. Then return to the present moment. This may be difficult initially, but the more you practice, the more you can notice, accept, and control your thoughts, then translate those skills into your professional and day-to-day life.

Step Three: Adapt Your Biology

Biology is next. Why do we focus on biology after discussing the importance of aligning with your presence? Would it not make more sense to work up some motivation in your mind first?

We learn about presence first because everything you do should arise from presence and awareness. If you're not aware of how you're feeling, how you're doing, or how you show up in life, you won't know you have something to improve in the first place. If you are up in your head and start aligning with all your negative stories and thoughts (your ego), you will be incapacitated. Once you come back into awareness that you are here in this moment with limitless possibilities right before your eyes, you can work and take action on your next step.

We want to jump into working on and improving your biology to give yourself the energy and the focus to do many other things. If you're feeling tired, sick, sleep-deprived, or irritable, how can you possibly have the energy to start working on anything else? It takes an immense amount of willpower to push through and ignore these biological imbalances in order to spend time on your work or other interests. Being in this kind of state diminishes your sense of self, leaks into your work, and brings you down. It influences your relationships, undermines your performance, and affects your decisions. But it doesn't have to be that way.

It's time to consciously create and maintain high-functioning biology to help you be at your best. You work on your biology because it's an enabler of becoming the best version of yourself.

You can't do your best if you aren't at your best.

What You Can Do Right Now

It's time you take action on improving your biology. If you circled any of those kryptonites, these are some of the things you want to focus on correcting: sleep deprivation, poor food choices, obesity, insulin resistance, addictions, drugs, gut imbalances, nutrient imbalances, alcohol, sugar, a sedentary lifestyle, and poor self-care.

There are several domains to talk about when it comes to optimizing your internal environment, your biology. Out of all of them discussed below, make sure to find the one that resonates with you and start taking action immediately.

1. Self-Care

One of the most critical actions you can take to focus on your biology is self-care. Self-care is the continuous process of caring for your physical and emotional needs. The emotional/psychological aspect of it will be discussed later. The central aspect is genuinely protecting and nourishing your own body. Self-care is not just about getting enough sleep, getting all the nutrients you need, or being rested and relaxed. Going to the doctor for regular health check-ups or even simple concerns is part of self-care. It is about examining what you put into your body and what you can do to help your body function at its prime. It is about getting the right amount of sleep every day to let your body reset itself. Furthermore, it's about taking advantage of what your body can do by challenging yourself with extraneous exercises or by simply taking a walk. Appreciate your biology and put the work into making you feel your best self.

When our bodies do not feel their best, our days do not go as well as we would have liked. If we don't put enough time into knowing our bodies and treating them right, it seeps into our everyday lives. Our work isn't the best it could be. Our relationships are not as positive and intimate as we would like. Therefore, I challenge you to recognize your biology and to put your body first.

2. Nutrition

One kryptonite that many people face today is not providing their bodies with the proper nutrition they need. The main problem with nutrition is that many people do not know what precisely their food contains or what they should change in their diet. Everyone's nutritional needs can be different, depending on allergies or how the body breaks it down, but ideally, we want to aim for whole, nutritious, fresh foods, preferably cooked the same day. If we eat meat, we want to make sure the animal was ethically raised and well cared for, because why would you want hormone-pumped, low-quality meat that might do you more harm than good? Also, look out for any preservatives, additives, or processed ingredients, although it's becoming more challenging to avoid those.

In modern-day society, many diets and nutritional trends have mixed results. The thing is, no single trend or diet works for everyone. Therefore, the first thing that you can take action on right now is to identify and eliminate your personal kryptonite foods. These are foods that your body has trouble breaking down or does not respond well to. The problem is that even if you eat perfectly nutritious meals, if you consume your kryptonite food, it will undermine your efforts to get your body to its optimal performance.

Common kryptonite foods include sugar, gluten, dairy, eggs, soy, nuts, seafood, wheat, shellfish, corn, and caffeine. The biggest kryptonites for many people tends to be sugar, dairy, or wheat. To identify your personal kryptonite foods, try an elimination diet, where you eliminate one possible kryptonite food from your meals every day for about a week (though longer is recommended). This allows you to see if this food is your kryptonite food by examining how you feel with it, comparing how you feel without it, contemplating if you need it in your diet, and then making a decision. If you notice positive changes when you eliminate a particular food, then eliminate it permanently. Then, try the next possible kryptonite food, and so on. You could also try an elimination + reintroduction diet, such as Whole 30. These usually consist of eliminating most of the possible kryptonite foods completely and then reintroducing them one by one over time. This approach is more effective, but also takes more time and discipline.

The most important goal to seek from inquiring about your nutrition is to develop a positive, healthy relationship with food and with your body. Unhealthy eating habits often stem from flaws in these relationships. Many people eat out of stress or boredom, creating an association between food and emotional relief and thus causing unhealthy relationships and outlets. Even obsessions with healthy eating can be a problem, so finding a good balance is essential.

A healthy balance comes largely from being mindful of your body and acknowledging its imperfections. Being skinny, thick, or muscular is not the goal. The goal is to feel your best, feel your body work optimally, and be happy with yourself today and tomorrow. Finding the best nutritious foods can be a challenge, but finding your kryptonite and the foods needed for you to perform at your best is an investment into your future self that is so worth it.

3. Sleep

We sleep for about a third of our lives, so why do we take it for granted?

Sleep is an unconscious activity that must occur with high quantity and quality in order to experience optimal brain function. Sleep allows our brains to make room for new memories, flushes out metabolic toxins from our central nervous system through the glymphatic system, and allows proper brain function the next day. The brain has many jobs in the human body, and sleep is essential for letting your brain perform the best it can.

One important aspect of sleep that many people do not consider is the quality. Sleep quality depends on the amount you get of each type of sleep, including rapid eye movement (REM) and non-REM sleep, and if you are following your biological clock, called your circadian rhythm.

The type of sleep you get is vital because REM sleep is essential for memory consolidation. It takes about 90 minutes after we fall asleep to get into REM sleep. We don't stay in REM sleep constantly. We go through a cycle of non-REM to REM sleep, but the longer we sleep, the faster we can get into REM sleep and the longer we stay in REM mode. Therefore, sleeping 7.5 or 9 hours is the best sleep duration. These specific amounts are ideal because getting into REM sleep takes about 90 minutes and a cycle of REM to non-REM typically takes 90 minutes, so it is important to sleep in 90-minute intervals. This strategy provides maximal REM sleep and prevents you from waking up groggy in the middle of a cycle.

Another thing to consider is that sleeping from 10 A.M. to 7 P.M. does not make you feel as rested as sleeping from 10 P.M. to 7 A.M. because of your biological clock. This biological clock is known as your circadian rhythm (*circa-* means "approximately" and *-dia* means "day"). Hence, our biological clock is about a day long. This circadian rhythm is controlled by the suprachiasmatic nucleus located in your brain's hypothalamus. The hypothalamus is the master regulator of your body, controlling hormone release, gene expression, and more.

The hypothalamus also receives light signals, which tell your body to stay awake when light is present. When your eyes are not exposed to light, it instead releases melatonin through your pineal glands to make you feel tired and motivated to sleep.

Humans are diurnal animals, meaning our circadian rhythm is naturally set to keep us awake when the sun is out and keep us asleep at night. Since the hypothalamus tries to follow a diurnal schedule, your body also functions best if you live as a diurnal creature. This is why working the graveyard shift is a health hazard, because you're forcing your body to work against itself.

The problem nowadays is that it is easy to stay awake and live the lives of nocturnal animals since we are surrounded by light – light from our phones and other electronics, city lights, and lights from stores open 24 hours. This light contains significant blue light, which suppresses the release of melatonin from the pineal gland. That's why if we stay on our phones in bed, it takes longer to fall asleep.

The easy way to fix your sleep schedule and optimize brain and body function is to follow your body's natural rhythm. You can do this by limiting the amount of light (especially blue light) you are exposed to after the sun goes down. Open the windows so that sunlight will wake you up naturally in the morning. Avoid caffeinated drinks after noon. Do not drink alcohol before you fall asleep, as it disrupts your sleep quality. Do not eat a large meal less than 4 hours before bed, as this will also disrupt the quality of your sleep by making your body work on digestion while you sleep. Avoid extraneous exercise less than 2 hours before you sleep because exercise releases hormones that excite your body instead of relaxing it. Try to relax an hour or two before bed to allow your body and mind to start to calm down and feel sleepy.

Remember that sleep should be a gradual softening and quieting of our mind and body. Give yourself the best internal and external environment in which to sleep. If you struggle with getting good quality sleep, falling asleep, or staying asleep, I recommend that you examine your internal and external environments. This can be done by visiting your doctor, determining if there's stress affecting you, and reassessing any habits during the day that could be contributing.

Indeed, the biggest kryptonite of sleep is stress. Focus on managing stress by talking about it with a therapist, practicing presencing through meditation or other methods, and otherwise diffusing any troubling thoughts that come to your mind. It is essential to check in mentally with yourself every day and to give yourself the relaxation you need so that you can sleep. Improving your sleep and making it a priority will bring you better outcomes in everyday life.

4. Physical activity

When I talk about activity, I'm not telling you what specific exercises you should do. An activity can be walking around the neighborhood, swimming in the pool, or simply stretching. The main idea is that we should be living an active lifestyle.

An active lifestyle does not have to revolve around going to the gym or running every day (unless you love doing that!). I am simply advocating against a sedentary lifestyle, to the extent that your body allows it. A lifestyle is considered sedentary if you spend eight or more waking hours sitting or lying down. Our main goal is to live an active, engaged, and fulfilling life. Many people find this type of life through sports and exercise, but it can be found in everyday life, too.

The easiest way to ensure that you stay active is through having a schedule for working out. Working out can be in many different forms, of course, such as boxing, running, or dancing. As long as you move your body and break a sweat, it is a workout. Your schedule does not have to include working out every single day or for hours at a time. The key is to schedule a time for activity rather than to wait for your schedule to open up.

Many of us complain about not having enough time to exercise, but even scheduling a chunk of time to stand rather than sit can be beneficial. It's not all about working out – just get your body moving! Our bodies are made to be active. Lymph fluid and all the blood in our veins require muscle activation to flow smoothly.

In our modern lifestyle, many of us don't recognize activity as a priority. Our priorities usually include being productive, making money, and living a relaxing life after we've finally retired. But our health doesn't wait for us to catch up after we retire. If we don't take care of our bodies now, we'll develop a crippling amount of problems down the line.

So, if you're physically able to, a great workout is a high-intensity interval training (HIIT) workout, which only takes around 20 minutes. There's no need for long, low-intensity workouts if a HIIT workout provides the same, if not more, benefits in less time. There are hundreds of HIIT videos online, including beginner workouts to get started. If you want more specific instructions to start improving your fitness in a mindful way - without spending your life in a gym - refer to the previous chapter "Get Fit at Home."

Of course, it's a problem if you are not active enough, but it's also a problem if you are overly obsessed with being at the gym and working out constantly. It's about finding the right balance and not having to constantly worry about being active. Use deliberate activity to help energize your body and all the other aspects of your life.

5. Supplements

Supplements, and the use of them, is a dual-edged sword. On the one hand, taking the right kinds of supplements can help provide your body with the nutrients that it needs so that you feel energized and ready to tackle more significant problems. Using supplements can help speed up recovery and provide results much faster than you usually would get. A great example is nourishing your gut microbiome. You can start cooking better meals and eating entirely whole foods while also taking a dense probiotic to help facilitate a healthier gut

341

microbiome. On the other hand, if you don't know how to use supplements properly, it could easily harm you and your progress. So, we'll be looking at some beginner's mistakes when it comes to supplements and see what we can learn from them.

The biggest problem is that many people use supplements who don't actually need or benefit from them. Many people buy supplements because of fancy marketing or because it promises some kind of dramatic result. Before even considering supplements, we need to ask ourselves if other parts of our biology are well taken care of. Are you dealing with your pressing kryptonite first?

Imagine someone buys thermogenic, weight loss supplements to help them lose weight. And while you might say, "what's the harm in buying supplements like that?", this can actually cause tremendous damage if used incorrectly. Taking a closer look at this person, their diet is all over the place. It's filled with sugary snacks, fast food junk, and eating at all hours of the day, indicating an unhealthy relationship with their diet. Their sleep is also out of order. They sleep in the afternoon in small intervals and stay awake through the middle of the night.

Typically, weight loss pills include caffeine. When taken at night, they stimulate your brain and rob you of restorative sleep. Poor diet and poor sleep both contribute to weight gain, so if this person had just spent their time fixing these issues, there wouldn't be a need to buy weight loss pills. So, when considering supplements, first ask yourself, "Do I genuinely need them, or do I actually need to improve some of my life choices and habits?" If something out of your control makes it so you do really need them, you need to be clear about what you want them for. Is it for general health? Is it for your low iron levels?

Lack of quality in supplement choices is another issue. There are so many supplements out there that have vitamins, minerals, and micronutrients that aren't easily absorbed. An example of this is a magnesium supplement. Magnesium comes in many different forms, the most common of which is magnesium citrate. However, this large molecule is hard for our digestive system to absorb and usually stays in the gut. Through osmosis, the magnesium citrate molecules pull water from your body and end up acting as a laxative for you. This is why you'll also see magnesium citrate sold as a laxative. More absorbable forms of magnesium are magnesium glycinate, magnesium threonate, and magnesium malate. Be wary of the bioavailability of vitamins and minerals in your supplements and do your research on them.

It's important to know that there are two types of supplement companies. The first is pharmaceutical, which is what doctors usually prescribe to their patients because of the high quality and strict regulations. Pharmaceutical-grade supplements are research-backed and offer the best bioavailable vitamins and minerals. They're also made in facilities that follow strict guidelines in cleanliness to avoid contamination and harm patients. Contrast that with commercial supplement companies, which generally have cheaper products, but also have little regulation and poorer quality.

Nowadays, pharmaceutical-grade supplements are becoming more and more available online for the general consumer. It's a lot easier to find and purchase them using a smartphone or computer. Just search "pharmaceutical grade supplement companies." You'll find many domestically based. When it comes to buying supplements, quality *always* beats quantity.

Lastly, the key to enjoying all the benefits of your supplements is to actually take your supplements. Many people buy them only to put them away in a cupboard and forget about them. Don't make this mistake. It's a waste of time and money. Set a reminder or leave the supplements out somewhere that you frequently see so that you can take them when needed and reap the benefits.

Step Four: Correct Your Psychology

At this point, you should have loads of energy to tackle more critical aspects of your life. After taking care of your biology and working from presence, the next step is to work on your psychology. As I define it, your psychology is the culmination of thoughts and experiences that ultimately manifests itself into how you show up in the world.

When working on your psychology, a general rule of thumb is that once it starts working well for you, your psychology will automatically update and improve. And just like with biology, if we're not in conscious control of our psychology, it will be in control of us. That's perfectly fine if it enables you to become the best version of yourself. If your relationships are great (including with yourself) and you're succeeding at your workplace, then maybe you don't need to change anything. For many people, though, their psychology is their kryptonite. It's an enormous obstacle getting in the way of their desired outcomes.

Let's dig a little deeper into your psychology so that you have an idea of what is and isn't working for you. Your psychology includes your beliefs, thoughts, stories, narratives, emotional patterns, and attitudes. Some of these aspects serve you well, and, obviously, some of them don't. A lot of these are conditioned behaviors developed when you were growing up, which were meant to protect you. But when we start living from our conditioned, reactive behaviors, we start living unconsciously, unaware of life.

This unconscious living controls you and every moment that you're engaged in. That's no way to live an optimal life, so learning how to escape that unconscious, reactive state and start living from a responsive state is a foundational skill that everyone should learn. Learning how to be in presence and access it when you need to is a great place to start. Once you start doing this, you set the foundation for building a healthy psychology for yourself. Below, we'll discuss how you can build on that foundation to alter your psychological state for the better.

What You Can Work On Right Now

In this section, we'll focus on the kryptonite of distractions, living in the head, addictions, toxic relationships, fixed mindset, trauma, inner critic, present moment resistance, untrained memory & attention, emotional suppression, obsessions, busyness, isolation, unmet emotional needs, poor/lack of boundaries, and poor self-care.

There are a few psychology domains that will help alleviate your kryptonite if you work on them. Find the one that needs extra attention for you and take the first step there. It might seem a little strange at first since we've been so conditioned to go against taking care of ourselves, but trust that this process will make you a better person.

1. Self-Care

As important as it is in biology, it is imperative to focus on self-care psychologically. Self-care is about checking in with yourself mentally and talking to someone when you need it. Genuinely caring for yourself is rooted in self-kindness and acceptance of self. It is a *commitment* to check on yourself and give your heart, mind, and soul everything they need. This is why it is crucial first to accept where you are and what kryptonite you may have.

Find out what is holding you back from your best self, especially your unhelpful thoughts and emotions. Then, acknowledge them and let them go. If you aren't able to accept the good and the bad thoughts so that you can take care of yourself, it'll hold you back in life.

We all live with an inner critic that drives our thoughts and influences our actions, but it doesn't have to control us. That inner critic undermines your abilities and keeps you rooted in your ego. It's the gremlin on your shoulder telling you, "You can't do it." To first practice self-care, you must *acknowledge* and *confront* your inner critic to allow you to work at your optimal performance.

When you hear this inner critic speaking and notice that it is telling you unhelpful things (judgemental, violent, critical), here is a simple solution that I would like to offer you since it has helped me with my own inner critic. As soon as you hear your inner critic speak out at you:

1. Take a deep breath into your lower belly.
2. Smile a warm and loving smile.
3. Say wholeheartedly, "I see you, and I accept you."

In the beginning, this inner critic will tend to try to fight you, but don't give in! Accept your inner critic, give it space, and let it go. It takes some practice, but soon that inner critic will go silent. We so often spend hours and hours fighting with our inner critic that we're used to making it fight us back. But once you allow it some space and allow yourself to hear what it's saying without attaching yourself to the content, it doesn't fight back. It loses power. It doesn't hold you. And instead of going against your thoughts and fighting every piece of yourself, you can finally live with your inner critic and accept yourself as a whole.

2. Mindset

We all have different beliefs about ourselves, the world, and how we should do things. This also includes beliefs about our capacity to learn, change, and adapt to the environment around us. Some of these beliefs help us to grow and become better versions of ourselves, while, of course, others are very unhelpful.

A natural step of self-improvement is to teach ourselves and develop a healthy mindset towards change. We need to learn how to disengage with stories about why we can't change and create a new story for ourselves that will bring us into a growth mindset.

One way to deal with unhelpful stories is through diffusion, where you take the story that you repeat in your head, and give it some space. If that story is something like, "I can't have an amazing relationship because I'm ugly," then slowly say that phrase word by word and focus on the space between the words. Take your time to do this as you also pay attention to how your body feels. Your goal is for that story to hold little or no power over you. By giving it space, you get to question why it's in your head and explore where it comes from. Also, be very in tune with how your body feels throughout this process and learn from what you observe.

Some things to look out for is how your body reacts negatively or positively. Do you tense up and feel your body getting sweaty after going through the exercise? Or do you start to calm down the longer you practice this? Dig a little deeper and see where these negative reactions are rooted in your body and your memories. This is where you can start sifting out the events that have led up to this unconscious, reactive response and work on correcting it.

In the end, we want to cultivate a mindset that drives and motivates our commitment to learning and discovering new things. This won't be an overnight journey. Take it one day and one step at a time. It can be as simple as a mental reminder to be open to the possibilities before you and to take prompt action on what you learn.

3. Emotions

Emotions are what make us who we are. They're the life force that brings personality into every conversation. They're the bridge to a rich and beautiful life. But when we're not in charge of our emotions, our emotions are in charge of us. And when our emotions are in charge of us, it often turns into a huge disaster. It turns *us* into a huge disaster.

One straightforward example of emotion turning us into a disaster would be anger. Everything we do is influenced by emotion, so imagine what life would look like if anger dominated everything that you did. People you once loved would look like enemies to you, and it would feel as if everyone was against you. Much like the Hulk, you'd be living a disparity between how you act and how you feel, and the damage can clearly be seen throughout all of Manhattan.

It all starts to change when you work from presence, which is why learning and practicing presence comes first. You must understand that working from the present moment, including being aware of your body, is the way to make controlled changes. When you're emotional, notice how your body is. Are your hands or jaw clenched? Is your head drooping down? Is it getting hot somewhere in your body?

Take a moment to notice these sensations and practice a centering exercise around this. As you practice centering and mindfulness, your body will more easily and more naturally relax into a present and calm state. Try it even when you're not feeling intense emotions because it will be easier to remember and develop the habit during those times. Practice often. If you practice this skill only once in a while, it'll be like performing brain surgery on someone only once every ten years. There would be no continual upkeep of skill or proficiency, and it just wouldn't work out well. Make sure you frequently practice being aware of your emotions and how your body feels and see what happens as a result.

You always have a choice whether or not you will act on your emotions. Physiologically, the lifespan of an emotion is only about ninety seconds. Emotions lasting any longer than that are usually extended by the stories, thoughts, and beliefs you tell yourself that keep your body pumped and running. That means that there's going to be a space where you can focus on your body and let those stories, thoughts, and beliefs pass away. The more frequently this occurs, the easier your brain adapts to this new situation, making it easier to control your emotions. Overall, it's going to be a long journey of going back to presence, being aware of your body, and shifting into a state that better serves you, but you can do it, and it's worth it

4. Self-Discipline

Self-discipline is a tough subject for many people, especially since self-discipline is often seen as a very strict, tough, and narrow way of living. In this case, it's hard to become more positive when we feel as if we need to be tougher on ourselves. In fact, the key to self-discipline is to be kind to yourself. It's about giving yourself gentle reminders to go in the right direction. Some people approach self-discipline as a harsh punishment, which takes a toll on their psychology over the long run. You don't need to be harsh to yourself to be successful. Become successful by being kind to yourself.

Remember that the point of self-discipline is to develop consistency. Consistency in life is the key to making a huge impact. If you're not practicing a skill or habit consistently, it won't give you the best results. This is where most people lose their patience and find a less-effective solution that's quicker and easier.

To get consistency and self-discipline down, you need to be clear on what you hope to achieve in the first place. Clarify what matters most, what your priorities are, and what gets in the way of all those things. That way, you know what you need to get rid of, and you know where you need to focus daily. If you're not practicing consistently, it's either because you don't know what your priorities are, don't know what matters most, or let distractions get in the way.

5. Communication

What do you usually define communication as? Many people see communication as a conversation with another person, yet they miss an entire gold nugget of opportunity by operating with this definition. Communication starts as listening. Listening to others with strong curiosity and intent evokes and invites deep connection with them.

We can't communicate with someone when we're up in our heads, thinking about our upcoming response, the next deadline, or whatever it may be. We can't listen if we're not present and engaged with the person, and therefore we can't communicate effectively. We practice in presence and do all these various exercises so that we can become aware of what's going on around us and effectively interact and respond to everything that happens.

Also, people often struggle with how to deliver our words when we try to communicate. We don't want to scream at others, demanding respect, which happens all too often in relationships. We want to treat others with the same respect that we would want ourselves, which is centered on kindness. You can be kind in your words while still being firm. You can be direct, yet accommodating, to the other person. You can maintain healthy boundaries for yourself in a conversation while also maintaining kindness and respect in your tone.

Don't let others play with your emotions while you play the screaming game. It would be more productive (and pleasantly surprising) to have full control of your emotions and speak empathetically, factually, and directly. Take this example:

"You NEVER do the dishes when you get home! I'm stuck with cleaning everything and I'm absolutely sick and tired of doing all these chores while you sit around not helping!"

"Hey, I get that you're upset because it seems like I never do the dishes. That would bother me, too, if I were you. I'd really like to understand your feelings and know how to improve, but I can't do that if we're not speaking accurately about each other. Do you think it's true that I *never* do the dishes? Would you agree if I said that I do the dishes *sometimes*? If yes, what would you like me to do to make this situation better?"

Usually, you would get one of two answers. One being "Yeah, I'd agree with that. I'd really like it if you did the dishes *more* often when you came home..." This is excellent; by controlling your emotions, you're starting to resolve the conflict and, more importantly, the underlying issue. Or you get number two: "I DON'T KNOW!" This shows that there has been quite a lot of damage done in the past, either by you or from other experiences. In this situation, when emotions are taking control of the conversation, you need to disengage: "I really want to work this out with you, but we can't if we aren't able to communicate well and work together to come up with a solution because our emotions are getting in the way. So, I'd like to take some time to cool down and come back to this in 30 minutes with a level head."

Effective communication arises from being present and aware of your body and surroundings. Tend to your own needs and make sure that your emotions are not in control of you. Then, speak truthfully and kindly, grounded in presence.

Step Five: Rebuild Your Environment

The last but equally important step is to change your environment. This section is last because it's not as urgent as fixing your biology or psychology, but it is no less crucial in creating a more positive lifestyle and developing your optimal self.

In this section, you'll see that small changes in your environment can have profound outcomes on your health. The environment that you're living in right now has such a massive influence on every aspect of your wellbeing. So, when you start to consciously change your environment to suit your needs, you'll amplify all of your other efforts, and reduce your chances of exposing yourself to kryptonite.

We can't wholly eradicate kryptonite or a bad habit through just one environmental change alone, but we can certainly minimize its effects. Let's explore some of the things that you can change in your environment right now that will have the most significant effect on your health and wellbeing.

What You Can Change Right Now

You can alleviate a lot of kryptonite by altering your environment. Whether in your workplace, your relationships, or your performance, these small changes can make a huge difference.

1. Light

Light energizes us in the morning when we take a walk outside. It keeps us awake, lights up our homes, and makes us more productive. But light can also rip away our energy if we don't know how to use it correctly.

Many of us are almost constantly connected to gadgets and devices that emit blue light. As already mentioned, this blue light keeps us awake and alert by suppressing melatonin production, a hormone that helps you fall asleep. Many of us also have this blue light shining into our eyes late into the night, robbing us of quality sleep. This could be in the form of the television, computer, keyboard, an air freshener, or even a power surge with a light on it.

Cover up anything that emits blue light in your room with some tape so that it can't mess with your sleep cycle. If you're on your computer, download F.lux software or turn on night mode so that it gives the computer background an orange tint and eliminates blue light. That chance helps mitigate the effects of being on the computer and reduces strain on your eyes.

To get the highest quality sleep possible, ensure that your devices and anything that emits blue light are shut off around two hours before you sleep. Light from the outside during nighttime can also cause trouble, so I recommend blackout curtains. Keep your room as dark as possible while you sleep, with little or no light at all. Then light things up as the sun rises.

2. Sound

When you think of noise pollution, the traffic outside your window may come to mind. Noise pollution can be detrimental to those sensitive to noise. For everyone, it can affect stress levels, sleep, and many other aspects of ourselves. You also need to be aware of the kind of noise or stimulation that you expose yourself to daily. Violence, screaming, arguing, drama, and anything that negatively stimulates you could have harmful effects.

Think about this in the same way you think about feeding your biological body. What can you eat that will give your body energy and nutrients to function at its best? Similarly, what shows and sounds are you exposing yourself to that nurture your psychology and mindset? Are you playing anything that enhances your kryptonite or undermines your connection to presence? If so, that's the right place for you to start making changes.

Blackout curtains can help keep the noise down if you live in a busy area. Noise-canceling headphones also help, assuming your music volume is reasonable. Be sure to question what you expose yourself to or listen to. Is it helping you become a better person?

3. Water

Many of us are dehydrated throughout the day, but mistake that feeling for hunger. Another common mistake is that we reach for something sugary or tasteful instead of plain water. By replacing your sugary drinks and alcohol with just water, you can make a huge difference to your energy levels and change your body's physiology.

For some people, this change could be difficult. It might have to be an acquired taste that comes over time. In some places, the available water tastes unpleasant. Get a decent water filter or buy bottled water and keep that on hand. Drink water when you think you're hungry and reassess whether you're hungry or just thirsty.

Keeping a large water bottle with you encourages frequent drinking and good hydration while eliminating the need to buy any drinks throughout the day. A one-liter bottle is usually enough to keep me hydrated from the morning to the afternoon, but experiment with how much water your body needs.

4. People

As you become conscious and aware of your surroundings and yourself, you'll notice that you behave in certain ways in certain environments. The people around you influence how you perceive life and how you behave. Start looking for patterns related to the people you're around.

What people do you usually connect with? Are you picking up traits that are similar to the people you're around? What's the impact of these people on your life and your health? Do you feel supported, safe, and challenged by the people around you, and if so, who encourages that? If not, what can you do to set boundaries around people who are negative influences?

Much like food in our bodies, social groups can be helpful or toxic to your health. Being with people that enjoy causing drama and starting fights creates a toxic environment for you and undermines your psychological health. When you start taking control of your environment, especially the people with whom you surround yourself, you'll realize that you can surround yourself with people who support, challenge, and nourish you. You're not obligated to be with anyone, even family members, which are the hardest to separate from. You get to choose who you want to be with.

You have to transition from the mindset of *needing* to be with people to *wanting* to be with people. It can be a difficult boundary to create for yourself, but it makes a whole world of difference. Eventually, you'll reach a point where you want to build a community of people who bring out the best in you while you also bring out the best in them.

5. Nature

Last, spending time in nature has a powerful calming effect. Whether going for a walk, hike, or run, it brings a groundedness to your body. It's a place where our thoughts can wander but also be present with nature itself.

For many of us, it's extremely therapeutic and a vital part of our lives.

Many studies show positive effects on us and our productivity when we're exposed to nature. Having a plant at your desk and looking at it every once in a while, relieves stress. We seek to have a healthy relationship with nature and use it to enhance different parts of our lives.

So ask yourself, what's your relationship with nature? Do you benefit from going out into nature? How so? How can you use time outdoors to help you? People tend to ignore the idea of going out into nature because it doesn't seem productive, but that is simply wrong and is not the mindset you want when it comes to your self-care. Go out and spend the time to take care of your psychology and stress – it will be a massive game-changer and will positively shift your perspectives on productivity, self-care, and happiness.

Conclusion

With that, I hope that this guide has given you enough direction to pinpoint what you need to focus on the most in order for you to optimize your performance. If you want a more in-depth analysis of the topics discussed in this chapter and a more thorough explanation of life hacks to push your limits an extra 10%, you can find a link to my book *Optimized: The Blueprint to Health* on the resource page for this chapter at www.superhumanplaybook.com. In that book, I share everything I've learned over the years that could help you address and fine-tune even *more* aspects of your life you may not even have realized could be affecting you.

This is only a quickstart guide on what you can do to optimize your health right now. We've discussed many different aspects of our lives that we tend to become out-of-sync with, and I hope that reading this made you realize that there are parts of yourself that you would love to spend a little extra love and attention on. I wrote this in hopes of revealing some of the key details you need to know about yourself so you can take action.

Even when times are tough, remember to check-in with yourself. Know that there will always be opportunities to choose a better path.

Make Yourself a Priority

Jan Hellwig – Frankfurt Germany

Jan is a software developer and Superhuman Academy Coach. Using the SuperLearner methodology, Jan rapidly advanced in his career and personal goals and comfortably reads over 60 books per year.

Start at the beginning

This playbook is intended for a wide audience, from those just starting their self-improvement journey to die-hard life-hackers. If you are a member of the former group, it is understandable to feel a little overwhelmed at this point. Now that you have had a chance to read the stories and recommendations from all the other authors, I want to give you one more principle and review the fundamentals, to help you get started. The ideas and strategies in this book won't help you until you decide you are worth helping. So, with that in mind...

Do you have your priorities in order?

Have you ever:

- Set a goal, only to not have the time to work on it?
- Failed to save money because you've spent it on things that were a waste later on?
- Wanted to be fit but never had the motivation to work out?

If you answered 'yes' to any of the above, it's time to make yourself a priority.

It's natural to get sidetracked when "life happens", but you can take steps to reduce this. If you want to always have enough time to spend on the things you want to achieve, you need to reorder your priorities.

Put yourself first

On commercial flights, the cabin crew always reminds parents to secure their own oxygen masks prior to helping their children, in the event of pressure loss. The message is obvious and well-taken: in order to give your full attention to those in need, you must first take care of yourself. Chances are, your kids won't know what to do if you pass out first. Outside of this context, this principle is forgotten to the disservice of everyone. If applied nearly universally, we would all be better off.

Treat your goals as needs instead of luxuries. This is self-care, not selfishness; you can't sustainably help others if you don't take care of yourself. By putting yourself first, you can then give generously without resentment or bitterness from perpetual self-sacrifice. Doing what you need for your goals first stops any outside factors from preventing you. Willpower is depleted over time, so by saving self-care and self-improvement for last, you are setting yourself up for personal neglect.

From a financial perspective, putting yourself first means automatically transferring money into a dedicated savings account every time you get paid *before* paying the bills etc. *Pay yourself first.* Even if you start with a small sum, it will accumulate over time (and you can always increase the amount if you want). If your goal is fitness-related, commit to working out first thing in the morning before checking emails on your phone. If you give your time, energy, and resources away before you take care of yourself, your unmet needs will compound and hang over you, and you will not only become ineffective at helping yourself, you will be unable to help others. Once you decide you are worth helping...

Don't rely on willpower

If you put yourself first, you will have more willpower to spend on self-improvement, but willpower is still a fickle thing. I first learned this lesson from the book *Willpower Doesn't Work* by Dr. Benjamin Hardy.[31] He argues your willpower will not last throughout the day; at some point, you start to give in to your cravings and make decisions contrary to what you want to achieve. As much as I wish this wasn't the case, I can think of many personal examples to support that claim. It doesn't always refresh day-to-day either. You have probably gone through weeks, or even months, when it feels like you start each day with an empty tank. It is unrealistic to expect to be able to will yourself across the finish line for every complex or long-term goal you want to achieve.

The solution? Make it difficult to do anything that *doesn't* align with your priorities. Hardy calls these friction

365

generators "Forcing Functions".[31] It's a fitting name; the idea is to force yourself to do what you know you should do, but might not feel like doing at that moment.

If your goal is to eat healthier, a good Forcing Function would be to remove all the unhealthy food from your home. If you need to go to the store first, those cookies will be less tempting than if you need to walk into the kitchen. The more time it takes to think about it, the less likely you will do it.

Make Success the Default

Forcing Functions make it harder to do the *wrong* things, but how can you make it easier to do the *right* things? One method is to perform any benign features of a task ahead of time, to minimize the amount of effort required to perform the main activity. For example, if your goal is to work out regularly, you could sleep in your exercise clothes and put your running shoes next to your bed. When you wake up the next day, you only need to put on the shoes and off you go.

Or, to reuse the healthy eating example, put a bag of carrots where the cookies used to be. You already have the habit of checking that cabinet when you want a snack, make that habit work for you! It's still tempting to buy chocolate at the supermarket, but resisting once while shopping is easier than doing it several times every day at home.

Schedule it

If you use a calendar (and you should), whether digital or on paper, block off time to work on your goals. One of the most common mistakes people make is to leave open space in the calendar and just intend to use that "free time" for self-care and improvement. Nature abhors a vacuum. If it is open on your calendar, life will find a way to fill it. Don't let your circumstances decide for you, schedule "you time" so you won't forget, and protect yourself from saying yes to other things that take time away from your goals. If you use a digital calendar you can keep your goals at the forefront of your mind by setting up notifications on your smartphone.

Personally, I sync my calendar across all of my devices, so even if I don't have my phone, I still get a reminder for all necessary things. By the way, not everything is worth setting notifications for, but that's a topic for another time.

Track your Progress

"What gets measured gets managed," is a popular quote often accredited to author and management consultant Peter Drucker (he never said that, but that's a different story).

While it's not possible to measure everything, many goals benefit from being able to track relevant metrics

There are endless amounts of apps available to track everything from financial transactions to reading habits and nutritional intake. You can also go old-school and take notes on paper. The important part is finding key performance indicators that show how you are progressing towards your goals.

By tracking these metrics, you can see exactly where you are and compare your progress over time. Looking back at your old data can be a great motivation as it shows how much you have improved.

For me, what I have achieved so far is more important than staring at a goal that might still be far away. The goal itself might be a huge motivator, but the long, rocky road leading up to it can be intimidating. Being able to look at how far I've come helps to balance that.

Get support from others

If you are the only one aware of your goals, you run the risk of being a pushover. You are too partial to your own excuses. If you have someone to hold you accountable, a friend at the gym or a coworker who wants to hear your daily progress at lunch, you will think twice before you skip. Your reputation is now on the line.

Telling others will also help you because they can now support you. This is true for people that you spend the most time with. And who knows, maybe they can join you? Team efforts are often more fun, and the accountability is priceless. Preparing healthy meals may be more work than throwing a pizza in the oven, but what if you use this time to cook and spend quality time with your partner instead?

Summary
1. Put yourself first.
2. Don't rely on willpower.
3. Make success the default.
4. Schedule it.
5. Track your progress.
6. Get support from others.

Whether you are new to self-improvement or you have just gotten off track, remember the fundamentals and make yourself a priority.

Conclusion

If you are reading this book, it is possible you have read many books like it on your self-improvement journey. As a SuperLearner, you are always seeking out new ways to better yourself, help others, or get a "competitive edge." Perhaps you have shelves lined with books like this one, written by top performers, telling stories of struggle and success, imparting secrets to transformation that anyone can apply. Have you applied them?

There is a reason this book is titled the *Superhuman Playbook* and not the *SuperLearner Playbook*. To be a SuperLearner is to ask and to seek, relentlessly. A SuperLearner *learns.* Every Superhuman is a SuperLearner, but not every SuperLearner is a Superhuman. To be Superhuman is to do more than learn. To be Superhuman is to *act upon what is learned.* Many a great mind has gone unnoticed by history for lack of action. A Superhuman cannot help but change the world because they change themselves. There is a reason this book is titled the *Superhuman Playbook* and not the *Superhuman Textbook* (other than marketability). Text is for study; plays are for *execution.* The number one pitfall of would-be Superhumans is inaction. Knowledge never manifested in action is worthless. It goes to the grave without ever seeing the sun. Don't add this book to your bookshelf to prove to your friends that you read. You don't need any more trophies for mental exertion; you need to act.

Before you skim through the end matter and close the back cover, I have one more challenge: If you want to be Superhuman, flip back to the chapter that scared you the most. Read it again. What is the source of your fear? What uncomfortable action does it compel you to take?

Consider the person you want to be, the Superhuman version of you.

Would that person take this action?

If the answer is yes, do it.

Not tomorrow, not next year, now.

The future of your world depends on it.

References

1. Steel P. The Procrastination Equation. Pearson; 2012.
2. Pychyl TA. Solving the Procrastination Puzzle: a Concise Guide to Strategies for Change. New York: Jeremy P. Tarcher/Penguin, a member of Penguin Group (USA); 2013.
3. Fogg BJ. Tiny Habits: The Small Changes That Change Everything. Boston, MA: Houghton Mifflin Harcourt; 2020.
4. Waitzkin J. The Art of Learning: a Journey in the Pursuit of Excellence. New York, NY: Free Spirit; 2008.
5. Ferriss T. Real Mind Control: The 21-Day No-Complaint Experiment. The Blog of Author Tim Ferriss. https://tim.blog/2007/09/18/real-mind-control-the-21-day-no-complaint-experiment/. Published January 16, 2020. Accessed August 21, 2020.
6. The History and Evolution of SMART Goals. AchieveIt. https://www.achieveit.com/resources/blog/the-history-and-evolution-of-smart-goals. Published December 19, 2019. Accessed August 21, 2020.
7. Parkinson's Law. The Economist. https://www.economist.com/news/1955/11/19/parkinsons-law. Accessed August 21, 2020.
8. Markowsky G. Physiology. Encyclopædia Britannica. https://www.britannica.com/science/information-theory/Physiology. Published June 16, 2017. Accessed August 21, 2020.

9. Elrod H. The Miracle Morning. the Not-so-Obvious Secret Guaranteed to Transform Your Life before 8 AM. Place of publication not identified: Hal Elrod; 2013.

10. Welcome to the Official Wim Hof Method Website. http://www.wimhofmethod.com/. Accessed August 21, 2020.

11. Jeannerod M. Mental imagery in the motor context. Neuropsychologia. 1995;33(11):1419-1432. doi:10.1016/0028-3932(95)00073-c

12. Clear J. Atomic Habits: an Easy and Proven Way to Build Good Habits and Break Bad Ones. London: Cornerstone; 2019.

13. Rubin G. The Four Tendencies. Hodder & Stoughton; 2018.

14. Sutherland JJ. The Scrum Fieldbook: Faster Performance. Better Results. Starting Now. London: Random House Business Books; 2019.

15. Mogilner C, Chance Z, Norton MI. Giving Time Gives You Time. Psychological Science. 2012;23(10):1233-1238. doi:10.1177/0956797612442551

16. Baumeister, R. F. (1991). Meanings of life. New York, NY: Guilford Press.

17. Bisin A, Hyndman K. Present-Bias, Procrastination and Deadlines in a Field Experiment. 2014. doi:10.3386/w19874

18. Forehand, M., Bloom's taxonomy. Emerging perspectives on learning, teaching, and technology, 2010. 41(4): p. 47-56.

19. Armstrong, P., Bloom's Taxonomy. Vanderbilt University, 2010.

20. Overbaugh, R.C. and L. Schultz, blooms-taxonomy-handout.pdf.

21. Coan, M., Research Guides: Information Literacy: Guide for Students: What is Information Literacy?

22. Cunningham, D. and S.L. Shablak, Selective Reading Guide-O-Rama: The Content Teacher's Best Friend. Journal of Reading, 1975. 18(5): p. 380-382

23. Cohen, M., Apply the Pareto Principle to Reading a Book | Marlies Cohen. 2016.

24. Kang, S.H., Spaced repetition promotes efficient and effective learning: Policy implications for instruction. Policy Insights from the Behavioral and Brain Sciences, 2016. 3(1): p. 12-19.

25. Ukko, J. and M. Saunila, The role of reflection in facilitating and assessing innovativeness. Journal of technology management & innovation, 2013. 8(4): p. 170-176.

26. Hilden, S. and K. Tikkamäki, Reflective Practice as a Fuel for Organizational Learning. Administrative Sciences, 2013. 3(3): p. 76-95.

27. Spaced repetition, in Wikipedia. 2020.

28. Spaced Learning 101 | Teaching Commons.

29. Hanyi Xu, Laurent Bègue och Brad J. Bushman, "Washing the guilt away: effects of personal versus vicarious cleansing on guilty feelings and prosocial behavior" In Frontiers in Human Neuroscience - Embodiment and the Human MNS, doi: 10.3389/fnhum.2015.00500, (March 2016) s. 87-91.

30. Kimberly LaMothe. 2015. Why we dance. A philosophy of bodily becoming. New York: Columbia University Press.

31. Hardy B. Willpower Doesn't Work: Discover the Hidden Keys to Success. London: Piatkus; 2019.

32. The 100 Most-Spoken Languages in the World

33. NORBERT SCHMITT, XIANGYING JIANG, WILLIAM GRABE: The Percentage of Words Known in a Text and Reading Comprehension; The Modern Language Journal, 95, i, (2011) The Percentage of Words Known in a Text and Reading Comprehension

34. Marc Brysbaert*, Michaël Stevens, Paweł Mandera and Emmanuel Keuleers: How Many Words Do We Know? Practical Estimates of Vocabulary Size Dependent on Word Definition, the Degree of Language Input and the Participant's Age; Front. Psychol., 29 July 2016 | https://doi.org/10.3389/fpsyg.2016.01116

35. Learn any language &. Learn Any Language. https://fluent-forever.com/. Accessed August 21, 2020.

36. It is time to triple your memory! Magnetic Memory Method - How to Memorize With A Memory Palace. https://www.magneticmemorymethod.com/. Published March 26, 2020. Accessed August 21, 2020.

37. Major System mnemonic technique database, list and generator. https://major-system.info/en/. Accessed August 21, 2020.

38. Chris Buck & Jennifer Lee. Frozen II [DVD]. Walt Disney Animation Studios, Walt Disney Pictures; 2019.

39. Alcohol: Balancing Risks and Benefits. The Nutrition Source. https://www.hsph.harvard.edu/nutritionsource/healthy-drinks/drinks-to-consume-in-moderation/alcohol-full-story/. Published 2020. Accessed August 16, 2020.

40. Mongan D, Hope A. Social consequences of harmful use of alcohol in Ireland. In: Health Research Board; 2009.

41. @JamesClear. Time spent working hard is often better spent identifying where the bottleneck is located. Working hard on the wrong thing leads to frustration, not progress. https://twitter.com/JamesClear/status/1257345454196523010. Posted May 4, 2020.

42. Peugh J, Belenko S. Alcohol, drugs and sexual function: a review. J Psychoactive Drugs. 2001;33(3):223-232.

43. Goodwin DW, Powell B, Bremer D, Hoine H, Stern J. Alcohol and recall: state-dependent effects in man. Science (New York, NY). 1969;163(3873):1358-1360.

44. Lowe G. Alcohol and state-dependent learning. Subst Alcohol Actions Misuse. 1983;4(4):273-282.

45. Overton DA. State-Dependent Learning Produced by Alcohol and Its Relevance to Alcoholism. In: Kissin B, Begleiter H, eds. The Biology of Alcoholism: Volume 2: Physiology and Behavior. Boston, MA: Springer US; 1972:193-217.

46. Petersen RC. Retrieval failures in alcohol state-dependent learning. Psychopharmacology. 1977;55(2):141-146.

47. Sanday L, Patti CL, Zanin KA, et al. Ethanol-induced memory impairment in a discriminative avoidance task is state-dependent. Alcohol Clin Exp Res. 2013;37 Suppl 1:E30-39.

48. Devineni AV, Heberlein U. Preferential ethanol consumption in Drosophila models features of addiction. Current biology : CB. 2009;19(24):2126-2132.

49. Kiefer SW, Dopp JM. Taste reactivity to alcohol in rats. Behav Neurosci. 1989;103(6):1318-1326.

50. Peru YCdPRL, Ojelade SA, Penninti PS, et al. Long-lasting, experience-dependent alcohol preference in Drosophila. Addict Biol. 2014;19(3):392-401.

51. Scinska A, Koros E, Habrat B, Kukwa A, Kostowski W, Bienkowski P. Bitter and sweet components of ethanol taste in humans. Drug and Alcohol Dependence. 2000;60(2):199-206.

52. Yamaki N, Matsushita S, Hara S, Yokoyama A, Hishimoto A, Higuchi S. Telomere shortening in alcohol dependence: Roles of alcohol and acetaldehyde. Journal of psychiatric research. 2019;109:27-32.

53. W.H.O. Global Status Report on Alcohol And Health. Geneva: World Health Organization;2014. 978 92 4 156475 5.

54. Miller JW, Naimi TS, Brewer RD, Jones SE. Binge drinking and associated health risk behaviors among high school students. Pediatrics. 2007;119(1):76-85.

55. Oscar-Berman M, Shagrin B, Evert DL, Epstein C. Impairments of brain and behavior: the neurological effects of alcohol. Alcohol Health Res World. 1997;21(1):65-75.

56. Koob GF, Colrain IM. Alcohol use disorder and sleep disturbances: a feed-forward allostatic framework. Neuropsychopharmacology. 2020;45(1):141-165.

57. La Vignera S, Condorelli RA, Balercia G, Vicari E, Calogero AE. Does alcohol have any effect on male reproductive function? A review of literature. Asian J Androl. 2013;15(2):221-225.

58. 7 ways alcohol could be affecting your fitness without you realising. TheJournal.ie. https://www.thejournal.ie/effect-of-alcohol-on-sports-fitness-hse-3286347-Mar2017/. Published 2020. Accessed August 16, 2020.

59. Traversy G, Chaput JP. Alcohol Consumption and Obesity: An Update. Curr Obes Rep. 2015;4(1):122-130.
60. Linton A. How Much Does Drinking Really Cost?. The Balance Everyday. https://www.thebalanceeveryday.com/what-lifetime-of-drinking-costs-4142309. Published 2018. Accessed August 16, 2020.
61. American Alcohol Expenditures | Delphi Health Group. Delphi Behavioral Health Group. https://delphihealthgroup.com/american-alcohol-expenditures/. Published 2020. Accessed August 16, 2020.
62. McDermott J. Drunk shopping 2020: Americans spend almost $44.9B | finder.com. finder.com. https://www.finder.com/drunk-shopping. Published 2020. Accessed August 17, 2020.
63. Booth BM, Feng W. The impact of drinking and drinking consequences on short-term employment outcomes in at-risk drinkers in six southern states. J Behav Health Serv Res. 2002;29(2):157-166.
64. Buvik K, Moan IS, Halkjelsvik T. Alcohol-related absence and presenteeism: Beyond productivity loss. Int J Drug Policy. 2018;58:71-77.
65. Corte CM, Sommers MS. Alcohol and risky behaviors. Annu Rev Nurs Res. 2005;23:327-360.
66. Castaneda R, Sussman N, Westreich L, Levy R, O'Malley M. A review of the effects of moderate alcohol intake on the treatment of anxiety and mood disorders. J Clin Psychiatry. 1996;57(5):207-212.
67. Murphy GE, Wetzel RD. The lifetime risk of suicide in alcoholism. Arch Gen Psychiatry. 1990;47(4):383-392.

68. Holmes A, Fitzgerald PJ, MacPherson KP, et al. Chronic alcohol remodels prefrontal neurons and disrupts NMDAR-mediated fear extinction encoding. Nat Neurosci. 2012;15(10):1359-1361.
69. Geiger BB, MacKerron G. Can alcohol make you happy? A subjective wellbeing approach. Soc Sci Med. 2016;156:184-191.
70. Appleton A, James R, Larsen J. The Association between Mental Wellbeing, Levels of Harmful Drinking, and Drinking Motivations: A Cross-Sectional Study of the UK Adult Population. Int J Environ Res Public Health. 2018;15(7).
71. Mäkelä P, Raitasalo K, Wahlbeck K. Mental health and alcohol use: a cross-sectional study of the Finnish general population. Eur J Public Health. 2015;25(2):225-231.
72. Cranford JA. DSM-IV alcohol dependence and marital dissolution: evidence from the National Epidemiologic Survey on Alcohol and Related Conditions. Journal of studies on alcohol and drugs. 2014;75(3):520-529.
73. U.S. Department of Health and Human Services, Substance Abuse and Mental Health Services Administration, Center for Behavioral Health Statistics and Quality. National Survey on Drug Use and Health 2016 (NSDUH-2016-DS0001). Retrieved from https://datafiles.samhsa.gov/. Accessed April 14, 2020.
74. Danaei G, Ding EL, Mozaffarian D, et al. The preventable causes of death in the United States: comparative risk assessment of dietary, lifestyle, and metabolic risk factors. PLoS medicine. 2009;6(4):e1000058.
75. Sacks JJ, Gonzales KR, Bouchery EE, Tomedi LE, Brewer RD. 2010 National and State Costs of

Excessive Alcohol Consumption. Am J Prev Med. 2015;49(5):e73-e79.

76. Ramage A, Fairbairns R. The 28 Day Alcohol-Free Challenge. Bluebird; 2017.

77. Hershow RB, Zuskov DS, Vu Tuyet Mai N, et al. "[Drinking is] Like a Rule That You Can't Break": Perceived Barriers and Facilitators to Reduce Alcohol Use and Improve Antiretroviral Treatment Adherence among People Living with HIV and Alcohol Use Disorder in Vietnam. Subst Use Misuse. 2018;53(7):1084-1092.

78. Prentice DA, Miller DT. Pluralistic ignorance and alcohol use on campus: some consequences of misperceiving the social norm. J Pers Soc Psychol. 1993;64(2):243-256.

79. Hemingway L. I Need To Stop Drinking!. Freedom Publishing; 2013.

80. Duhigg C. The Power Of Habit. New York: The Random House Publishing Group; 2012.

81. Willink J, Babin L. Extreme Ownership: How U.S. Navy SEALs Lead and Win. Sydney, N.S.W.: Macmillan; 2018.

Printed in Great Britain
by Amazon

59796101R00221